HOW DO YO

The old wooden school a
oak chair sat forlornly but proudly before the new computer
station in the center of the classroom.

WHICH IS CORRECT?
Everyone should wear their seat belt.
Everyone should wear her or his seat belt.

WHAT IS WRONG WITH THIS SENTENCE?
Scratching and biting, the veterinarian gave the rabies shot
to the owner's cat.

DO YOU NEED AN APOSTROPHE?
In a democratic society, the people's needs are respected.

FIND THE ANSWERS FAST.
IT'S AS EASY AS ABC
WITH THE NEW DICTIONARY FORMAT
OF THE . . .

21st CENTURY GRAMMAR HANDBOOK

— 21ST —
CENTURY
GRAMMAR
HANDBOOK

Edited by

THE PRINCETON LANGUAGE INSTITUTE

AND

JOSEPH HOLLANDER

Produced by The Philip Lief Group, Inc.

A LAUREL BOOK

Published by
Dell Publishing
a division of
Bantam Doubleday Dell Publishing Group, Inc.
666 Fifth Avenue
New York, NY 10103

Published by arrangement with
The Philip Lief Group, Inc.
6 West 20th Street
New York, NY 10011

ISBN: 0-440-21508-0

Printed in the United States of America
Published simultaneously in Canada
April 1993
10 9 8 7 6 5 4 3 2 1

CONTENTS

How to Use This Book

The *21st Century Grammar Handbook* is designed to give you direct and rapid answers to your questions about how to write or speak correctly. It is arranged like a dictionary: Its entries are in alphabetical order, covering not only grammar rules and examples of correct and incorrect usage but specific words or terms that often cause errors. It includes entries for *be*, *is*, *am*, *are*, *was*, and *were*, as well as the special names and terms used in English classrooms to analyze and categorize how these words work. The *21st Century Grammar Handbook* is constructed to help you find solutions quickly and directly even if you don't know classroom grammar terminology.

You can also use the *21st Century Grammar Handbook* to improve your writing and speaking overall—to identify the areas in which you are weak or need pointers and then to find all the entries that will help.

To find answers to immediate problems you are having with your writing or speaking, simply look up the word or words that are bothering you. For example, to find out whether you should use "who" or "whom," just look under *who*. You will discover right and wrong examples, an explanation of why the rules work the way they do, and suggestions for other entries to look at if you need more information.

But what if you know something is wrong but don't know exactly what the problem is or what it is called? Then look at the next section of this book: "How to Know What You

Don't Know." Here you will find a listing of the most common writing and speaking problems along with suggestions for places to look for answers. The list asks some questions that will help guide you to the places where your problems will be solved simply and swiftly.

If you don't find a match for your problem by looking through this section, then try to look up words that are similar to the ones that are causing you difficulty or that you think are okay in your sentence but that might be hiding errors: Look under *and* or *is* or *that* or *comma* or *-ly* or *s*. Then follow the suggestions for looking at related entries until you have identified what's wrong and how to fix it. If you still can't find what you don't know, try the entries on very broad topics like *rules*, *style*, *bland writing*, and similar subjects. There you will find not only specific answers to immediate problems but many hints about other areas you might consider to find the root of your difficulties.

If you do know the name of the grammar category or term with which you need help, you can look in the entries for the full citation and also find related entries on the subject that interests you.

To teach yourself better grammar and writing or speaking, first take the self-assessment quiz called "How Good Are My Grammar, Writing, and Speaking?" It will help you identify weak spots in your statements, places where tips and tricks will help make your writing or speaking stronger and more effective, and ways to avoid common pitfalls and take advantage of your stylistic strengths.

In each entry related subjects are highlighted in *italic type*. Examples are set off in quotation marks and clearly marked as RIGHT or WRONG.

How to Know
What You Don't Know

This list contains the most common errors and confusions that beset writers and speakers. It is designed to highlight the most likely places for you to look for answers to your questions. Be sure to check entries for similar words or terms as well as for the things in your statement that seem correct to you but that might in fact be what is causing problems. Remember that the *Handbook* includes entries for general problems like *bland writing*, *rules*, and *style*. Each of these entries includes not only solutions to immediate problems but ideas about where else to look in the book for help or answers.

The list of topics to look at is not alphabetical for each problem but in order of where you are most likely to find specific answers to specific problems.

1. SPELLING: How do I know a word is spelled wrong? See *spelling*, *dictionary*, and *languages*.

2. RULES: Do I always have to follow them? See *rules*, *style*, *dialect*, *grammar*, and *standard English*.

3. RULES AGAIN: How do I know when I've broken them? See *editing*, *revision*, and *audience*.

4. PUNCTUATION: Who cares? See *comma*, *period*, *quotation mark*, *question mark*, *exclamation point*, *colon*, *semicolon*, *conjunction*, *clause*, *sentence*, *ellipsis*, *bracket*, *symbol*, and *hyphen*.

5. VERBS: What are they, and how do I use them? See *be*, *is*, *am*, *was*, *were*, *are*, *will*, *would*, *should*, *shall*,

tense, *verbs*, *conjugation*, *clauses*, *agreement*, and *fragments*.

6. PRONOUNS: When do I use "who" and "whom" or "she" and "her"? See the entries for the specific words as well as *pronoun*, *personal pronoun*, and the related grammatical listings.

7. NOUNS: What are they? See the entries for *noun*, *proper noun*, *names*, *title*, *capitalization*, and suggested related topics in those entries.

8. CONJUNCTIONS: How do parts of sentences get linked together? See the entries on *conjunction;* specific conjunctions like *and;* and *parallelism*, *emphasis*, *clause*, and so on.

9. MODIFIERS: "Good" and "well" drive me crazy. Look them up, along with *adjective*, *adverb*, *comparison*, and many other subjects.

10. CONFUSING WORDS: What is the difference between "their" and "they're" and "there"? Look them up, and see the entry for *homonym*.

11. SEXIST AND OFFENSIVE LANGUAGE: When should I call a woman "Ms." or "Miss" or "Mrs."? All these words are listed, and there are entries on *sexist language*, *titles* of people, *names*, and many related subjects.

12. USING NUMBERS: Is it the "23rd Precinct" or "Twenty-third Precinct"? Look under *numbers*, *cardinal number*, *ordinal number*, and related topics.

How Good Are My Grammar, Writing, and Speaking?

Mark any errors you find in the following sentences, each of which is numbered. The answers follow and are listed by the number of the sentence. Look for possible mistakes and whether your solutions are the right ones for making the sentence more accurate or better written. Other things to think about when you write or speak are noted as well. Be careful; there are some tricky things in the samples.

SAMPLES

1. I didn't know who to give the book to.

2. She completed the operation, and then walked out of the operating room.

3. A doctor is supposed to keep his hands clean.

4. Its clear whats gotta be done.

5. Speaking of grammar, errors are to common to worry about.

6. In the spring the birds begin to sing and the bees begin to sting.

7. Joans book is called, "How To Write Better."

8. I read the book, that is about grammar, and writing.

9. There is great value to an university education but it is weak.

10. The cases of sexual harassment which is common bothers me.

11. Predominant forms of transgressive behavior, deviance that is selfgenerated, and retrogressive emotions.

12. Examples are given so that help can be provided where it is needed.

THINGS TO THINK ABOUT

Remember that *italicized words* refer to entries in the *Handbook* you should look at for answers, details, and explanations. Keep in mind as well that the samples are purposely tricky sentences that are not meant to embarrass or fool you but to help you identify as many areas as possible that you should pay attention to when you write or speak.

ANSWERS

1. **I didn't know who to give the book to.** In this *sentence*, "*who*" is not right. In fact it should be "whom" because you should use the *objective case* of a *pronoun* before an *infinitive* ("They asked me to improve.") and because "*who*" can also be seen as the *object* of the *preposition* "*to*" that dangles at the end of the sentence.

But it might not be as obvious that there are other things in this sentence that don't meet the formal requirements of *standard English* or that could be written more clearly or carefully. First, a *contraction* like "didn't" may not be acceptable if the *audience* for this statement sets very high, formal standards for writing. It's better to use "did not" if this sentence is to appear in a school paper, scholarly publication, or some similar place.

The dangling preposition "*to*" might confuse some readers or offend those who apply grammar rules strictly. Better to edit or revise this sentence along these lines: "I did not know to whom to give the book." Of course, you can't edit words you've already spoken, and you might feel that the people who are going to read this sentence will understand you perfectly and either not notice or not care about your "errors." But be sure you know your audience will be that tolerant, and be aware that informal *style* is not always appropriate. See also *dangling modifier, editing,* and *revision.*

2. **She completed the speech, and then walked out of the lecture hall.** No *comma* is needed before a *compound predicate* like "completed . . . and . . . walked." Overuse of *punctuation* is as much an error as underuse, and it can lead to a very heavy or boring *style.* Also see *and* and *predicate.*

3. **A doctor is supposed to keep his hands clean.** Not all doctors are men, so the *possessive* pronoun "his" is misleading and lacks *agreement* with its *antecedent.* This *sentence* should be revised to something like: "All doctors should keep their hands clean." Or: "A doctor should keep her or his hands clean." This is an instance of *sexist language* or offensive language. See also *pronouns, gender,* and *revision.*

4. **Its clear whats gotta be done.** This information *sentence* would not be considered appropriate in most

written communications except perhaps a personal letter. The most glaring error is "gotta," which would be just as wrong if it were "got to." Formal, *standard English* requires "must," "should," "has," or a similar construction: ". . . what should be done."

Two *apostrophes* are missing from *contractions*: "It's" (compare the *possessive* pronoun "its") and "what's." And in more formal *style* contractions might not be appropriate, although this *rule* is less rigid than it used to be. Here is a possible *revision* that would meet most standards: "It's clear what has to be done." Change "It's" to "It is" to satisfy the most rigorous *audience*. See also *possessive* and *pronoun*.

5. **Speaking of grammar, errors are to common to worry about.** The first verbal phrase ("Speaking of grammar") is a *dangling modifier* or *misplaced modifier* that has no clear *antecedent,* or referent. "Errors" were not speaking of grammar, nor was anything or anyone else in the *sentence*. Moreover, the form of the phrase does not show whether it is an adjectival usage (modifying a *noun*) or an adverbial construction (modifying a *verb*; surely the phrase does not refer to "*are*"). Most readers will actually "understand" this sentence on a first and rapid reading, but any closer attention will lead to puzzlement, the need to reread and try to figure out what is meant, and a loss of *clarity* and *efficiency* of communication. See also *adjective*.

You can avoid *bland writing* or weak writing by starting sentences with phrases instead of noun *subjects*. But you need to be careful that the phrases are constructed properly and refer clearly to something or someone appearing soon after in the sentence.

The first "*to*" is also wrong; instead of the *preposition* "*to*," its *homonym*, the *adverb* "*too*," is required here.

The *preposition* "*about*" at the end of the sentence is not dangling since it is an integral part of the verb. Dropping it would make the sentence unintelligible, while *revising* to add an *object* or inserting a pronoun object would make the sentence very stilted.

The whole sentence could be rewritten as follows: "When one is talking about grammar, errors are too common to worry about." If the last preposition troubles you because it seems to be dangling, try: "When the subject is grammar, errors are too common to cause worry." See *revision* and *editing*.

6. **In the spring the birds begin to sing and the bees begin to sting.** A *comma* should be inserted after "*sing*" because the two *clauses* in this sentence are independent. Modern *usage* permits the dropping of such commas between short independent clauses, particularly in less formal or journalistic writing. If you are striving for a racy effect, need to save space by cutting down on *punctuation,* or want to defy authority a bit, the comma could be left out, but not in most classroom work or more formal writing.

7. **Joans book is called, "How To Write Better."** "*Joan's*" is a *possessive* that requires an *apostrophe* before the "*s*" (as do all singular *nouns* in the possessive *case* no matter how they are spelled: "Gus's book"). But the *comma* before the *quotation marks* isn't necessary because what follows is not someone's speech but a *title* of a work. Book titles are usually underlined or italicized rather than being set off in quotes. Within *capitalized* titles of works, *conjunctions, prepositions,* and the "*to*" of *infinitives* are

not capitalized. The rules of capitalization are complex and flexible, depending on the purposes of your writing and your *audience*. See also *possessive* and *italics*.

8. **I read the book, that is about grammar, and writing.** The choice of the definite article "*the*" is probably poor since there are many books about grammar and writing: "a book" would likely be better. *That* is a *relative pronoun* used to introduce a *restrictive phrase* or *restrictive clause*; *nonrestrictive phrases, nonrestrictive clauses,* or *appositives* are not set off by *commas*. "Which" could be used here with a comma to make a nonrestrictive clause, but the sentence then wouldn't make sense (try it). The best revision might be: "I read a book about grammar and writing." This is less wordy and solves the pronoun problem by eliminating the pronoun altogether.

The final comma (after "grammar") is not needed since there are only two words in this *series*; standard English requires a comma before "*and*" only in series of more than two elements: ". . . a book that is about grammar, usage, and writing." See also *phrase, clause, a,* and *standard English*.

9. **There is great value to an university education but it is weak.** The indefinitive article "*an*" is wrong because "university" begins with a consonant sound. Only words that begin with vowel sounds should take "an" ("an owl," "*a* one-time offer," "a university," "an unclean house").

There should be a *comma* between the two independent *clauses* that are joined by the *conjunction* "*but*." However, something must be done about "*it*." There is no clear *antecedent,* or referent, for this *pronoun,* and therefore, what is weak is completely unclear. Since "university" is a *noun* serving as an *adjective* in this sentence, and since the sentence begins with the weak opening "There is," which presents no clear *subject,* the reader could assume "it" has something to do with "value," "university," or "education" (see *expletive*). Whatever assumption a reader makes, time will be lost trying to figure out what is meant, and *clarity* will never be achieved.

It is not wrong to begin sentences with vague opening *phrases* like "It is" or "There is." But overreliance on them can lead to boring, unclear statements, particularly if later pronouns in such sentences are not given clear antecedents. *Revision* of this sample sentence requires going back to square one and rethinking what it is you have to say before setting pen to paper.

10. **The cases of sexual harassment which is common bothers me.** Here a *nonrestrictive clause,* properly introduced by "which," needs to be set off by *commas,* and the main *verb* ("bothers") should be *plural* to agree with the *subject* ("cases"): "The cases of sexual harassment, which is common, bother me." The sentence is now grammatically correct, but *editing* or rewriting would help eliminate the *awkwardness* of a plural subject separated from its verb by a singular *clause*: "I am bothered by the cases of sexual harassment, which is common." Although this change creates a *passive* construction, the sentence is clearer. See also *that* and *agreement*.

11. **Predominant forms of transgressive behavior, deviance that is selfgenerated, and retrogressive emotions.** Although there is a *linking verb* ("is") in a restrictive dependent *clause* in this set of words, the example is not a *sentence* since it lacks a main *verb*. The

compound word "self-generated" should also be hyphenated. See *is, hyphen, restrictive clause,* and *fragment.*

Another problem here is the heavy *vocabulary,* made up mainly of words derived from *Latin.* In some professional or technical contexts, such display of learning might be acceptable or even expected. But in most common communication, it is better to use fewer long, abstract words. Of course, there are some concepts so complex (like scientific ideas) that they defy expression in ordinary words. But if you are not a scholar or scientist or if it is possible your statements will not be read exclusively by specialists able to penetrate *jargon,* write as clearly and simply as you can. And even if you are an expert, you might try to find language the uninitiated can understand and enjoy. See *scientific language* and *clarity.*

12. **Examples are given so that help can be provided where it is needed.** There are no grammatical errors in this *sentence.* However, it does contain three *passive* verbal constructions. Not only do passives tend to weaken writing *style* by removing actors or *agents* from sentences, but they also add words and make it somewhat harder to find referents and *antecedents.* A possible *revision:* "We give examples to provide help where you need help." This sentence could be criticized for addressing an assumed reader ("you"), but it is more direct, shorter, and clearer than the sample.

If you review all the italicized words, terms, and ideas in the answers, you will not become an expert in grammar or stop making mistakes in writing or speaking. But you will gain some insight into the possible deficiencies in your

statements and some ways to identify them quickly so that
you can seek further help in the *Handbook*. That help—plus
care, attention, and constant rethinking and revision—will
go a long way toward making you a more accurate, better
writer.

A

A, an. "A" and "an" indicate single, uncertain objects and are, therefore, called "indefinite *articles*." Like most words that say something about *objects* (modify them in the broadest sense), they usually come directly before the word they describe (*noun* or *adjective*): "a dog," "an orange cloud."

When the word these articles comes before begins with a consonant sound, use "an" to describe or modify it; when the word begins with a vowel sound, choose "a." If the word that follows begins with a *number* or an *abbreviation* or an acronym, then choose "a" or "an," depending on the way the word is said out loud: if it sounds as though it began with a vowel, choose "an"; if it sounds like a consonant, choose "a." For example, these are correct choices: "a 100-megabyte disk," "an EKG reading," "an mflop."

The *rule* of choosing "a" or "an" according to the *spelling* or pronunciation of the word it comes before can lead to some confusion when different groups of people write or say a word differently. For instance, some British speakers do not pronounce the "h" of words like "humble," leading them to say or write "an humble home." Most American speakers and writers do not drop "h" and do not use "an" before words that begin with "h" in most cases. However, this Britishism does continue to appear in the most formal English, especially in the case of "historical." Some American writers prefer "an historical study" to avoid possible confusion with "ahistorical study." If the group to which you are addressing your words prefers this construction, it is acceptable to break the more generally followed rule stated above. See also *modifier* and *British English*.

Abbreviation, acronym. If possible, avoid abbreviations or acronyms—letters used to stand for words or clusters of words—in your writing if you are unsure your readers will understand them. To ensure *clarity,* spell out any acronym or abbreviation the first time you use it and show the way you will shorten the word or *phrase* in *parentheses:* "We will examine how the central processing unit (CPU) works." If there are many such instances in your writing, you might include a *list* of abbreviated terms or the acronyms used so that readers can check similar or less frequently used terms.

Many of these clusters have become so common they don't need explanation: company names like "IBM," commonly used words and abbreviations, such as "etc.," and many symbols or signs like "$," "%," and "&," can sometimes be used without further clarification. But when it is possible those who read or hear you won't know what you mean, help them with a fuller treatment of the abbreviation or acronyms you use.

Another group of commonly recognized shortened versions of words includes *numbers* and *symbols:* "There are 400 snakes in that pit."

Efficiency or length considerations are common reasons for using abbreviations or acronyms. Technical writing is often full of long names for things that must be repeated to ensure accuracy and clarity. Shortening these terms can save a great deal of space. A computer manual, for example, that repeats "central processing unit" a few thousand times will be much longer than one that uses "CPU." Some also argue that it is more efficient or quicker to read abbreviations and acronyms. That is so if you have first made sure your *audience* knows what you are shortening, and how.

If you are writing or speaking to people who are used to or even demand the use of acronyms, then follow the local *rules* and use them to save space or show you are part of the group.

Finally, remember that acronyms and abbreviations are treated as sound clusters when deciding whether to put "*a*" or "*an*" before them—use "*an*" if the shortened form usually is pronounced with a vowel sound ("an LED readout") but "*a*" if the pronunciation begins with a consonant sound ("a 100° day") no matter how the acronyms, abbreviations, numbers, or symbols are spelled.

You can find explanations of the proper use of the following terms in the entries for each abbreviation or acronym: *A.D.*, *A.M.*, *B.C.*, *ca.*, *cf.*, *Co.*, *dollars*, *Dr.*, *ed.*, *e.g.*, *et al.*, *etc.*, *hr.*, *ibid.*, *i.e.*, *lb.*, *loc. cit.*, *Ltd.*, *min.*, *Mr.*, *Ms.*, *N.B.*, *op. cit.*, *percent*, *Ph. D.*, *P.M.*, *q.v.*, *sec.*, *St.*, and *U.S.* See also *contractions*.

About, around. In *standard English* "about" should be used instead of "around" to mean approximately. WRONG: "He is around six feet tall." RIGHT: "He is about six feet tall."

Above. *Preposition* governing the *objective case*: "The balloon is above me."

Accent. In our multicultural, international age, we encounter more and more words from other *languages* that use accent marks. And more and more it becomes correct grammar to apply accents to names, words, and so on that come into English from other languages or that we use as we address those whose first language is not English.

If you are doing business with a company or person whose name has an accent, your correspondence will show more consideration and most likely be better received if you include accents. On the other hand, if you are uncertain how the name or word appears in the other language, omitting an accent is usually not very offensive or confusing to the person who is being addressed. If you are dealing with individuals or organizations that choose to use an accent in their names, then it is probably best to show the mark in all your correspondence.

Please look under the specific language for common accents and their use (*French, German, Spanish,* etc.).

Accept, except. Do not confuse these two words that sound almost alike (near-*homonyms*). "Accept" is a *verb* that means to allow, tolerate, receive. "Except" is a *preposition* that means besides.

Accusative case. See *objective case*.

Acronym. See *abbreviation*.

Across. *Preposition* governing the *objective case*: "The pedestrian walked across the street."

Active voice. English is said to have two voices: active and *passive*. These grammatical terms denote two ways of forming *sentences* or two ways of thinking about and expressing action. While it is not necessary to know the distinctions of the grammatical categories (except in English classes), it is critical to understand the difference between the two forms of expression, when to use or avoid them and what the choice of one or the other suggests about your writing and you.

In the active voice, a sentence or idea conveys the fairly simple and direct sense of a *subject* acting on an *object* by preserving a *noun, verb,* noun structure: "The bat hit the ball, and Dukie chased it." While active voice sentences can become much more elaborate and the sense of "action" can become quite remote ("Gaseous products of distillation amalgamate ionizing forces . . ."), the basic structure is still something acting or having an effect on something else.

In the passive voice, usually signaled by the presence of an *auxiliary* verb like "*is*" linked to the main verb, the sentence is turned around from the active pattern—the thing that is somehow the object or focus of the verb is its subject, while the thing or person that does the action moves into a *prepositional phrase*: "The ball is hit by the bat." Thus, the passive voice shifts the emphasis of the sentence from actor to recipient of action.

Standard English dictates that the active voice is preferred to the passive since it is a simpler, more direct form of communication. This is true only to a certain extent, but it is a handy *rule* to follow: Avoid the passive voice where possible to give your speech or writing more direct force, *clarity,* and simplicity.

But like all rules, this one has many exceptions. There are many instances when the passive voice allows a subtle distinction or is otherwise the preferable form of saying something. And for some *audiences* it is more or less mandatory. Much scientific and scholarly writing is done in the passive voice because many scientists and scholars feel that removing themselves—their specific personalities and predilections—from the focus of the sentence lends their ideas "objectivity." They believe that the sentence "I saw the bacteria grow" is more personal, more subjective, and more likely to be read as a single, nonverifiable action than "Bacteria were observed to grow" (see *scientific language*).

When you speak to or write for a scholarly or scientific audience, you may prefer to violate the active-passive rule in order to adopt the more common passive, "objective" style. However, this stylistic preference has been subjected to many questions and doubts in recent times. Thus passive constructions are no longer so much the rule as the preference of scholarly and scientific writing, which has come to recognize that the observer, actor, or agent whose role is obscured by passive constructions still takes part in and influences activities reported in the passive voice. Writing or speaking in the active voice seems to make that presence more explicit, hence clearer.

A.D. This *abbreviation* stands for the *Latin* words "anno Domini" and means "in the year of the Lord" or the time since the birth of Christ. It is added to dates to distinguish where they fall in the commonly accepted Western dating system. The abbreviation is usually not spelled out, precedes the whole date, and appears in capital letters with *periods*. Using *lower case* or dropping the periods is acceptable in many *styles* and less standard writing, though A.D. and B.C. ("before Christ") usually appear in more formal works, where the standard *rule* should be followed. See *capitalization*.

Adjective. Words or *phrases* that add qualities to *nouns* are called adjectives. Few are usually needed to convey the essential attributes of the things, people, or places about which we are talking or writing. However, many writers and speakers pile up too many adjectives before nouns, thus weakening their writing by obscuring or thinning out their intent. Using too many adjectives can lead to a weak *style* or *bland writing*.

Adjectives normally come before the nouns they apply to or modify. Quite commonly they stand in the *predicate* of simple *sentences*: "The house is red." When more than one adjective is used to qualify something, the adjectives can be separated by *and* or by *commas*: "the red and white house"; "the tall, strong, and athletic singer." If the "and" is omitted between two adjectives of equal weight modifying the same thing, a comma separates the *modifiers*: "The tall, athletic singer ran." If two adjectives modifying a noun are not of equal weight or would not normally require "and" to make the meaning clear, then no comma need be inserted: "a tall French singer said." The distinction between these two cases is often not very clear, and the choice of using the comma between adjectives is up to the writer, who may be indicating the relationship between the modifiers by putting in or leaving out the comma.

To indicate the qualities of adjectives, use *adverbs*: "the bright red house." Only adjectives can apply to nouns, and only adverbs can qualify adjectives (and *verbs* or other adverbs). It is a common mistake to use adjectives to modify verbs or adverbs to modify nouns. When the qualifying word stands near a noun or verb, the mistake is fairly easy to notice. But when the modifier stands alone in the predicate of a sentence, errors are more likely. RIGHT: "I drive a fast car." "I drive rapidly." WRONG: "I drive rapid." Some specific adjectives and adverbs that are particularly troublesome are treated in separate entries: "*good*" and "well," "*bad*" and "badly," "*real*" and "really," and so on.

The most common problems with adjectives or adverbs in predicates come from using *linking verbs* like "*is*," "looks," "*seems*," "appears," "*sounds*," "*smells*," "tastes," "*feels*." All these words can be followed by adjectives or adverbs to make correct sentences. But the meaning will dictate which kind of modifier to use. If you are stating the qualities of a thing or person (noun), then the word in the predicate should be an adjective no matter how far away the noun being talked about might be located: "The expert who spoke at our meeting, held on March 25 at an alternate location (because the usual hall was being used by someone else), looked feeble." This is a weak, wandering sentence, but it makes the point.

If you want to indicate the quality of action taking place—even if that action is embodied in bland linking verbs—then use an adverb, again, no matter where the verbs, nouns, or other adjectives in the sentence fall: "The expert who spoke looked, perhaps because we weren't in our usual location, feebly at me."

Adjective *phrases* work the same way as single-word adjectives but are made up of more complex ideas expressed through combinations of more words, including, possibly, almost all other *parts of speech*. In the long, weak sentence about the feeble speaker, the *clause* that begins with "who spoke" functions as an adjective modifying "expert"; the participial clause that begins "held on" is an adjectival phrase modifying "meeting."

Nouns can also be used as adjectives: "computer program." This is a simple way of conveying a more elaborate relationship in fewer words than "program written for the computer." Take care not to use too many nouns as adjectives in a string because your *audience* will have trouble finding the end of the string and knowing what is modified by what: "Desktop computer writing correction programs are useful." Such strings can often be broken into *prepositional phrases* or other kinds of phrases that are easier to follow: "Desktop computer programs for correcting writing are useful."

Adjectives indicate qualities that may be more or less present in the thing they modify. This property is called *comparison* and is treated in a separate entry; see also *more, superlative, good, better, best, bad, ill, little, many, much, some,* and *worse.*

Adverb. The properties of *adjectives, verbs,* and other adverbs are conveyed or described by adverbs. Many adverbs signal their role by ending in "*-ly,*" but not all do: "He spoke rapidly and well."

Adverbs cannot modify *nouns* or stand alone in *predicates* where they refer to nouns. WRONG: "The lecturer is angrily." RIGHT: "The lecturer is angrily gesturing," "The lecturer is angry." While "angrily" in the WRONG example seems incomplete and probably incorrect to most readers, some adverbs can stand alone after verbs (though not usually after the *linking verbs* "*is,*" "*seems,*" "appears," "looks," "*feels,*" "*sounds,*" "tastes"): "The lecturer speaks well." Confusing pairs of adjectives and adverbs are treated in separate entries. See, for example, *good, bad,* and *real.*

Because they are often marked in some way (such as having an "*-ly*" ending) and can modify so many different kinds of words or *phrases,* adverbs can appear in many places in a sentence. They therefore must be used with care to ensure that they clearly indicate what word or phrase they are qualifying. To help make decisions about adverb placement somewhat easier, a number of *rules* have evolved over the years. These guidelines are useful but are also commonly bent or broken by the best writers and speakers.

The first rule is that of the *split infinitive*: Do not put an adverb between "*to*" and the verb it commands. This rule would make the phrase "to boldly go" substandard. Many people will associate these words with a popular television show and will feel that alternate phrasing would be odd: "boldly to go" or "to go boldly." While it is best to follow this rule in most cases, if the resulting sentence or phrase strikes you as awkward, stiff, or simply pretentious, then abandon the rule for fluidity's sake.

The second rule is to avoid dangling adverbs that don't bear a clear relationship to the word or phrase they modify. Generally, this is a rule that should be observed more firmly—revise your writing when possible to make sure what is being modified is clear. However, the broad qualifier (like "generally" in the preceding sentence or the conjunctive "however" at the beginning of this sentence) can sometimes float about to good or at least passable effect in a less formal sentence or where it does little harm. Moving such semidetached adverbs can create subtle changes in meaning or *emphasis,* however. So care should be taken to consider whether an adverb has been "dangled" so that your *audience* is misled. See *dangling modifier, modifier, awkwardness, conjunctive adverb,* and *revision.*

Like adjectives, adverbs can indicate comparative degrees of a quality or property: "more concretely, most concretely." Almost all adverbs form the comparative and *superlative* by adding "*more*" or "*most*" before the adverb. But there are a few irregular *comparisons* of adverbs: see the entries for *better, best, ill,* and *worse.*

Advice, advise. These two words sound almost alike (near-*homonyms*) but are quite different *parts of speech* with dissimilar meanings. "Advice" is suggestions or guidance given to someone when he or she is "advised" by someone else. The first word is a *noun,* while the second is a *verb.*

Advise. See *advice.*

Affect, effect. Commonly confused, these two words have different meanings despite their somewhat similar sound (near-*homonyms*). "Affect" is both a *noun* and a *verb*. As a verb it means to influence how a thing happens or is experienced; as a noun it has to do with emotions and attitudes and is used principally in psychological texts. "Effect" is also both a noun and a verb: the noun means the result or outcome of some action, while the verb means to make something happen. Just as the noun "affect" is little used in ordinary speech or writing, so "effect" as a verb is not very common. In most cases, the right choice for a verb is "affect," and the right choice for a noun is "effect": "Poverty has a bad effect on people; it affects them adversely." "The prisoners effected their escape, revealing little affect in the process."

African American English. See *black English*.

Afro-American English. See *black English*.

After. *Preposition* governing the *objective case:* "The dog ran after her." *Adverb* of time: "That happened after."

Against. *Preposition* governing the *objective case:* "The politician worked against us."

Agent. The *subject* of a sentence is often the agent of some action, the person or thing that does something.

Agreement. Perhaps the most common and most glaring grammatical errors come with matching the various elements of sentences—*subject* with *verb,* and *pronoun* with *antecedent.*

While the *rules* for properly pairing verb and noun and referent and pronoun are fairly simple, a number of common writing problems (usually inattention or carelessness) too often fracture these important links in *sentences*. The rules of agreement should be treated consistently by all writers because they spell out how readers and listeners should make the connections we want them to between key concepts. If the rules are broken, so are the logical bonds of our ideas, and our *audience* is left adrift to wonder what we mean.

To understand agreement, recall that *nouns* and pronouns can vary in *number* and *person*.

Number simply means that there may be one or more things or people who perform an action in a sentence—who are its subject. If a noun is the subject, it can be singular—one actor or agent—or plural—more than one agent. Verbs usually change their forms for singular or plural subjects: "One elephant trumpets, but two elephants trumpet." Normally, singular verbs with noun subjects add "*s*" or "es" to their simple or normal forms to show that the subject is singular. English retains this form of marking the number of verbs in order to ensure that subjects and verbs clearly indicate agreement.

Person and *gender* are properties of pronouns, which can be used to stand in the place of nouns in *sentences*. Pronouns can indicate not only number but gender ("he," "she") and whether the subject (person) is the same being as others in the sentence: "I," "you," "we," "they," "he," "she," "it." English does not indicate gender distinctions in verb forms (*conjugation*), but it does retain some verb forms that match only with certain persons of subject pronouns: "I am," "we are," "it is." More important, it has a rich array of pronoun forms that must match the person and number of the words the pronouns replace or refer to (their antecedents).

The process of taking into account the number and person of a sentence's subject and fitting those to the correct verb form is called agreement. Why is it sometimes difficult?

Sentences come in many shapes and sizes. Sometimes subjects are rather far from the verbs with which they must agree. Some nouns and pronouns can have different or varying numbers or persons. The number of such words is small, but some of them are tricky to work with. All these factors and others can complicate the process of making verb and subject agree. Let's look at some specific examples of problems.

AGREEMENT OF SUBJECT AND VERB

REMOTE SUBJECT. It is easy to fall into the trap of making a *verb* agree with the closest *noun* even though that word is not the *subject* of the *sentence*. WRONG: "The book containing lists of names and addresses often include errors." RIGHT: "The book . . . includes errors." WRONG: "Many people standing in the line around the theater is impatient." RIGHT: "Many people . . . are impatient." Only careful rereading and revising will catch and correct these errors. Note that many nouns that end in "*s*" are *plural*, but not all. "People" is a plural word. There are also many singular words that end in "s": "electronics," "physics," "mattress," and so on. And remember that some verbs do not form third-*person* singulars with "s": "the man has"; "the woman is."

TITLES OR WORDS AS SUBJECT. *Titles* of works or words treated as things in themselves agree with singular *verbs* even if they contain *plurals* or compound *subjects*: "*War and Peace* is a novel in which war and peace are the subjects discussed." " 'Words' is the plural of word."

INVERTED SUBJECTS. One way to enliven *sentences* is to change the expected *order of words* by putting the *verb* first—to invert the sentence. When you flip verb and *subject,* be sure that the verb agrees with the following *noun* or *pronoun* subject rather than any preceding nouns or pronouns: "Near the cat stand five pigeons." A form of *inversion* is to begin sentences with a general word like "there" and "*is*" or "*are*." It is tempting and a common mistake to begin all such sentences with the singular verb, although the following subject is often plural. WRONG: "There is five pigeons near the cat." RIGHT: "There are five pigeons near the cat."

SUBJECTS LINKED BY "AND." In most cases, *subjects* that consist of two or more *nouns* or *pronouns* linked by "*and*" are *plural*. However, in some cases the pairing of words with "and" indicates a unity so tight that the words are meant to be a single thing and thus agree with a singular form of the verb: "Bacon and eggs is a traditional breakfast." "The bacon and the eggs are on the plate."

SUBJECTS LINKED BY "OR," "EITHER," "NEITHER," AND
"NOR." *Subjects* tied together by the *conjunctions* "*or,*"
"*nor,*" "*either,*" and "*neither*" are not of equal weight.
The *verbs* that follow such compound subjects agree with
the second *noun* or *pronoun* of the linked pair: "Either my
roommates or I am going to flunk out." "Neither the cows
nor the horse stays out in the rain." Generally, the *plural* of
the pair should be the second subject linked and followed by
a plural verb to avoid leading an *audience* to think plural
first and then have to shift into singular later. A singular
subject linked to a plural and followed by a plural verb
somehow sounds more natural to an audience used to
finding more than one subject, however linked, followed by
a plural verb.

SUBJECTS THAT CAN BE EITHER PLURAL OR SINGULAR. Some
collective nouns that stand for groups of things or people
can be treated as either singular or *plural* subjects. American
English normally takes these words to be singular and
matches them to singular *verbs* unless special *emphasis* is
being placed on the activity of the individuals in the
collective, in which case they can be joined to a plural verb.
It is probably better to rewrite such plural use of collectives
rather than make your *audience* wonder what you mean.
But if a collective in the plural sense seems the best way to
convey your idea, such agreements are possible: "The team
plays well on weekends." "Today the team are going to
their homes for a rest." The second *sentence* is grammatically defensible, but it seems a bit forced in modern
American English. (*British English* usually treats such

collectives as plural, making a correct American plural construction sometimes seem like an affectation of British "refinement.")

INDEFINITE PRONOUN SUBJECT. Some *indefinite* pronouns ("*another*," "*anybody*," "*anyone*," "*each*," "either," "everyone," "everything," "*much*," "*neither*," "*nobody*," "no one," "*nothing*," "*one*," "other," "somebody," "someone," and "something") agree with singular *verbs*, while others are treated as *plurals* ("both," "few," "*many*," "others," "*several*"), and some can be used in both ways ("all," "any," "enough," "*more*," "most," "*none*," and "*some*"): "All of the paint spills, and all of the children mop it up." Note that the singular indefinites may be followed by *prepositional phrases* with plural *objects* but still take singular verb forms: "Each of the cats is white."

RELATIVE PRONOUN AS SUBJECT. In dependent *clauses*, *relative pronouns* can refer to either *singular* or *plural* things or people (*antecedents*). The *verb* in the clause agrees with the antecedent: "The car with the four doors that is near me has trouble starting." "Picasso is one of the artists who have an inflated reputation." "Picasso is the one among all those artists who has the most exaggerated reputation."

PREDICATE NOUN VERSUS SUBJECT. Sentences with *linking verbs* should have the *verb* agree with the *subject* and not with the following *predicate noun* (word or words after the linking verb), even if the subject is not the same *number* as the predicate noun: "Artists' reputations are a subject of controversy."

AGREEMENT OF PRONOUN AND ANTECEDENT

Pronouns replace or refer to other words, which usually come before them in *sentences* (*antecedents*). In more complex sentences it takes care to distinguish which words the pronoun relates to and to match them in *number* and *person*. For example, in the previous sentence "them" refers to "words" and, therefore, is third-person plural. If the sentence had said "which word the pronoun relates to," then the proper pronoun would be singular third-person: "*it*."

Problems in making the proper links between pronoun and antecedent commonly arise in distinguishing plurals from singulars, collectives, and *indefinites*. There is also the issue of *gender* to examine.

The use of "*he*" as a generic pronoun that represents both men and women has come to be viewed as restrictive of women and prejudicial. For instance, a sentence that reads "A doctor should keep his instruments clean" ignores and excludes women who are doctors. This sentence can easily be changed by using a more accurate construction: "A doctor should keep his or her instruments clean." Remember to consider your *audience* and always choose appropriate pronouns. This subject is discussed more fully in the entry on *sexist language,* where ways to avoid prejudicial or offensive constructions are also examined.

When antecedents consist of more than one word linked

by "*and*," we have a tendency to assume that the words referred to are *plural* and to follow them with plural pronouns. Sometimes this assumption betrays us: "Dogs and cats have their special traits." "Each dog and cat has its special traits." In the first instance "and" does link a plural antecedent; but in the second sentence, "and" is less important than "each," which is an indefinite pronoun that is singular. The subject in the second sentence means "each dog and each cat taken by itself as a single thing." That is why "each" agrees with a singular *verb* and takes precedence over the seemingly plural antecedent linked by "and."

Similar problems occur with indefinites or collectives as antecedents since these words can vary in number. All of the following sentences are correct: "All of the people had their favorites." "All of the paint poured out of its can." "The orchestra was proud of its performance." "The orchestra shifted in their chairs."

Antecedents linked by "*or*," "nor," "*neither*," "either," and the like also require care in determining person and number. Remember that it is the second element in pairs linked by these *conjunctions* that governs agreement: if a singular word is joined to a plural word by "or," for instance, the plural word dictates that the following pronoun must be plural: "The boy or the men will call their elephant." Avoid writing sentences that link a plural antecedent and a following singular one with "or" because such sentences often sound awkward: "The women or the girl will call her elephant." Rewrite such sentences to make clear who is doing what: "The women will call their elephant, or the girl will call hers."

Appositives—nouns or pronouns that add information to other nouns or pronouns—also must agree in person, number, and *case:* "The president awarded the medal to Smith, teacher of the year." See the entry on appositives for more examples and details.

Ain't. "Ain't" should appear only in informal speech, correspondence, or humorous writing. No *standard English* statement should include it.

All ready, already. "All ready" is a compound adjective *phrase* that means someone or something is totally prepared. "Already" is an *adverb* that means before or previously. See also *adjective.*

All right. A compound adjective *phrase;* it is not spelled "alright," a *colloquial* form used only to report or record less than standard speech. See also *adjective.*

All together, altogether. Don't confuse "all together"— everyone or everything assembled or at the same time ("the giraffes were all together")—with the *adverb* "altogether"—completely or totally ("the giraffes were altogether edgy").

Allude, elude. Although these words sound about the same (near-*homonyms*) they mean different things. "Allude" means to refer to or note in passing. "Elude" means to evade or escape.

Allusion, illusion. These near-*homonyms* (sound-alikes) differ in sense. "Allusion" is a reference to something, while "illusion" is a deception or misperception.

All ways, always. Like many *compound words* using "all," "all ways" differs from a similar merged form of the two words—"always." "All ways" means in all possible manners, while "always" means for all time or every time: "The freelancer is always trying all ways to make a living."

Along. *Preposition* governing the *objective case:* "The boat sailed along the coast."

A lot. Never "alot."

Alphabet. See individual *languages* for their alphabets and how to alphabetize words in them. See also *alphabetization*.

Alphabetization. Two systems exist for putting words into alphabetical order, and both of them are correct. Choose the one that is commonly used by your *audience* or that you find better suits your purposes.

    Word-by-word alphabetizing arranges lists of words by letter order until a space is reached in a *compound word,* at which point it arranges all words that begin with the first word of the compound by the order of the word that follows, and then moves on to the next word, compound or not. For example, in word-by-word alphabetizing "fire dog," "fire screen," and "fire station" would come before "fireboat," "firehouse," and "fireside," since each of the compounds of "fire" plus another word after a space is seen as a category of "fire."

In **letter-by-letter** alphabetizing spaces are ignored, with the result that the words in the example in the previous paragraph would be alphabetized as follows: "fireboat, fire dog, firehouse, fire screen, fireside, fire station." Both methods of alphabetization ignore *hyphens* and other internal *punctuation* of words or names. This book is arranged by the letter-by-letter method.

There are elaborate procedures, *rules,* and customs for specialized alphabetizing systems used by scholars, libraries, *dictionaries,* and for other purposes. If you need to work in such a system with a long list of terms that present difficult ordering decisions, then it is best to follow the standard guides or in-house documents that are used to resolve alphabetizing problems.

Already. See *all ready.*

Also. An *adverb* always spelled as one word, never "all so."

Altar, alter. This *homonym* pair (sound-alike words) combines a *noun* and a *verb.* The noun "altar" is a sacred place or platform, while the verb "alter" means to change: "The sexton altered the altar by lowering it."

Alter. See *altar.*

Although. A *subordinating conjunction*: "Although you speak the truth, I still don't trust you."

Altogether. See *all together*.

Always. See *all ways*.

Am. The first-person singular, present tense of *be:* "I am." "I am writing." Also see *agreement, auxiliary, conjugation, number,* and *person*.

A.M. This *abbreviation* of the *Latin* phrase "<u>ante meridien</u>" means before noon. It is used to distinguish times from the two halves of the day where a twelve-hour clock or system of time notation is common.

Where twenty-four-hour clocks are used, the abbreviations A.M. and P.M. are not used, since there is no possibility of confusing one in the morning with thirteen in the afternoon. Since English speakers who write in twenty-four-hour systems still tend to say "one in the afternoon" rather than "thirteen," the abbreviations still creep into speech even where the twelve-hour clock is no longer used.

The standard use of these abbreviations has them follow the time, in small capital letters, and with *periods. Lower case* and no periods are acceptable in many *styles* and in less formal writing, though you should avoid confusion with the *verb "am."*

Among, between. The *preposition* "between" is used only when you are talking or writing about two things or people. "Among" links more than two things or people: "I split the assignment between John and Joan." "I divided the task among Joe, Jean, and Jim."

This simple *rule* changes if there are more than two

things or people that are conceived as separated into natural or logical pairs: "There are four bridges between the three islands." Writing "There are four bridges among the three islands" would suggest that the three islands shared four bridges that might or might not link one to the other, while the initial example means that the bridges run from one island to the next.

An. See *a*.

And. The *coordinating conjunction* "and" links two or more things or people, *phrases, clauses,* or other grammatical, logical, or natural entities. Usually, the things that "and" puts together are of equal weight or significance ("coordinate"). Avoid the construction "and/or" unless the logic of a statement must be extremely precise.

A *comma* usually comes before "and" when it links more than two *nouns, pronouns, adjectives, adverbs,* phrases, or other words or groups of words that are not independent clauses: "The man, the woman, and the boy looked at the pond, the duck standing on the shore, and the large, red, and shiny umbrella." This poor, *run-on* sentence illustrates the use of the comma in several instances of a *series* joined by "and," and it shows why most *standard English* styles prefer to retain the second comma in such series—to make it clear what belongs to each series and when a new series begins. However, many *styles* prefer the economy of dropping the second comma in a series (particularly newspapers and often business writing). Adopt the style that is most likely to suit your *audience*.

Commas also appear before "and" when it introduces an independent clause: "The woman looked at the duck, and the man stood on the shore." Be sure not to use a comma before "and" when it links compound *verbs* or compound *subjects*, adjectives, *predicates,* and so on. WRONG: "The man, and the woman looked longingly to sea." No comma is needed in this sentence.

Traditionally, writing teachers and guides have warned against starting *sentences* with "and." But many good writers commonly do so to good effect. Just as too strict observance of this *rule* limits your flexibility in writing, so overindulgence in breaking it is not wise. Too many sentences that begin with "and" can indicate a failure on your part to think through the logical and grammatical connections between your thoughts and the way you express them. And it can get boring.

An other, another. Distinguish between the *compound word* "an other" (which means "a different": "You saw a heron, but I saw an other one") and the *indefinite* pronoun "another" (which means one more of the same kind or number: "You saw three herons, and I saw another three"). See *pronoun*.

Another. See *an other*.

Antecedent. It is important to keep in mind the *number* and *person* of words to which *pronouns* refer or which they replace—their "antecedents"—so that you ensure they

agree. Many grammatical mistakes are made because antecedents are not carefully determined. See *agreement*.

Anybody, anything. These *indefinite* pronouns are third-
person singular. Note that ''any body'' is a phrase referring
to some physical being and is not the same as ''anybody,''
which means any person: ''Anybody can see that any body
lying on the floor is a murder victim.'' See *pronoun*.

Any one, anyone. Don't confuse ''any one''—a phrase
referring to any single thing or person—and ''anyone,''
which is an indefinite pronoun that agrees with third-*person*
singular *pronouns* and *verbs*. ''Any one of the people will
know the answer.'' ''Anyone knows that answer.''

Anyone. See *any one*.

Anything. See *anybody*.

Apostrophe. Apostrophes are *punctuation* marks used to
form *possessives*, *contractions*, and a few *plurals*. Be
careful not to use apostrophes where they are not needed.
    Possessives are formed by adding an apostrophe and ''*s*''
to singular or collective words, or plural words that don't
end in ''s,'' no matter how they are spelled (''Zeus's
thunderbolt,'' ''the boss's idea,'' ''the team's captain,''
''children's manners'') or by adding an apostrophe to plural
words that do end in ''s'' (''dogs' fleas''). Possessive
pronouns don't use apostrophes. See *collective noun* and
collective pronoun.
    Contractions use apostrophes to replace omitted letters

("don't," "can't"). No matter how many letters are dropped from or changed in a contraction, only one apostrophe appears to mark the shortening of the word ("will not" becomes "won't").

Plurals are usually formed by adding "*s*" without an apostrophe to words ("elephants," "1990s," "three capital Ds"). However, in some cases this might prove confusing, and an apostrophe is added before the "*s*": "Ph.D.'s," "A's are good grades," "I's are thin letters," "Look at the x's on the graph."

Appositive. When *nouns* or *pronouns* do not convey enough information on their own, other nouns or pronouns are sometimes put next to them to add identity or information to the initial words. The added nouns or pronouns are said to be "appositives": "The car, a Ford, was slow"; "My accountant, Smith, said she would help"; "Tolstoy's novel *War and Peace* is long."

Note that some of the appositives in the examples are set off by *commas* while others are not. The distinction being made here is between a *restrictive phrase* and *nonrestrictive phrase*, one of the most confusing and troublesome concepts in *grammar*. Most simply put, nonrestrictive phrases add information that is not essential to the sense of a sentence while restrictive phrases provide more specific, required information. Thus in the examples, the car is slow no matter what its brand name, which is added to clarify the *sentence* but which does not introduce any information that affects the basic notion of a slow car (presumably not all Fords are slow and some cars of other brands are slow). Similarly, the accountant's offer to help does not depend on her name, which is nonessential, additional information in this sentence. But the name of Tolstoy's novel is required to distinguish it from his other works; therefore, no comma appears to set off the appositive *War and Peace*.

Appositive pronouns need to agree with their *antecedents* in *gender*, *number*, and *case*: "The doctor helped all of us, Jane, Jim, and me. She, the doctor, applied all possible remedies, all her tricks of the trade, and her solid scientific knowledge. We gave her a check, our form of payment." See also *agreement*.

Elaborate appositive phrases or *lists* can be set off from the nouns or pronouns they supplement by *colons*, as we have done with many of the examples in this book: "We presented the instances in which one uses apostrophes: possessives, contractions, and some plurals."

Appraise, apprise. These near-*homonyms* (sound-alikes) are often confused. "Appraise" means to estimate a value of something. "Apprise" means to inform or keep informed.

Apprise. See *appraise*.

Arabic. There are many systems for representing Arabic language words in English letters. Consult a reliable source book or the style guide in force for your *audience* to be sure of the preferred method for rendering such names as "Qaddafi" ("Gaddafi," "Quadaffi," "Kadafi") and "Koran" ("Quran," etc.). If someone has expressed a preference that his or her name be spelled a certain way, that request should take precedence over any *rule* or *style* book.

Some figures from the Arab world's past and some places have been given Western names or versions of their names that have become accepted in English: Avicenna ("ibn-Sina" in Arabic) and Mecca ("Makka"). The choice of which form to use depends on your audience's expectations—you might abandon the common English form for the Arabic when writing for Arabic specialists, nationals, or the like.

Capitalization, punctuation, and other grammatical concepts are also represented in different ways in different systems of transliteration that bear greater or lesser resemblance to Arabic originals, depending on one's writing purpose and point of view. Some systems represent sound rather accurately, while others strive for letter-by-letter accuracy, and so on. All systems struggle with the *accents* (also called "diacritical marks") that represent breathing points and sounds in Arabic. Some transliterations become quite complex and are suitable only for scholarly writing or linguistic treatises. Others simply omit this important feature of the languages. Whatever you choose or need to use, be consistent and sensitive to your audience's need for authenticity versus visual or graphic complexity. See *languages.*

Are. The second-*person* singular and first-, second-, and third-person plural *present tense* of "*be*": "we are," "you (singular or plural) are," "they are." "You are reading." Also see *agreement, auxiliary, conjugation, number,* and *person.*

Are, our. In some speech *dialects* these words sound more like each other than in others. But they are still commonly confused by writers who might not say or hear them as the same. The first is a *verb* form of "*be*" (second-*person* singular and all forms of the plural *present tense*), while the second is a *possessive* pronoun (first-person *plural*): " 'Are our homes in danger?' we asked."

Around. See *about*.

Article. "*A*," "*an*," and "*the*" are articles. They come before *nouns* to indicate degrees of definitiveness: "a house, the house." See entries for the specific words for more information on their use, *spelling*, and meaning.

As. The *subordinating conjunction* "*as*" should not be confused in *standard English* with the *preposition* "*like*." "*As*" introduces *clauses* rather than simple noun *objects*: "I see it as you do." Often the *verb* in the clause that follows "*as*" is omitted: "The consultant acted as a troubleshooter [would]." Dropping the verb makes it appear that "*as*" is a preposition followed by a *noun*; for that reason, people sometimes make the mistake of using "*like*" when the *conjunction* "*as*" is called for. This sometimes also leads to misuse of pronoun *cases*. WRONG: "The speaker talks like me." RIGHT: "The speaker talks as I do." See *pronoun*.

The confusion of "*like*" and "*as*" has become so common that the grammatically correct *usage* sometimes sounds stilted or affected. If your writing or speaking seems to suffer from this distortion, adopt the form that makes you more comfortable or that fits your *audience* better. But for formal moments, the standard *style* is the better choice.

Sentences like "He was frightened as this was his first visit to the dentist" are not acceptable because it is unclear whether "as" refers to time or causation. Was he afraid because this was his first visit to a dentist, or was he frightened on the occasion of his first visit to the dentist? The distinction is perhaps minor in this example, but it should be made clear in other sentences by using words like "because" or "when" instead of "as." See also *simile*.

Asian languages. The many languages of Asia are often written with different characters than are used in English, which means that there are differing ways of representing words and names in those languages in English. Follow appropriate or accepted *style* guides, *rule* books, and so on, allowing personal preferences to overrule any system or approach. If a person named Ching prefers to be called "Qing," so be it.

Note that some countries have expressed preferences for certain spellings ("Beijing" has largely replaced "Peking," for instance, along with "Mao Tse Tung" giving way to "Mao Dsedong" or other versions). And countries have changed their names ("Cambodia" became "Kampuchea") and names of cities within them ("Saigon" to "Ho Chi Minh City"). Consult up-to-date references to make sure you are using the most recent and appropriate *spellings* for your *audience* as well as consistent and sensible *capitalization, punctuation*, and so on. See *languages*.

Assure, ensure, insure. These words are commonly confused because they are similar in sound and *spelling*. But they differ markedly in meaning and proper use.

"Assure" means to convince or promise. "Ensure" means to make certain or safe. "Insure" means about the same as "ensure," but it is most commonly and properly used to refer to specific protection of items or people for money: "To ensure that our children will be well provided for, we will insure each other and our property."

Asterisk. The asterisk *symbol* (*) can be used to mark special parts of writing: indented or separated *paragraphs* for *emphasis;* footnotes or endnotes; or subdivisions of chapters, *lists,* or other segments of writing. Don't overuse asterisks—their role is to be a special marker, and specialness disappears with repetition. Asterisks also should not be used in place of the strings of three or four periods called *ellipses,* which indicate omitted words in *quotations.*

At. *Preposition* governing the *objective case:* "Kim threw the stick at him." Don't add "at" to "where" statements unless it has an *object.* WRONG: "Where is it at?" RIGHT: "Where is it?"

Ate. See *eat.*

Audience. Audience means the people to whom you are speaking and writing, whether a single person well known to you or humankind through the ages to come.

Most of us write or speak a good deal in business or public relationships, toward which many of the points in this book are directed—the general, standard readers and speakers of English who are interested in hearing or reading what you have in mind as clearly, briefly, and efficiently as possible. You undoubtedly address many other audiences in your daily, personal, educational, and other lives. In each instance you need to consider with care who your audience is and what set of grammatical *rules* they will expect you to observe in your communications with them. If you don't know your audience personally—because it is too big, hidden from you behind business or bureaucratic titles, or simply because you have not yet had a chance to meet with it or figure out who its members are—then your best choice is to follow the rules of *standard English* as closely as possible.

If you don't know your audience, you run the risk that those who hear or read you will see grammatical mistakes or attempts to play with the rules of grammar as evidence of your inability to speak or write clearly or correctly. Perhaps as important, those who detect grammatical errors in your statements will have to waste time figuring out just what you meant to say or how you meant to say it. Grammatical errors thus certainly fail to meet one of the goals of ordinary communication—efficient transmission of information— and they probably undermine *clarity* and brevity as well. We sometimes recognize that our writing or speaking doesn't meet audience expectations when those we address don't respond as we want.

It is true that many rules of *grammar* are less than absolute, open to interpretation, and flexible, depending on circumstances and your stylistic and personal preferences. But all such invitations to bending or breaking the rules of standard grammar have to be weighed against how such departures from common practices will be taken by your audience. If you are completely confident that a substandard construction like "ain't" will amuse or be tolerated by those who listen to or read you, then use the word. If you are at all uncertain how such a word—or any other mistake or deviation from standards—will be received, then stick to the rules.

Briefly put, audience is the single greatest determining factor in your choice of rules to observe, twist, or abandon. Be very sure of your ground—of your skill as a writer or speaker, which amounts to your ability to judge and properly address your audience in an appropriate *style*—if you choose anything but the strictest observation of grammatical rules.

Auxiliary. *Verbs* are often made up of more than one word. The verb words in such clusters break down into main verbs and helping verbs, which are also known as "auxiliary verbs." The most common auxiliaries are "*be*," "*can*," "*could*," "*have*," "*may*," "*might*," "*must*," "*shall*," "*should*," "*will*," and "*would*." "Be," "*do*," and "have" and their various forms can also be main verbs.

Auxiliaries combine with many verb forms to produce *tenses*, the *passive* voice, *moods*, and other verb phrases and effects. See also *voice, main form*.

A while, awhile. "Awhile," an *adverb*, modifies *verbs*. "A while," a compound of an *article* and a *noun*, cannot modify verbs but can be the *object* of prepositions: "The law will stand awhile, which means that in a while it might be repealed." See *modifier*.

Awhile. See *a while*.

Awkwardness. There is no clear definition of "awkwardness." It is simply something felt or noticed by a writer or *audience* in speech or writing. If you sense it in your work, look for some common symptoms:

- *Subject, verb,* and *subject complement* are far apart or not clearly linked together.
- *Clauses* do not tie neatly and clearly together because they are too long or too wordy.
- The *antecedents* of *modifiers* or *pronouns* are unclear, remote, or not linked carefully and clearly to each other.

Many other mistakes contribute to awkwardness. Try reading sentences aloud to listen for mistakes, then try other versions of sentences to see if they sound and work better. See *editing* and *revision.*

B

Bad, badly. "Bad" is an *adjective* and can therefore only modify *nouns*; "badly" is an *adverb* that modifies only *verbs*: "This really is a bad manuscript, but I feel badly about its rejection." See *modifier*.

Badly. See *bad*.

B.C., B.C.E. These *abbreviations* stand for "before Christ" and "before the common era," and they refer to the time before the birth of Christ. They are added to dates to distinguish where the dates fall in the commonly accepted Western dating system. These abbreviations are usually not spelled out, follow the whole date, and appear in capital letters with *periods*. Using *lower case* or dropping the periods is acceptable in many *styles* and less formal writing, though *A.D.* ("anno Domini" or after Christ), B.C., and B.C.E. usually appear in more formal works, where the standard *rule* should be followed. See *capitalization*.

In many Western cultures, years are counted forward from the birth of Christ to the present ("A.D. 1989 was four years ago"), while years are counted in reverse order back from that date into so-called prehistory ("426 B.C. is a later date than 537 B.C. but comes before A.D. 426"). Of course, non-Western cultures don't all see time this way, and even many Western cultures use alternate systems. Jews (or at least some Israelis) use the Hebrew calendar that sets the beginning of time at the Creation, which took place, in their view, about 5,500 years ago. Some people prefer not to date time from the birth of Christ but accept the commonest Western dating system by adding C.E. and B.C.E. (after the "common era" or before it) to dates.

B.C.E. See *B.C.*

Be. "Be" is the *main form* of the common *linking verb* and *auxiliary*. In its many forms it is probably the most used verb or verb form in English, often overused in *bland writing* or weak writing. Because its *conjugation* is irregular, "be" is also frequently misused. See *agreement* and *irregular verbs*.

The forms of "be" are

	SINGULAR	PLURAL
Present tense		
First *person*	I *am*	we are
Second person	you *are*	you are
Third person	he/she/it *is*	they are
Past tense		
First person	I *was*	we were
Second person	you *were*	you were
Third person	he/she/it was	they were

The *future tense* is regular ("I will be . . ."); the present *participle* and *gerund* are "being"; and the past participle is "been."

Errors in the use of forms of "be" are quite common.

Some contend that many such "errors" are in fact dialectical *usages* that should not be seen as incorrect (see *dialect*). However, any statement in *standard English* or that is likely to be judged by your *audience* by the standards of formal English should not contain either errors or dialectical forms. Thus "I be here" might be admissible in some specific circumstances that accept dialect or nonstandard speech or writing, but such constructions should never appear in everyday business, school, or other common communications. Also see *black English*, *grammar*, *rules*, and *style*.

As a linking verb, "be" and its forms suggest some sort of general equality or equivalency between the *subject* of a *sentence* and its *complement* rather than some action the subject does to an *object*: "The dog is a puppy" rather than "The dog bites a cat." The words "a puppy" in this example are a *predicate noun* in the nominative *case*. These grammatical definitions are important only when you are dealing with *pronouns* in the predicates of sentences with linking verbs like "be." Pronouns change forms from *nominative* to *objective case,* and you should, according to the rules of grammar, follow a linking verb with a nominative: "It is I." "The group that will do the project is we." The problem with this rule is that usage has changed so much that strictly correct constructions like "It is I" have come to sound pretentious in many circumstances.

Depending on the audience you are addressing, you need to choose how closely you will follow the rule of putting nominative pronouns after linking verbs. In a college paper, follow the rule strictly. In other communications, you might well follow usage that is less stringent. Better, revise the sentence to avoid facing the problem and perhaps causing your audience to wonder about what you have said or written: "It is Jane." "We are the group that will do the project."

Beat, beat, beaten. An *irregular verb* in its main, *past tense*, and past *participle* forms.

Beaten. See *beat*.

Became. See *become*.

Because, because of. As a *subordinating conjunction*, "because" links dependent *clauses* to main or independent clauses and defines the relationship between the clauses as causal. Be sure that clauses you link with "because" actually have a cause-and-effect linkage, and be sure not to start too many *sentences* with "because" (because it gets boring after a while and because the conjunction "because" commands readers or listeners to accept your view of causality, which they may not agree with or may come to resent).

Note that "because of" is usually used to indicate causation in which a clause is seen as the effect: "The day loomed long because of the many tests we had to take." When the effect is a *noun* directly followed by a *linking verb* like "*be*," cause-and-effect relationships should be indicated by "due to": "The long day will be due to many tests to be taken."

Because of. See *because*.

Become, became, become. An *irregular verb* in its main, *past tense,* and past *participle* forms. See *linking verbs.*

Before. *Preposition* governing the *objective case*: "The teacher stood before us and lectured." *Adverb* of time: "The guide got there before him."

Began. See *begin.*

Begin, began, begun. An *irregular verb* in its main, *past tense,* and past *participle* forms.

Begun. See *begin.*

Behind. *Preposition* governing the *objective case*: "In the photograph the statue stood behind her."

Below. *Preposition* governing the *objective case*: "The shark prowled below him."

Beneath. *Preposition* governing the *objective case*: "The earth shook beneath him during the quake."

Beside, besides. Although *usage* no longer makes so clear a distinction between "beside" (next to, alongside of) and "besides" (in addition to, moreover), *standard English* prefers that the words not be confused: "I sat beside the door. Two other people besides me sat beside the door." While "beside" is sometimes acceptable in the sense of "in addition to," "besides" is a clearly incorrect spelling in the sense of "next to."

Besides. See *beside*.

Best. The *superlative* degree of *good* is "best": "That is the best of the three examples." "The rose smells best of all the flowers." Don't confuse "best" with "*better*"— "best" is used when more than two things are being compared, while "better" compares only two things to each other.

Better. The comparative degree of "*good*" is "better": "That is a better example than the other one." "The rose smells better than the lily does." When *comparisons* are between an individual and a group of several others seen as a unit or collective, use "better" rather than "best" or "best of": "The fiddler plays better than all the other musicians." "The fiddler is better than the rest." Don't confuse "better" with "*best*."

Between. See *among*.

Beyond. *Preposition* governing the *objective case*: "The process was beyond him."

Bit. See *bite*.

Bite, bit, bitten. An *irregular verb* in its main, *past tense*, and past *participle* forms.

Bitten. See *bite*.

Black English. African-Americans sometimes speak and write in one or more *dialects* that are lumped together under the term "black English." Like any dialect, black English is acceptable only in nonstandard statements. But also like any dialect, black English is not clearly distinct from *standard English*, nor is it always clear under what circumstances dialect or standard English should be used. As with all *grammar* and usage *rules*, apply those of standard English whenever you have any doubt that the standards of dialect might be taken as defective or deficient.

Bland writing. Although weak or bland writing is not strictly a grammatical or *usage* problem, it does violate one of the key principles of this book: serving the *audience* for your statements with *clarity*, brevity, and *efficiency*. Bland writing is often clear, concise, and economical in its presentation of ideas or information. But it also lulls readers or listeners into inattention, so that they sometimes lose track of what you are trying to convey. Thus clarity can be obscured, brevity can be lost to repetition, and efficiency vanishes.

There are no simple *rules* for avoiding bland writing, and the purpose of this book does not provide for a long exploration of the symptoms, causes, and cures for dull writing. But keep in mind that overuse of "*be*" and other vague *linking verbs*, repetition of the same constructions or patterns of writing, and heavy reliance on either very simple or very complex sentences can produce bland writing. Consult guides for writers, *style* manuals, and similar sources for more help in enlivening your writing; and remember that you have a duty to keep your audience interested as well to meet their need for correct, clear, brief, and effective communication.

Blew. See *blow*.

Block quotations. In most nonacademic writing *quotations* can be set off simply by enclosing the quoted words in *quotation marks* and proper *punctuation*. However, at times your *audience* will not be easily able to grasp where a long quotation starts or ends, or whether what they are reading is in fact still part of a long quotation that started sometime ago but may or may not have ended.

A simple strategy in writing to ensure that longer passages are clearly marked is to indent them, making a "block quotation." Such blocks can be introduced by simple phrases like "Smith said" followed by a *comma* or *colon*, some space to set off the block, and then the indented passage. Or some small part of the quotation can appear in unindented text along with transitional words that introduce the block: "The speech was brilliant. 'Ask not,' Kennedy said,

> what your country can do for you. . . ."

Block quotes are not surrounded by quotation marks. If the block includes quotations of words from someone other than the original speaker, those passages are set off by quotes:

> Professor Brown liked the speech. The academic repeated one of the most memorable statements in it, "Kennedy said, 'Ask not what your country can do for you,' and then he moved on to other topics. I liked that." The professor then talked about the meaning of political speeches.

If your audience will be interested in the source of your block quotation, the simplest way to present it is in *parentheses* directly after the passage:

> . . . but what you can do for your country (Kennedy, *Collected Speeches*, p. 79).

There are other more elaborate procedures and rules in various systems for indicating the source of a quotation and showing it in a document. Consult a *style* manual or writing guide recommended by your school, business, or agency if you need to adopt a specific system of citing or presenting sources for block or other quotations.

Block quotation is a form of *emphasis* that can be applied to your own words in a written document. Indented passages stand out even if they are not quotations from others.

Blow, blew, blown. An *irregular verb* in its main, *past tense*, and past *participle* forms.

Blown. See *blow*.

Bold type. Darkened, thickened letters in print are called ''bold'' or ''boldface.'' Such letters often appear in *titles*, captions, and similar places where *emphasis* is desired to call attention to something. The alphabetical subjects in the entries throughout this book appear in bold type.

Both . . . and. The *correlative conjunctions* ''both . . . and'' are used to link two equal things or people: ''Both Mary and John give excellent speeches.'' No *comma* should stand before "and" in this construction, and the agreeing *verb* should be in the *plural*. See *agreement*.

Bracket. The squarish *punctuation* marks ([. . .]) used in some circumstances to set off added or supplementary material are called "brackets." Their main function is to indicate a secondary level of enclosure of *sentence* elements within *parentheses*: "The value of gold ($350 [2,100 francs] on September 4) has a close relationship to inflation." If it is possible to avoid such complex constructions, which are hard for readers to follow unless they are used to such a *style* (as scientists are), you should do so.

Brackets are also used (usually in more scholarly writing) to insert words into *quotations* that weren't there in the first place but that the writer thinks are necessary to make the quotation comprehensible to the reader: "Kennedy said, 'Ask not what your country can do for you but [ask] what you can do for your country.' " The purpose of such insertions is usually not to indicate opinions about the matter being quoted but to supply bridge words or other aids to the reader. Avoid using brackets to set off criticisms or other views of quotes. WRONG: "He said, 'Ask not [well, why shouldn't we ask?]. . . .' " Move such commentary to separate sentences, allowing the source of the ideas you want to annotate the courtesy of having his or her say before your thoughts intrude on the statement.

Break, broke, broken. An *irregular verb* in its main, *past tense,* and past *participle* forms.

Bring, brought, brought. An *irregular verb* in its main, *past tense,* and past *participle* forms.

British English. *Standard English* in America differs from correct English in Great Britain (as well as in Australia, Canada, India, New Zealand, and other parts of the world where English is the first, official, or common language). It is usually seen as an error, an affectation, or a substandard performance to apply the standards of one English where another is commonly accepted. But, as with the lines between *dialect* and standard speech, the boundaries between national or regional versions of English are often fuzzy and subject to the constraints of *audience* preferences and the speaker or writer's skill at playing with conventions and expectations.

In general, the simplest *rule* to follow is: When in doubt, strictly observe the standards of your native language or version of English. Attempts to emulate British or other non-American versions of English can prove embarrassing to you or insulting to your audience. Of course, when you are in another country, you must adopt some of its *usages* and *vocabulary* in order to be understood. Insisting on American standard English when talking to an Australian waiter is just as pointless as trying to sound like a British lord or lady if you aren't one.

Broke. See *break.*

Broken. See *break.*

Brought. See *bring.*

Build, built, built. An *irregular verb* in its main, *past tense,* and past *participle* forms.

Built. See *build.*

Burn, burned, burned. An *irregular verb* in its main, *past tense,* and past *participle* forms.

Burned. See *burn.*

Burst, burst, burst. An *irregular verb* in its main, *past tense,* and past *participle* forms.

But. The *coordinating conjunction* "but" links two more or less equivalent things, people, or parts of a *sentence*: "I watered the flowers but not the plant." "The flowers bloomed, but the plant eventually died." When two *nouns, pronouns,* or *phrases* are joined by "but," no *comma* comes before the conjunction. When two independent *clauses* connect with "but," as in the second sentence in the example, a comma comes at the end of the first clause. *Series* of more than two things or clauses joined by "but" should have a comma before "but": "I came, I saw, but I didn't conquer."

Buy. See *by.*

By, bye, buy. Don't confuse the *preposition* of agency or time "by" ("The work is being done by Chris; it will be finished by ten.") with its *homonyms* "bye" (a short version of "good-bye," or not having to take part in a round of competition: "The high-ranking tennis players get a bye in the preliminaries and don't have to play.") and "buy" (purchase). Note that "buy" has irregular forms in the *past tense* and past *participle*: "buy, bought, bought." See *irregular verbs*.

Bye. See *by*.

C

Ca. This *abbreviation* of the word "circa" means "almost," "about," or "approximately." It is properly used primarily in footnotes or endnotes or highly technical writing and is best avoided in the main text of *standard English* writing or speaking. Replace it with one of the words that define it or one of their *synonyms*.

Came. See *come*.

Can, may. Distinguish carefully between "can," which refers to physical ability or opportunity to act, and "may," which suggests permission or potential to act: "J. R. can act (has the ability to do so) and may appear in the next production (it is possible J. R. will appear)." "If J. R.'s parents allow it, J. R. may appear (if J. R. gets permission)."

Can't. The *contraction* of "can" and "not" or "cannot" is "can't." It shouldn't be used in most formal writing.

Capitalization. As with so many grammar *rules,* those for capitalization are both simple and complex, both rigid and flexible, and subject to the demands of *audience* or circumstances.

The complexity stems from the large number of possible applications of *upper-case* letters; the flexibility comes from the use of larger upper-case letters for *emphasis* as well as to mark the many standard properties of *nouns* that require capitalization; and the adjustments to the expectations of your readers lead to choices among, as well as careful application of, the rules that follow. The standards below are comprehensive, but more variants and possibilities can be found in *style* manuals and writing guides designed for specific circumstances like scholarly writing, business documents, government papers, and so on. Consult the guide that is appropriate to your needs.

First Words

English *sentences* normally begin with a capital letter. So do sentences of quoted speech: ''The poet said, 'This is fine.' '' First words of lines of poetry often also start with capitals, although the fact that lines of poetry are not all sentences may lead writers to start some lines with *lower-case* letters. Personal taste or preference can also lead to a decision not to capitalize first lines of poetry.

First words of whole sentences that follow a *colon* are often capitalized: ''We can summarize the rule as follows: There is no need to capitalize every line of poetry.'' Whole sentences contained within other sentences and set off by *dashes* or *parentheses* are not capitalized: ''State the capitalization rule—the rule is clear—and follow it.'' Whole sentences set off on their own within parentheses are capitalized: ''That is the rule. (Some authorities disagree.)''

Titles, captions, headings, and similar clusters of words used to label things or to display or emphasize words also usually start with capitals. There is more flexibility about whether words that follow in such displays are capitalized, with elements of type design and other considerations of *style* coming into play. The larger size of capital letters is also often a way to contribute to the display property of word clusters that stand apart from other text, and therefore, capitalization is a common device in such text fragments.

PROPER NOUNS—NAMES

When people's *names* include *titles,* both are usually capitalized: President Bush, Terrence Cardinal O'Connor, Professor Harner, Dr. Slade, Aunt Sue. But the titles alone are commonly not capitalized: "In Washington I saw the president." To show respect for the offices represented by titles, some writers capitalize the titles whether used with a name or not, while other writers use *lower-case* letters.

Rules and variations for capitalization of such parts of names as "de," "von," "ap," "ter," "bin," "ibn," and the like are too complex to review here. Check sources for the language from which such names come as well as personal preferences.

Capitalization of things or abstractions is used at times when personification is intended: "when Nature brings her warm rains" or "as Death unleased his fury." However, personification may assign stereotypical characteristics to common words (as in the examples above). Guard your writing against such biases, however subtle. See also *sexist language.*

TRADEMARK NAMES. Many objects or products have trade names that are usually capitalized: Chevrolet, Honda,

Coke, and Xerox, for example. While it is not uncommon
to refer to colas or photocopies in general as "cokes" or
"xeroxes," the trademark holders aren't very pleased with
such usages because they think a capitalized use suggests
the trademarked product and might lead to sales. In more
formal writing, especially when rights to products and their
names can be an issue, it is necessary to preserve commercial capitalization. When in doubt as to whether a name is
trademarked, refer to a style manual that lists brand names.

GEOGRAPHICAL NAMES. Places, geographical or topograph-
ical features that are named, and large segments of the
world are usually capitalized: Denver, the Mall (in London,
not the local shopping center), Morton Street, Lake
Naivasha, the Rift Valley, the Western Hemisphere, the
West. When you refer to places without a proper *name,* use
lower case: "When I was at Lake Naivasha, I noticed that
the lake is becoming polluted." Similarly, city, state, or
county names are usually capitalized in official form and
order but use lower case in less formal order: "the Republic
of France"; "the French republic." And compass directions
are not capitalized when they do not stand for a region:
"The rider headed west." "The rodeo rider lit out for the
West."

SCIENTIFIC NAMES. *Latin* scientific names of animals and
plants have the genus, the first word of the name, capitalized
(and are usually in *italics*): "*Bucephala clangula clangula.*" However, for common names of creatures and
plants, capitalize only those parts of the names that are
proper nouns in their own right: "Barrow's goldeneye."

Astronomical bodies with specific names are capitalized: "the Milky Way," "Mars." But generic terms such as "planet," "galaxy," and the like are *lower case*: "comet Kohotek," "the Spider nebula."

ETHNIC NAMES. Names of groups of people with established cultural or geographical identities are usually capitalized: "Yanomama," "French," "Asian," "Native American," "Portuguese." Words referring to more generic populations are usually *lower case*: "black," "white."

NAMES OF ORGANIZATIONS. Like place names, these *proper nouns* are capitalized in formal use and *lower case* in less formal or less complete usage: "New York City Council," "city council," "the council"; "Touchstone Company," "the company." National governmental bodies often retain capitals: "United States Congress," "the Congress"; "the House of Commons," "Commons." Political parties and movements usually capitalize only the specific name and not the words "party," "movement," "bloc," and the like: "Democratic party."

NAMES OF PERIODS OR TIMES. Calendar *dates* are capitalized but not seasons: "November," "fall." Larger segments of time that are named are capitalized, but centuries are not: "the Middle Ages," "the thirteenth century." Many such periods that include words like "era," "age," or "period" are not capitalized unless they include a proper name: "colonial period," "Victorian era," "nuclear age." Some widely recognized periods are often capitalized: "Stone Age."

NAMES OF EVENTS. Usage varies widely, although capitalization of important events is common: "Industrial Revolution," "Battle of Britain."

RELIGIOUS NAMES. Names of the deity, saints, holy persons and their titles, holy writings and their major divisions, rites or services, important religious concepts or events, churches and synagogues, and denominations and sects are usually capitalized, especially by participants in specific religions.

NAMES OF VEHICLES. Specific names of airplanes, ships, trains, and other vehicles are usually capitalized (and in *italics* or underlined): "*Enola Gay,*" "*Challenger,*" "*Bismark.*" Makes, brands, classes, and types of such vehicles are usually just capitalized: "Polaris submarines," "T-10 tanks."

TITLES OF WORKS

WHOLE WORKS. *Titles* of whole books, magazines, newspapers, plays, musical works, paintings, sculptures, long poems, radio and television programs, and movies are usually capitalized (and in *italics*): "*War and Peace,*" "*Los Angeles Times,*" "*Goodfellas,*" "*Mona Lisa.*" Within such titles *coordinating conjunctions, prepositions, articles,* and the "*to*" of *infinitives* are in *lower case* if they are not the first word of the title: "*A Moon for the Misbegotten,*" "*To Kill a Mockingbird.*"

WORKS THAT ARE PARTS OF LARGER WHOLES. Chapters of books, articles in periodicals, acts or movements of plays or musical works, and the like follow the same capitalization rules as whole works, but they are usually set off in *quotation marks* or simply by capitalization alone: "Chapter 2," " 'People in the News' in the *New York Times*," "Act 4." Terms like "chapter," "act," and so on are not capitalized when they are not specific parts of a specific work: "I read Chapter 2, the chapter on grammar." "It is a good chapter."

PRONOUNS

The first-*person* singular *pronoun* "I" is normally capitalized. Other pronouns are usually *lower case*.

EMPHASIS

Despite all the rules just set out, virtually any word can be capitalized to give it added weight or *emphasis*. Current usage favors the use of *lower case* where possible, so overuse of this flexibility should be avoided.

The *interjection* "*O*" adds emphasis in the somewhat archaic *phrase* "O gentle Queen!" and is capitalized. Note that the interjection "*oh*" is not.

HYPHENATED WORDS

When hyphenated words are capitalized, special problems arise. Formal usage requires that the second element in a hyphenated *compound word* be *lower case* if it is of lesser weight than or modifies the first word: "French-speaking Population." Both words are capitalized when the two elements are essentially equal (or if the second is a proper noun or adjective): "Post-Impressionism." Defining equality of weight or *modifiers* versus nonmodifiers is a tricky business. See *hyphen*.

It is often acceptable to capitalize both elements of hyphenated compounds. This is particularly so when capitalization is used for *emphasis* or display, as in captions or headlines. (When hyphenated words are not compounds but parts of a single word—"self-reliant"—capitalize only the first element: "How to Build Self-reliance.") The examples that follow are neither exhaustive nor set in concrete— interpretations vary. Each could be considered correct as shown, depending on its use and the writer's intentions. No one reading these examples as they are written or with different combinations of capital and lower-case letters could misunderstand them: "Non-Western," "Worker-Management Alliance," "Nineteenth-Century History," "Junior-College Courses," "Caring for Two-year-olds," "Buying a Medium-size Car," "Toxin-carrying Train Derailed."

Cardinal number. The common forms of *numbers* are called "cardinals": "There are three people here." Depending on style, cardinals can be spelled out, as in the previous example, or written in figures: "Look, 222 bassett hounds!" See also *ordinal numbers*.

Case. The grammatical category "case" names the functions of *nouns* and *pronouns* in *sentences* and the forms such words take when they change to reflect their grammatical roles. It is not especially important to know what case means or what the various cases are, but it is critical to use cases correctly, particularly for pronouns, which commonly change form as they change case. Many of the most common *grammar* and *usage* errors are mistakes with case. (Other languages have much more elaborate case systems.)

There are three cases in English:

1. *Subjective* (or *nominative*), which is used for the *subjects* of sentences or *clauses,* as the *predicate* (or complement) of *linking verbs,* and as the *appositive* of any of the previous functions: ''I see him, and he sees me.'' ''Who sees whom?'' ''The person who sees is the subject, and the person seen is the object.'' ''The viewer's eyes are her instrument of vision.'' The underlined words are all in the subjective case.

2. *Objective* (or *accusative*), which is used as the *object* of a *verb,* verbal construction, or *preposition* and as the appositive for any of these functions: ''The thing that is seen moves you or leaves you cold.'' ''People believe what they see; they trust their eyes; they trust them too much.'' The underlined words are all in the objective case.

3. *Possessive,* which is used to indicate ownership: ''His eyes are blue, and hers are green.'' ''Her vision is as bad as his, and they must always wear their glasses.'' ''Nature's ways are unavoidable, yet people's ability to adapt is remarkable.'' The underlined words are all in the possessive case.

Look at entries for specific pronouns to find the proper forms of these words in cases and more examples of how they are used correctly and incorrectly. See also *capitalization, lower case,* and *upper case.*

Catch, caught, caught. An *irregular verb* in its main, *past tense,* and past *participle* forms.

Caught. See *catch*.

Censor, censure. These *homonyms* sound alike to some people but have different meanings. A "censor" is a person who checks things for acceptability and removes offensive matter, while "censure" is condemnation of someone for acting badly. The words are also *verbs*.

Censure. See *censor*.

Century. The word "century" is commonly miscapitalized and erroneously hyphenated in *compound words*. Centuries should appear in *lower case* unless they are parts of *titles* of works, captions, or being emphasized for some other reason: "It happened in the thirteenth century." They should not be hyphenated when they function as *nouns,* as in the example just given. When centuries are used as *adjectives,* they are hyphenated: "I read an eighteenth-century novel set in fourteenth-century Spain." When centuries are capitalized, as either nouns or adjectives, both elements of the compound are *upper case*: "Variations in Nineteenth-Century Grammar." See also *capitalization, hyphen,* and *emphasis*.

Cf. This *abbreviation* for "compare" or "see" should be confined to footnotes or endnotes and should not appear in the main text. Even in notes, it is better to use the English word rather than the *Latin* abbreviation.

Choose, chose, chosen. An *irregular verb* in its main, *past tense,* and past *participle* forms.

Chose. See *choose.*

Chosen. See *choose.*

Clarity. Just as it is impossible to define *"awkwardness,"* so it is difficult to spell out just what its opposite—clarity—is and how to achieve it in writing and speaking. The only certain test is to give your writing to people and ask if they understand it all quickly, completely, and easily. If they don't, chances are that it is not clear.

Today it is assumed that clear writing is *colloquial*—close to everyday speech in *style,* complexity, directness, and *vocabulary.* While this idea seems self-evident to all of us who live in the late twentieth century and is probably an adequate *rule* to follow, writers or speakers who try to convey very complex or unusual concepts might find these guidelines hard to follow. How do we describe what we understand about nature or technology in simple ways? See *scientific language* and work hard to make your statements clear in a time of confusion, bafflement, and shifting standards.

Clause. Clusters of words that include a *subject, verb,* and *object* or *predicate* but that are parts of larger *sentences* are called "clauses." In themselves, clauses work in more or less the same way as whole, simple sentences, but clauses often are linked by *conjunctions* of various kinds that make them operate within the larger sentence as *nouns, adjectives,* *adverbs,* or other *parts of speech.* When clauses assume the role of other parts of speech within a sentence, they must be in *agreement* with the other words or clauses they refer to or modify. As with most grammatical categories, you need not know the names of clauses, but you should use clauses correctly. Errors in agreement across clauses are frequent and glaring.

Since clauses let you build up complex and varied relationships between clusters of words and ideas, they help you avoid *bland writing* or weak writing. Clauses are an important element of *style* and therefore merit particular care in their use. Here is a review of the *rules* and pitfalls of using clauses.

INDEPENDENT CLAUSES

Many clauses are in fact whole *sentences* joined by *conjunctions* like "*and*" or "*but*": "Collins is a vice president, but Martell is a senior editor." Either clause in the example could stand by itself as a sentence; both are therefore "independent" clauses. There are no *rules* mandating *parallelism,* or balance, between independent clauses, but common sense says that ordinary language in ordinary moments does not mix wildly different elements. So independent clauses in most straightforward writing probably should be of roughly the same length, complexity, and *tone* or *style.* As with all such guidelines, there are many circumstances in which they do not apply and are best violated for effect or *emphasis.*

Dependent Clauses

When *pronouns* introduce or *conjunctions* join clauses in such a way that one or more of the clauses cannot stand alone as a *sentence*, the sentence is said to include both independent and dependent clauses. Those clauses that cannot stand alone (with their conjunctions) are the dependent ones: "When we have reorganized, Martell will be vice president." "When we have reorganized" is a *fragment* or dependent clause that means nothing by itself. The core of the clause ("we have reorganized") could be a sentence by itself, but the addition of the *subordinating conjunction* "when" makes the clause dependent.

Agreement

The key concern with clauses is *agreement* among their elements across *conjunctions,* particularly when clauses depend on others. Often the agreement that is needed extends beyond grammatical needs to logical concerns. That is, *subordinating conjunctions* cannot in themselves create the connection of meaning between clauses; there must also be sensible construction of the clauses to support the relationship suggested by the conjunction. WRONG: "When we have reorganized, Martell was vice president." Grammatically, this example could be considered correct, but the relationship between the *tenses* of the *verbs* makes no sense—the dependent clause suggests an action to come in the future, while the independent clause depicts a condition in the past. The two things don't go together. Many writers, however, fail to provide logical consistency or agreement between clauses and rely too heavily on the connecting power of conjunctions.

More formal grammatical agreement errors are also common. WRONG: "When Jones is vice president, their problems will be solved." The error is the lack of agreement between the singular nouns in the dependent clause and the plural *possessive pronoun* "their," which has no clear plural *antecedent* with which it can agree. The only way to avoid such errors is to reread, revise, and check everything you write to make sure clauses agree logically and grammatically. The more complex or longer the pieces of a sentence, the more careful you must be to preserve clear, sensible relationships between clauses. Having more than two clauses in any one sentence simply multiplies the need to pay attention to agreement among all the statement's elements. See also *revision, number,* and *plural*.

CLAUSES AS PARTS OF SPEECH

Remember that clauses can function in *sentences* as virtually any part of speech: noun, *adjective, adverb,* and so on: "What you are deciding bears on who will attend the meeting." The first dependent clause in the example ("What you are deciding") operates as a *noun* and the *subject* in the sentence; the second clause ("who will attend the meeting") is also a noun, but here it functions as the *object* of a *preposition*. It is important to treat clauses functioning as *parts of speech* in the correct grammatical way.

Cliché. Clichés are overused expressions of various kinds that have become worn out and should not be used in most *standard English* writing.

Just when an expression becomes tired and looses its expressive force is not clear, so the danger of clichéd writing is always present, particularly when writing contains hidden metaphors or similes. That is, what once seemed to be a fresh and interesting comparison may now have been used so often that we don't even recognize it as a metaphor or simile invented long ago to good purpose. We talk and write more or less automatically about aims and targets, for instance, without sensing the underlying metaphor of weapons and war that long ago shaped such expressions. While using such hidden images isn't wrong, one would do better to find new expressive means wherever possible to enliven one's writing. Clichés are, on the other hand, quick ways to convey a known or assumed bit of information or idea.

Co. This *abbreviation* stands for "company," "country," or "county." Like all such shortenings of words, it is acceptable in some business prose, but it is best to spell the word out fully in most formal writing.

Collective noun. Collective *nouns* are words that refer to groups of people or things: "orchestra" is a single word that names many people; a "pride" of lions or "handful" of pins similarly is one word representing many individual things. In standard American English, collective nouns are singular and agree with singular verbs: "The orchestra is playing." "The pride of lions sleeps under a tree." "A handful of pins sticks in your palm.'' In standard *British English* such words are often *plural*: "The orchestra are playing.''

Some collective nouns can be either plural or singular, depending on how they are used in a sentence: "A number of lions are sleeping under a tree." "The number of lions sleeping under the tree is small." See *agreement* and *standard English*.

Collective pronoun. Collective *pronouns* like "*none*" are generally singular and agree with singular *verbs*. But *standard English* is evolving in this regard, finding acceptable the use of "none" with *plural* verbs in many cases. See *agreement*.

Colloquial. Everyday speech and writing are called "colloquial," a word whose derivation suggests two important aspects of *grammar* and *usage*. "Colloquial" comes from *Latin* roots having to do with both talking and words; it evidently was used in ancient times to distinguish the formal, high *style* of communicating from the mundane, day-to-day language of the people.

While the ancients could perhaps make such a distinction clearly—between the way to talk or write in different, easily separated forums—in our age the "formal" and the "familiar" mix and blur. In part, the fuzzing of borders between high and low styles results from the twentieth-century literary trend toward incorporating speech patterns into written art (a trend not limited to but most marked in our age). More and more words were written in poems, stories, and novels as various populations spoke them, and more and more variants and violations of grammar *rules* and standards began to appear in print as a reflection of the looser way people speak.

Newspapers, magazines, and other public forms of communication led or furthered this deformalization of communication, as did the explosion of commercial and business writing that became more public in our age as education became universal, the working place became an acceptable topic of conversation and writing, and daily lives of all people took center stage in general.

With the emergence of the colloquial came the decline of the formal, standard, rule-driven ways of speaking and writing. Decline, but not disappearance. There are still many moments, places, and people that demand grammatically correct language. And, as is pointed out repeatedly in this book, the safest, clearest, most economical way to communicate is still *standard English* in most circumstances.

However, it is also true that violations of virtually every rule of English *grammar* in some way in speech and writing have been, quite rightly, rewarded with the loftiest recognition and prizes. Similarly, grammatically correct but stuffy, stilted, boring language has been, again quite rightly, mercilessly mocked in satire, comedy, and other forums. The demand to speak the common language, to make oneself understood to as many people as possible is profoundly democratic and pervasive in our society. It allows the colloquial to penetrate the high, formal style at will.

That means the choices available to writers and speakers today are immense, but guidance in deciding what is the right choice in the right circumstance is harder to come by. Perhaps that is a price of democratization of language. See also *dialect* and *language*.

Colon. The colon *punctuation* mark (:) sets off two more or less equal but quite distinct parts of a *sentence*. It can introduce *lists,* stand before full sentences that exemplify what previous *clauses* have delineated, or simply indicate that what follows illustrates what has gone before. Unlike a *semicolon,* which makes an abrupt break between segments of a sentence, the colon suggests that what follows is somehow equivalent to or illustrative of what has come before it. Here are some examples: "We saw the following: a car, a bridge, a horse." "Your order consists of two parts: the main shipment and the packaging." "The president made the following statement: 'Dear friends. . . .' "

Note that anything following a colon is not capitalized unless it begins a full sentence (as when a colon is used to introduce a *quotation*) or is a word that in itself requires *capitalization* (such as a *name*). Generally, a colon is not necessary if no punctuation or simpler marking is possible. Thus a listing of items need not be introduced by a colon ("We saw a car, a bridge, and a horse." "He said, 'Dear friends. . . .' "). Use a colon mainly when it is necessary to draw some attention to a separate but equivalent part of a sentence.

Come, came, come. An *irregular verb* in its main, *past tense,* and past *participle* forms.

Comma. The comma *punctuation* mark (,) has many uses, most of which are changing rapidly in modern *usage*. Where commas used to be necessary, they are no longer needed; where they never appeared, they now sometimes pop up. Some specific kinds of texts have firmer *rules* about commas than others; take into account the *audience* for which you are writing and its expectations.

The basic function of a comma is to separate two or more elements of a *sentence*. The elements might be *clauses* or *nouns* in a *list*: "The poet talked, and the painter listened." "The student wrote novels, poems, and plays." Note that newspaper and some other writing avoid the second comma in lists of three (or the last comma in longer lists that end with "something and something"). Most *standard English* accepts as correct lists that include the "serial comma" (as in the example). The decision about whether to use the last comma in a series will depend on the usage in the group you are addressing plus your own preferences. Whatever choice you make or is dictated to you, it is most important to be consistent: All lists should either contain or not contain the last comma in a *series*.

The first example above of two independent clauses joined by a comma and "*and*" seems less ambiguous but isn't. In today's writing, particularly in fiction or any other slightly less formal, more conversational prose, the comma between independent clauses is often omitted, especially if they are short, simple clauses. Just what constitutes "short and simple" is debatable and subject to individual interpretation, which means that it is not uncommon to find much longer clauses joined by "and" or "*but*" and without a comma. This probably will earn bad grades in a school paper and might cause grumbling or raised eyebrows in a business letter. But such omissions are found more and more commonly in academic publications and quite formal business writing as well. If you are unsure of your audience or the perception of such usages, err on caution's side and include the comma between independent clauses or in a series.

Commas are also used to separate many other sentence elements, which are listed below more or less in order of frequency of occurrence.

INTRODUCTORY CLAUSES

Longer *prepositional phrases, infinitive phrases,* or participial *phrases* that begin sentences or dependent clauses in introductory positions in sentences are often set off by commas: "In the best of times and in the worst of times, people look for help." "When it snows, the child skis." Just what constitutes "longer" phrases is a matter of judgment, and some writers feel safer setting off all introductory phrases with a comma: "In January, it often snows." Whatever judgments you make about which phrases to set off, it is most important to appear consistent in your decisions. See also *participle.*

QUOTED SPEECH

Phrases that show who said something that is quoted are commonly set off with commas as well as *quotation marks*: " 'Yes,' the teacher said." "The child whispered, 'What time is it?' '' '' 'Indeed,' Smith opined, 'there is reason for that.' '' Such commas always appear within the quotes if the speaker follows the quotation marks (unlike British usage). Longer *block quotations* can be introduced by a comma even though no quotation marks appear around the quoted speech: ''Kennedy delivered these remarks,

> Ask not what your country can do for you but what you can do for your country. . . .

He then went on to say other things.''

The comma before the word ''remarks'' in the last example could also be a *colon* or could even be omitted altogether. See also *quotation*.

DIRECT ADDRESS

Names of people directly addressed in a *sentence* are set off with commas: ''Chris, please apologize.'' ''It is clear, Sandy, that Chris will not apologize.''

PLACE NAMES

Addresses and other place *names* separate the elements of a location with commas: ''Casper, Wyoming''; ''Rosewell, NM''; ''Adelaide, Queensland, Australia.''

PARENTHETICAL PHRASES

While incidental or interjected words inserted into a *sentence* are best placed in *parentheses*, certain short *phrases* or stock phrases are commonly separated by commas. These phrases can be seen as kinds of *appositives*: "It is true, in my opinion, that prisoner is guilty." "This comes, no doubt, as a surprise to you." See also *interjection*.

APPOSITIVES

Words that are equivalent and stand together without connecting words or *phrases* are said to be in apposition. Such words or phrases are set off by commas: "The lawyer, a district attorney, spoke briefly." See also *appositive*.

DATES

Commas divide parts of *dates* when dates are written in month, day, year style: "November 23, 1963." When dates are written in other *styles,* the comma is usually omitted: "23 November 1963."

NUMBERS

American standard *usage* puts commas in *numbers* that are greater than 999: "1,000" or "$5,276,489.00." European usage differs, preferring *periods* where Americans put commas and commas where Americans put periods. Neither system puts commas into *dates*: "1963," but "1,963 years ago." In some tabular and scientific or business materials, commas do not appear in larger numbers.

TITLES

Titles that follow names are usually set off by commas: "Samantha Smith, Ph.D.," "Eliot Ness, Jr." Numerals following a *name* and titles before names do not need commas: "Dr. Jane Hart," "King George III."

CLARITY

It is sometimes helpful to add a comma where it is not required by any *rule* in order to make a sentence clearer. But take care not to put commas in just in case—they will confuse more than they clarify. RIGHT: "Coming in, in droves, they shouted greetings." Although no rule requires that the two "in's" in the example be separated by a comma, some readers will find the comma helps clarify the meaning. The sentence would probably be adequate without the first comma; the second is necessary. It is better to rewrite such sentences altogether. WRONG: "The guests, and the host came inside." "Jones gave it to one, and the other." "Smith said, that it was so." " 'Why not?' Kim asked." In all these examples there is no need for a comma, which if present is confusing. See also *clarity* and *revision*.

Common noun. Common *nouns* refer to objects or people in general rather than specific *names* by which individuals are known. A dog might have a name; the name is a *proper noun* (usually capitalized), while the word "dog" is the general, common term applied to the class of animals—a common noun. The distinction between proper and common nouns depends on their *usage* at any moment: something can be named "Dog," just as a word we most commonly think of as a name or proper noun (Baker) can function as a common noun ("The baker made bread."). See also *capitalization*.

Compare to, with. The distinction between these constructions is fading in all but the most formal writing. In very precise writing, one compares something to something else in order to suggest a similarity between the things: "The clerk compares the customer to a dragon." One compares something with something else to suggest that similarities between them might be found: "The clerk compared the customer with a dragon but found the customer was far less terrible than was thought."

Comparison. Expression of degrees of some quality is comparison. Grammatically, it involves the use of *auxiliary* words like "*more*" or "*most*" or the comparative or *superlative* forms of words ("faster, fastest"). Words that indicate qualities of things or actions are *adjectives* or *adverbs*.

Generally, words of one *syllable* form comparatives and superlatives by adding "*-er*" or "*-est*," while longer words form comparatives and superlatives by adding the auxiliaries "more" and "most": "longer, longest"; "more pleasurable, most pleasurable." Words of one syllable that end in "e" are made into comparatives by adding "-r" and "-st": "simpler, simplest."

Some irregular comparatives follow different patterns: "*good, better, best*." It is important to learn these patterns and not to add comparative elements to such words. WRONG: "more better." Note also *bad*, badly, *ill* (*worse*, worst); well (*better*, *best*); *many, much, some* (more, most); *little* (less, least—quantity; little, littler, littlest—size).

Note that two things or people are compared, but more than two (even implicitly) require superlatives: "The second runner is slower than the first one is." "The first runner is the fastest in the heat." WRONG: "The first runner is the fastest of the two."

Also be sure that all comparisons are complete: "The first runner is faster than the second runner is." WRONG: "The first runner is faster." Obviously, in the right context of preceding statements, the last wrong example could be acceptable—the point is to make sure that your reader knows what you are comparing to what even if the words aren't all there in the *phrase, clause,* or *sentence* that contains the comparative or superlative word. Comparative and superlative forms do not take a *hyphen*.

Complement, compliment. The first word denotes something that completes or adds to something else, while the second refers to words of praise: "The poem's dedication complemented the ode, which complimented the writer's achievements."

Compliment. See *complement*.

Compose, comprise. Things that compose something are the parts or elements that go into it. The entity or whole that is created by the things that compose it then comprises or embraces (contains) its parts. "Comprise" is used too often when "make up" or a similar simple construction would do better than this Latinism, which is also often confused with "compose." WRONG: "The car was comprised of many parts." This *usage* violates the strict meaning of the word "comprise." RIGHT: "The car was composed of many parts." Still stiff but technically correct. BETTER: "The car was made up of (had, contained) many parts." RIGHT: "Grammar comprises punctuation, spelling, and many other rules and opinions." See *Latin*.

Compound predicate. When two or more *verbs* are used in one *sentence* to describe the action a single *subject* takes, the verbs constitute a compound *predicate*. Compound predicates with two verbs joined by a *conjunction* ("*and*," "*but*," or the like) do not need to have a *comma* separating the verbs. WRONG: "In the spring bears emerge from hibernation, and search for mates." No comma is needed anywhere in this sentence, though it is a common error to insert one.

Compound sentence. Two or more independent *clauses*, however joined, constitute a compound sentence. Bear in mind that similar compound sentences should be joined in similar ways: with a *comma* and "*and*" or another *conjunction* or without such a comma—but consistently. Similarly, writers should take care with such sentences to be sure that *pronouns* are given clear *antecedents* across the joined clauses and that pronouns and *verbs* agree across the clauses (see *agreement*). UNCLEAR: "The teacher gave the student the book, and they were correct.'' BETTER: ''The teacher gave the student books, and they were the correct ones.''

Compound word. Two or more words that can stand independently are often joined in various ways to make compound words. It is important to recognize that such compounds are tricky to spell and to make into *plurals*. Some guidelines follow, but be sure to look up such words in the *dictionary* if you have any doubt about their *spelling*.

In grammatical terms, comparatives and *superlatives* made up of ''*more*'' or ''most'' and an *adjective* or *adverb* are compound words that are not hyphenated or ''spelled solid'' (as one word). They represent the simplest case of compounding and need not be of further concern to most writers. Some examples: ''more favorable,'' ''most appreciative,'' ''White House,'' ''standing invitation,'' ''quickly stated.'' No compounds of adverbs ending in ''*-ly*'' should ever have a hyphen, though this mistake is commonly committed. *Plurals* of these words are formed as one would expect, with only the more important of the words becoming a plural form: ''White Houses,'' ''vice presidents.''

Compounds that are hyphenated are more complex. First, you need to make sure that the word is in fact spelled with a hyphen. Many words form most of their compounds either with hyphens or without, but some combine both words into one solid word: ''self-starter,'' ''self-management,'' and ''self-conscious'' but ''selfless.'' Other compounds are hyphenated when they act as *adjectives* but not when they are *nouns*: "decision-making processes" but "good decision making is needed." To avoid leaving such discretion to writers or dictionaries or to stop puzzling combinations from cropping up ("The decision-making offices need good decision making"), some *styles* dictate spelling common compounds one way only. But controversy and variation persist: "database" is a solid compound in some styles, "open" (two words) in others, and hyphenated in yet others. Consistency should be your byword, as well as reliance on whatever authoritative sources are available to you—an organization style sheet or preferred dictionary.

Care should be taken, under whatever style is adopted, to make sure that compounds are hyphenated when leaving them open would cause ambiguity: "The free trade policy is in force in this country." Lack of a hyphen between "free" and "trade" in this sentence leaves the reader unsure if the policy in question has to do with free trade or if there is a trade policy that has become free somehow. Many readers will recognize free trade as a concept and compound the words mentally. But those who don't know about the history of economics and policy might be left to wonder, as will the more informed for whom the lack of a hyphen opens the door to guessing what you had in mind. Help everyone out with a hyphen.

Some compounds that are always hyphenated include many forms of *numbers,* like *fractions* and spelled-out numbers: "one-tenth, two-thirds, forty-six, three-year-olds." But numbers with the spelled-out word "percent" should not be hyphenated even when they are used adjectivally: "a 42 percent raise."

Plurals of hyphenated words add "*s*" to the critical word only: "self-starters," "sisters-in-law." But *possessives* of hyphenated compounds add an *apostrophe* and "*s*" to the end of the compounded string: "the sisters-in-law's gift" (treated as a singular possessive although the compound is plural because of the position of the first "s," which makes a plural); "Self-starters' rewards are great" (plural possessive formation because the plural "s" and possessive ending are in the same place).

Comprise. See *compose*.

Computer. Wondrous are the efficiencies and consistencies that can be gained by using a computer (word processor, spell checker, and grammar checker) in your writing! And woeful are the errors that overreliance on computers can produce!

Computers are useful writing tools because they can so easily copy, move, and check things. But they can also easily be made to move and copy things in the wrong places, leaving unwanted remnants of such cutting and pasting if we don't supplement the computer's speed and ease with care and attention in our writing, revising, and proofreading. It is so easy to move a character or space too much, leaving an inadvertently spliced word behind (or too many spaces or a *fragment* no longer wanted where a *phrase* used to be). And it is so easy to push the copy button more than once or too long, creating *redundancies* and other embarrassments.

But nothing is so seductively helpful and disruptive as the

spell checker. "Butt their canned bee errors in thus document—I spill chucked it trice!" True, but did you look with care to see if the properly spelled but completely inappropriate words were in the right order, had the right meanings, were not misused *homonyms* or other tricky words? (Look again at the quoted sentence. Virtually every word in it is the wrong one for the *sentence*. For example, "their" is spelled correctly but is grammatically wrong. It should be "there.") "In the big inning God created the word" is all spelled right, but it doesn't quite meet the highest standards of accuracy.

A *grammar* checker would also not find fault with the last mistaken example (rumored to have occurred in a famous and elaborate edition of the Bible). Your writing is probably less subject to inspection than the Bible, but it needs as much care to avoid such errors that cannot be caught (and might be generated) by a carelessly used computer.

So by all means write on the computer and benefit from its efficiencies and ability to help check for and maintain consistency. But don't believe for a minute that all those handy tools take the place of careful, attentive writing, revising, and proofreading. Otherwise, you might be in for a sore prize. See also *revision, editing, spelling,* and *dictionary.*

Conjugation. *Verbs* change forms to agree with their noun *subjects* and to reflect *tense, mood, voice,* and so on. The forms into which they change are called "conjugations." See also *noun* and *agreement.*

Most verbs change in regular patterns into their various

forms, but some are irregular in pattern and require memorization or checking of *grammar* references or other authoritative sources. There are few if any acceptable variants of conjugation forms, and it is very important to form verb *persons,* tenses, moods, voices, and so on absolutely correctly. Few errors are more glaring than improperly conjugated verbs.

See the entries for each tense, mood, voice, person, or *number* for proper *usage* of the forms outlined here. This entry discusses only the mechanics of conjugation, not proper use of the verb forms. See also entries for important specific verbs.

REGULAR VERBS

In the *present tense* regular *verbs* stay the same as their root (or main) form in first- and second-*person* singular and *plural* and in third-person plural, but they add "*s*" to the third-person singular:

I paint	We paint
You paint	You paint
He, she, it paints	They paint

Past tenses of regular verbs add "-ed" to the root form for all persons and *numbers:* "I, you, he, she, it, we, you, they painted." There are some variants, depending on the letter that ends the root form and where the accent falls on the word. Words that end in "el" and are accented on the first *syllable* ("travel") form the past as do other regular verbs:

"traveled." Words that end in "el" but aren't accented on the first syllable ("excel") add an "l" in forming the past tense ("excelled"). British spelling uses the double "l" for all past tenses of "el" root words, and some American *styles* adopt this variant *spelling*. For the most part, this style should be avoided in American writing.

The past tense form is also, in most cases, the past *participle*, which is used to form compound past and *future tenses*: "I have traveled, I will have traveled, I could have traveled." The same form often appears in the *passive* voice: "It was painted."

The regular present participle is formed by adding "ing" to the root and by following the same spelling *rules* as the past tense: "traveling," "excelling." This form is used in compound present and future tenses: "I am traveling, I will be traveling, I will have been traveling." See *gerund*.

Besides the indicative *moods* covered by the forms already listed, verbs form regular *imperatives*, which are the same as the root form and regular *subjunctives* or conditionals in the present, in the same way: "Paint the fence, Kid." "It is important that the kid paint the fence." Past subjunctives add *auxiliary* verbs: "It would have been better if the kid had painted the fence." See *irregular verbs*.

Conjunction. The words that connect pieces of *sentences* are called "conjunctions." The following list includes the most commonly used conjunctions. You should look at the entries for individual words to find any peculiarities in their *usage*, associated *punctuation*, and other tips:

and	neither . . . nor
after	*nevertheless*
also	next
although	nor
anyway	not only . . . but
as	now
as if	once
because	*or*
before	otherwise
besides	similarly
both . . . and	since
but	*so*
certainly	so that
either . . . or	still
even though	*than*
finally	*that*
for	then
furthermore	therefore
however	though
if	thus
incidentally	unless
indeed	until
in order	*when*
instead	where
likewise	whether . . . or
meanwhile	while
moreover	yet
namely	

The conjunctions are classified grammatically into several types, each of which has a separate entry in this book to give you some idea of how the category works and differs from the other sets of conjunctions. The grammatical types of conjunctions are *conjunctive adverbs, coordinating conjunctions, correlative conjunctions,* and *subordinating conjunctions.*

Conjunctive adverb. *Adverbs* that perform the role of conjunctions are called conjunctive adverbs; they link independent *clauses* essentially in the same way *coordinating conjunctions* and *subordinating conjunctions* do but suggest a stronger division of the *sentence* parts and are therefore accompanied by a *semicolon* as *punctuation*: "Lynch is brilliant; indeed, Lynch is a genius." The adverbs most commonly used as conjunctions are

also	*namely*
assuredly	*nevertheless*
besides (see beside)	next
certainly	now
finally	otherwise
furthermore	similarly
however	still
incidentally	*then*
indeed	therefore
instead	thus
meanwhile	undoubtedly
moreover	

Connective. See *conjunction.*

Conscience, conscious. Commonly confused, these words not only have different meanings but are different *parts of speech*. "Conscience," a *noun*, is a person's feeling for or sense of moral or ethical correctness—right and wrong. A "conscious" person is awake, aware, not asleep or otherwise knocked out. "Conscious" is an *adjective*.

Conscious. See *conscience*.

Consonant. The letters in the alphabet divide into two main types: consonants and *vowels*. Consonants are all the letters but "a," "e," "i," "o," and "u," from which they are distinguished by the way we produce their sounds when we speak. It is sometimes important to recognize consonants and vowels when you are deciding how a word breaks into *syllables* so that you can *hyphenate* it.

Continual, continuous. "Continual" things go on over longish periods but may stop and start. "Continuous" things don't stop and extend for fairly long times.

Continuous. See *continual*.

Contraction. Especially in less than formal or *standard English*, words are often shortened or contracted and combined into a single word: "Isn't it wonderful!"

While this happens in speech naturally and without recourse to any special conventions or treatments, in writing the decision to use contractions must be consistent with expected *style* and standards and must observe some rules of *spelling*.

Written contractions contain an *apostrophe* that indicates letters have been omitted form the shortened word or words: "cannot—can't," "should not—shouldn't," "she would—she'd." Just where the apostrophe falls can be hard to judge and may require the use of a reference source or *dictionary* to confirm. Be careful not to use more than one apostrophe even though more than one letter has been dropped or letters have been dropped in more than one place: "he could not have—he couldn'tve."

The last example illustrates the problem of standards and choosing whether or not to use contractions. Strictly speaking, no contractions, particularly elaborate ones like "couldn'tve," should appear in academic or otherwise formal writing. But increasingly, the highest, most constrained styles allow contractions as they come closer to spoken language, which is full of such elisions. No guidebook or reference can tell you whether to use contractions in what you write, but there are some points to consider. If you are unsure of the style expected of you, it is probably best to be cautious and avoid contractions. However, even in the most demanding styles, some uncontracted phrases may sound affected or pretentious. When you face such a situation, you might decide to yield to the temptation to allow a less formal, more speechlike contraction to creep into what you write.

A few contractions have become standard English, usually when archaic *phrases* have been contracted into commonly used forms: "five of the clock—five o'clock." Only the contracted forms of such words are used. See also *its, their,* and *your.*

Coordinating conjunction. Coordinating conjunctions link more or less equal parts of *sentences* in a rather direct and clear relationship: "X and Y," where "*and*" is the coordinating conjunction. The other coordinating conjunctions are "*but*," "*for*," "nor," "*or*," "*so*," and "yet." When using these conjunctions in your writing, you should make sure that the elements linked are relatively equal in importance, weight, and treatment. Coordinating conjunctions that separate independent *clauses* usually have *commas* before them: "The dog is three, and the cat is five."

Correlative conjunction. Correlative conjunctions function almost the same as *coordinating conjunctions*—linking more or less equal parts of *sentences*—but they come in pairs: "*both . . . and*," "either . . . or," "*just as . . . so*," "*neither . . . nor*," "*not only . . . but also*," "whether . . . or." "Both Robbins and Thornton speak French." "Just as Robbins speaks quickly, so Thornton, speaks forcefully." In most cases, correlative conjunctions joining independent clauses have *commas* before them, as in the previous example.

Cost, cost, cost. An *irregular verb* in its main, *past tense,* and past *participle* forms.

Could. "Could" is an important *auxiliary* verb: "I could do that if I wanted to. And pigs could fly." See *verb.*

Could of. Don't use "*of*" to stand for "*have*" in constructions like this.

Criteria, criterion. "Criteria" is the *plural* of "criterion." Its unusual form reflects its origins in Greek. Make sure "criteria" as a *subject* agrees with a plural *verb*. WRONG: "That is the right criteria." RIGHT: "Those are the right criteria." See *agreement*.

Criterion. See *criteria*.

Cut, cut, cut. An *irregular verb* in its main, *past tense,* and past *participle* forms.

D

'd. The letter "d" with an *apostrophe* before it is used to form *contractions* of *past tense* and other *auxiliary* verbs and *pronouns*: "he had—he'd," "I would—I'd." Avoid contractions in formal, *standard English* writing. See also *verb*.

Dangling modifier. One very common problem in writing concerns *adjectives*, *adverbs*, *phrases*, and *clauses* that are worded or located in sentences in such a way that they do not have clear, or any, referents or *antecedents*—they dangle somewhere without a clear relationship to any other part of the sentence: "Lying in the sun, the day was clear." In this example it is not clear who or what is lying in the sun—certainly not the day. You can detect problems like this in your writing only by rereading, checking, revising, and proofreading. You can solve such problems by putting the dangling words close to what they are talking about and by making sure that the relationship between that thing or person and the words describing it is clear and logical. Thus the sentence used in the example might become "Lying in the sun, I enjoyed the clear day," depending on what you intend to say. The point is to match clearly intention and expression.

Dash. The dash *punctuation* mark (—) is used to separate parts of a *sentence* that are more or less equivalent but that

have no words to link or join them (that lack *conjunctions*):
"The minister spoke of a book—the Bible—known to us
all." Here the dashes take the place of words like "that is,"
which could also be used to blend the concepts of "book"
and "Bible" together. *Clauses* can also be joined by
dashes: "The lecturer gave a speech—the audience listened
with interest." Again, the dashes stand for something like
"that is" and indicate a sort of contraction, or elision, of
the ideas or words in the sentence.

Since dashes are used where words might have been
supplied to specify a relationship, there is always the risk
that the dash will not clearly convey the nature of the
relationship or the things linked. Moreover, the things
dashes set off are usually interjected into a sentence rather
than being integrated into it with connective words. By their
nature, such *interjections* interrupt the flow of thought to
some degree (and often to good effect), and many of them
can prove distracting. For these reasons, most *style* guides
suggest restricted use of dashes.

Dashes can be typed as two *hyphens* with or without
spaces around them or as any solid line longer than a
hyphen. But using more than two hyphens is not preferred
in *standard English*.

Data. Although "data" is a *plural* form of the *Latin*
"datum" and since the singular is not used in *standard
English* except in the most erudite writing, this "plural"
noun has come to be used quite commonly as a singular,
especially when the topic is large quantities of information
seen as a collection: "The data on this subject is copious
and convincing." Many academic settings would find this

example substandard, but singular uses of "data" have spread with the growth of computers and information science.

Dates. There are several systems for expressing dates in writing. Which you use in your writing depends on the standards set in the community in which you are expressing yourself or by the *audience* to which you are addressing yourself.

The most commonly used date system is month, day, year. The full name of the month comes before the number of the day, a *comma* follows, and then comes the numbers of the year: "March 23, 1987." The number of the year is followed by a comma if the *sentence* continues or by any other *punctuation* mark that is appropriate at that point in the sentence: "On March 23, 1987, the contract took effect. But work began only on March 28, 1988—much later than anticipated. The completion date was March 22, 1999." The *numbers* are in figures, and they are not followed by letters to indicate that they are *ordinal numbers,* even though the date in the example is frequently pronounced as the "twenty-third of March." WRONG: "March 23rd, 1987."

If the day of the week is specified in this style, it can come before the date and is followed by a comma: "Friday, March 23, 1987" (because the day of the week and the numerical date are seen to be in apposition, as are the numerical date and the year; see *appositive*). The day of the week following the date is preceded by a comma and usually adds an *article,* since the following day is seen as an afterthought or *interjection*: "May 23, 1987, a Friday." No comma is needed if month and year alone are recorded: "It happened in March 1987."

An alternate system avoids the commas by placing the day number before the month and year: "23 March 1987." All the other *rules* noted above apply to this system, which is common in the military and other styles: "Friday, 23 March 1987."

In formal English it is preferred to spell out dates in one of the systems noted above. However, our digitized society more and more commonly also expresses dates in numbers alone: "5/23/87," "5-23-87," or some variant on these. Follow the style set or likely to be least confusing for the circumstances in which you are writing. If your audience includes British or European readers or writers, be aware that numerical notations of dates in Europe (and the United Kingdom) usually reverse the month and day from American usage: "23/5/87." In the now-boring example, there is no question that March 23 is meant because "23" can only be a day. But a European who writes "11/12/1992" probably means "December 11," while an American who wrote the same numbers would mean "November 12." See *A.D., B.C.,* and *century*.

Declension. The pattern of *inflection*—changes in word forms to reflect changed grammatical roles—for *nouns* and *pronouns* is called "declension." In nouns and pronouns, declensions list patterns of changes in *case*, *gender*, and *number*; pronouns can also be inflected (and therefore declined) in *person*. The declension for the personal pronoun in the *nominative* case is "I; you; he, she, it; we; you; they."

Degree. See *comparison*.

Demonstrative. Demonstrative *pronouns* are "*that*," "these," "this," and "those." They work the same way all other pronouns work, and they are used mainly to point at, identify, or indicate a *noun* (thing or person): "Do you see this picture?" "I saw that film." "The child read those comic books." "This" and "these" (*plural*) generally refer to things or people that are or are perceived to be closer or more immediate, while "that" and "those" (plural) indicate more remote nouns. Be sure that these pronouns agree in *number* with the words they modify or refer to. WRONG: "These are the picture I had in mind." Don't use "*them*" as a demonstrative pronoun. WRONG: "I saw them things." See *agreement, modifier,* and *antecedent*.

Dependent clause. See *clause*.

Dialect. The dialects or variants of English that ethnic, religious, regional, cultural, or economic groups speak are often highly prized by them as important signs of group identity or solidarity. Many people in such groups speak or write *standard English* in some circumstances but prefer to observe the standards and *usages* of their dialects in other, usually less formal, communications. However, keeping the two sets of grammatical and usage *rules* separate is often difficult, just as it is often hard to judge what parts of any standard apply in any specific instance. Perfectly sound constructions, *spellings*, pronunciations, and so on in one dialect or pattern of standards might indicate seriously defective education, intelligence, or taste in another.

Most standard English writing should, by definition, avoid dialect. However, it must be recognized that standard English is simply the dialect of preference among those who are or believe themselves to be in a position to dictate what the standards are or should be. Thus the choice of what standard to apply—what dialect to choose—at any moment is not as clear as one would hope. In general, it is safe to follow the strictures of any widely recognized *grammar* handbook or *dictionary* to produce an acceptable standard English. It is always a matter of judgment on the part of each writer to decide whether that dialect is suitable for the writing she or he is doing at the moment. See *colloquial*.

Dialogue. Recording others' speech directly is called writing in dialogue. Conventionally, *quotation marks* are used to indicate directly recorded speed: '' 'Hello,' he said.'' In this example, the directly quoted speech is contained in single quotes because examples in this book are contained in double quotes. Normally, dialogue appears in double quotes, while direct speech recorded within a dialogue is put in single quotes, as in the example. Directly quoted speech can also be indented and made a *block quotation* to indicate that the words of someone other than the author are being reported: ''The politician said

> I am, as usual, confused on this point, but I would say that it is possible. Actually, I'm not sure that it is possible, but I am guessing that it is. It's most probably probable.

The news conference ended shortly thereafter.''

Directly reported speech within an indented block appears in double quotes, but the block itself has no quotes around it. Normally the reported speech of each person who takes part in the dialogue being recorded is also set off by beginning a new *paragraph*:

> It was a dark and stormy night. Thunder crashed, and the rain poured down.
>
> "Wow," Chris said, "I'm scared."
>
> "Don't worry," replied Sandy, "We're safe here."

However, to save space in nonfiction writing, some briefer dialogues are reported without such paragraphing.

Note that *contractions* appear in the last example. Such less formal elements are common in dialogues, which are, after all, representations of more *colloquial*, informal, dialectic speech, rather than formal, standard writing. Dialogue—real or invented—thus presents the writer an opportunity to relax a formal style and introduce into a document more conversational elements and all the variants they entail. See *dialect, standard English,* and *quotation*.

Dialogue can also be reported less directly and therefore without quotation marks or other clear markers of speakers and speeches: "He said that he was scared." This is called "*indirect quotation.*"

Dictionary. The only way to be sure words are spelled correctly is to look them up in a dictionary. No dictionary is particularly better than any other, except that longer ones tend to have more words, examples, and explanations, which means you are more likely to find what you want.

Don't be fooled by finding a word in a dictionary. You might have found a correct spelling of the wrong word for your sentence. See the entries on *homonyms* (sound-alikes) and such words as "*their*" and "*to*."

Different from, than. The preferred *usage* is "different from" when a distinction is being drawn between things or people: "Old is different from young." Don't use "different than" unless you are introducing a *clause*: "That is different than I had expected." Or: "That is different from what I had expected."

"Differ with" means disagree and should not be confused with or used for "differ from" (be different).

Dig, dug, dug. An *irregular verb* in its main, *past tense*, and past *participle* forms.

Direct object. The *object* of a *verb*'s action is said to be its "direct object," while someone or something to which that action and object may be transferred is called the "*indirect object*": "The boss gave the bonus to Horton." "The bonus" is the direct object, and "Horton" is the indirect object.

Discreet, discrete. The first word refers to tact or prudence, while the second *adjective* means separate or separable: "People are discrete individuals who are sometimes discreet in their dealings with others."

Discrete. See *discreet*.

Dive, dived, dived. An *irregular verb* in its main, *past tense*, and past *participle* forms.

Dived. See *dive*.

Do. Besides its direct meanings (to perform or act), "do" is an *auxiliary* verb that combines with other *verbs* to change or intensify their meaning: "I do believe you are right." "It does not seem you agree." The first example borders on *dialect* and is the kind of *intensifier* that should not be overused.

"Do" is an *irregular verb*, forming its *past tense* and past *participle* in an unpredictable way (see *conjugation*): Present: do, does; past: did; past participle: done. These forms are important because they are commonly used with other verbs when "do" plays an auxiliary role: "I did not see him." Forms of "do" are also commonly confused or used wrong: "Jan done killed the bug." "Jan done it." RIGHT: "Jan killed the bug." "Jan did it."

Doesn't. The *contraction* of "does not," which should normally not be used in formal writing.

Dollars. Put a dollar sign before any amounts in figures, and indicate cents after a decimal: "$1.95." No additional spaces or *punctuation* is needed. When *spelling* out *numbers,* spell out "dollars" after the figures: "Ten dollars changed hands."

Sums of dollars can be singular if they are seen as lumps of money rather than individual bills: "A billion dollars is a lot of money."

If you are dealing with non-American dollars, you can distinguish between currencies by putting an *abbreviation* before the figure and dollar sign—"C$1.95," indicating Canadian dollars—or, preferably, by following the figure with a parenthetical expression of sufficient length to make the matter clear: "$1.95 (C)" or "$1.65 (Can.)." Dollars of various kinds are used in many countries, so you should be sure to distinguish between any countries that could be confused by single-letter abbreviations.

Don't. The *contraction* of "do not," which should not be used normally in *standard English* writing.

Double negative. It is wrong in *standard English* to include more than one word in a *sentence, clause,* or verb *phrase* that negates the element. WRONG: "He never did nothing." RIGHT: "He never did anything." Having double or multiple negatives in a sentence is a very common error, particularly when phrases or clauses are long and the negation of an early element is forgotten later. Only careful proofreading or revising can catch such mistakes and fix them. Since the error is particularly frowned on in standard English, it is important that you take care when writing to avoid such problems.

Down. *Preposition* governing the *objective case*: "The elephant blew water on Dave's head, and it dribbled down him."

Dr. This *title* is commonly written as an *abbreviation* rather than spelled out. Note that the *pronoun* following a reference to a doctor by name or in general is not automatically masculine: ''Dr. Smith picked up her bag.'' ''A doctor could forget his or her equipment.'' When referring to two married doctors, it is offensive to write ''Dr. and Mrs. Smith'' or ''Drs. John and Mary Smith.'' Put instead ''Dr. John and Dr. Mary Smith.'' The same point applies to coauthors or coinventors. See the entry on *sexist language.* ''Dr.'' is also an *abbreviation* for ''drive'': ''3789 West Brookdale Dr.''

Drank. See *drink.*

Draw, drew, drawn. An *irregular verb* in its main, *past tense,* and past *participle* forms.

Drawn. See *draw.*

Drew. See *draw.*

Drink, drank, drunk. An *irregular verb* in its main, *past tense,* and past *participle* forms.

Drive, drove, driven. An *irregular verb* in its main, *past tense,* and past *participle* forms.

Driven. See *drive.*

Drove. See *drive.*

Drunk. See *drink.*

Due to. See *because of*.

Dug. See *dig*.

During. *Preposition* governing the *objective case*: "The conductor coughed during the concert."

E

Each. "Each" is an *indefinite* pronoun that is always singular, even when it is followed by plural *phrases*: "Each of them is here." See also *pronoun* and *plural*.

Each other. See *reciprocal pronoun*.

Eat, ate, eaten. An *irregular verb* in its main, *past tense*, and past *participle* forms.

Eaten. See *eat*.

Ed. The common *abbreviation* for "edition," "edited (by)," or "editor"; "ed." belongs mainly in endnotes or footnotes and should be spelled out in most text rather than appearing in its short form.

Editing. Once you have written something for the first time, you need to go back several times to check for errors, appropriateness of *style*, and general *efficiency* of communication. This process of checking your writing is called "editing" or "*revision*." During editing, pay attention to your *audience* and make sure that it will understand you clearly, quickly, and simply. No piece of writing is complete until it has been edited at least once, and most work should be edited several times.

Effect. See *affect*.

Efficiency. It may seem odd to see a discussion of "efficiency" in a *grammar* book. But the whole point of grammar *rules* and discussions of *usage, style,* and so on is to make it clear how to say most directly and simply what has to be said. This book intends to help you communicate most efficiently with your *audience*.

Poetry, styles of other eras or for other occasions than simple communication, and the like might require or allow us to write or speak without concern for efficiency. Telling a story at great leisure and with elaborate digressions and meanderings, for instance, is an important part of all our lives at some moments and of many cultures' greatest glories. But most of the writing and speaking you do requires directness, *clarity,* and efficient communication.

Keep in mind that errors of *agreement* or mistakes with *antecedents,* poor choice of *vocabulary,* and so on keep your reader or listener from hearing or seeing what you mean most quickly and clearly. Such deficiencies in your writing or speaking thus hinder efficiency of communication. That is why it is important to master the rules of grammar and apply them strictly in most statements.

Besides looking up the words italicized in this entry, review the entries on *bland writing, editing,* and the related topics those entries mention for further guidance on how to achieve efficient communication.

E.g. This *abbreviation* stands for the *Latin* "exempli gratia," which means "for example." While it is a handy way to shorten text a bit, some readers will not be comfortable with the expression or might find it too academic. It is better to use the English "for example."

Elicit, illicit. These near-*homonyms* (sound-alikes) are different *parts of speech* and have different meanings. The *verb* "elicit" means to draw out or extract; the *adjective* "illicit" means illegal.

Ellipsis. The omission of text for any reason from a reported statement or incomplete thought is called an ellipsis (plural: ellipses).

It is normally represented by three consecutive *periods* with or without space surrounding them and separating them: "He said, 'The ten points to remember are . . . and don't forget them.' " If the ellipses come at the end of a *sentence,* a fourth period is added to represent the end of the sentence. This is particularly common when ellipsis are used to indicate a thought that is left incomplete or allowed to trail off: "But that is another story. . . ." Four ellipsis points also appear between sentences in *block quotations* when other sentences between them have been omitted.

Ellipses that come before other parts of sentences can be followed by other *punctuation*: "The four points are the nature of organization, the structure of firms . . . , and the management scheme."

Since ellipses represent the omission of text or the incompleteness of thought, they can present the reader with gaps in information or logic. Ellipses should therefore be used with care to preserve the sense of a quoted source and the full intent of the shortened sentence. Overuse of ellipses leads a reader to feel that a writer is manipulating a quoted source and probably changing its meaning or is not arguing or presenting a case cogently and completely. Finally, too many sentences that end in trailing ellipses can seem quite coy and off-putting—if there is more to be said, say it.

Elude. See *allude*.

Emigrate, immigrate. Both of these words derive from the *verb* "migrate," meaning to move, and refer to living beings changing their living place over fairly significant distances. The two commonly confused forms in this entry (near-*homonyms*) are verbs that denote human migratory movement out of someplace ("emigrate" from Europe) and to someplace ("immigrate" to America). Closely related are the *nouns* "emigration," "immigration," and "migration."

Emphasis. There are many ways to add emphasis to *sentences, phrases, clauses,* and whole statements. But their use should be resisted in most cases: If you have not presented your ideas clearly and forcefully enough through careful choice and *order of words*, it is unlikely that adding one of the emphasizing devices to your words will in fact make them any stronger. Still, there are moments when it helps your reader to stress what is important by using one of the following methods.

Underlining is a typographical device to indicate a particularly important part of a text. Needless to say, lots of underlined text is no more distinctive than no underlined text. With today's machines, many writers turn to other *typefaces* to do what underlining did on a typewriter—draw attention. But the presence of a lot of different typefaces in a document is usually more distracting than anything else, and an overabundance of *italic type*, *bold type*, and so on doesn't improve logic or expression.

Similarly, the addition of an *exclamation point* creates emphasis when it happens occasionally, but not when it is overdone. So don't do it too often!

Other *punctuation* marks commonly used to emphasize text are the *dash*, the *ellipsis*, and the *quotation mark*. All these marks have more legitimate uses than emphasis and should be used for those purposes more often than for emphasis. But it is true that an interjected or omitted phrase marked by dashes or ellipses is a sometimes handy tool, just as the "extra" quotation mark can call attention to a word that bears a bit of extra thought from the reader (see *interjection*).

It is also possible to use word selection and word order to stress a point or idea (which is close to saying write more forcefully rather than rely on the more mechanical devices noted above). Words that merit special attention might be moved from their more expected or common position to a comprehensible but slightly unusual place in a phrase, clause, or sentence to draw attention to them: "Going home is nice" is probably a stronger expression than "It is nice to be going home." The rearrangement of words need be no more dramatic or unusual than in this example to achieve adequate emphasis.

The simplest and strongest places for words to draw attention are at the beginning and end of phrases, clauses, and particularly sentences. Which is why most sentences begin with a *subject*—the thing you most want your reader to pay attention to—and end with an *object,* the next most important thing in the sentence. Right in the middle lies a *verb*—at the center of attention in its own way.

But sometimes more radical tools are needed: "Indeed, interjections—even wholesale *inversions* of word order— can come into play." Using a *conjunction* or other interjected word at the beginning of a sentence is a modest emphatic device. Similarly, starting a sentence with a word other than the subject can add point to the statement. Similarly again, *repetition* of words in key positions or repeated similar phrase or clause structures can pull a sentence or series of statements out of the ordinary and into the reader's focus: "Using inversions, choosing interjections, and writing for effect can add punch to your words."

Depending on how much pizzazz you are looking for or your *audience* can tolerate, you can resort to certain *rhetorical* devices that fairly scream your intent. "Hyperbole" is the intentional exaggeration of something to make a point: "There are millions of people here!" Exclamation points go quite naturally with hyperbole, which should be used with similar caution and restraint. So too with words that border on the limits of taste and acceptability by whatever standards are in force for your audience: *Expletives* of whatever degree of severity or slang can draw attention. Usually they are unwarranted, and always they risk causing dismay or disgust. But, damn the torpedoes, give it a try!

Expletives of the grammatical sort—sentences that begin with "*it*" or "*there*" and a form of "*be*"—have often been seen as a kind of emphasis, since they move the subject from its expected leading position in the sentence. However, any emphasizing effect such sentences might have ever had has long since been lost in overuse. These more formal expletives are now *clichés* of a sort and often emphasize only weak or sloppy writing.

Yet another device for emphasis is the sentence *fragment*, usually a grammatical error but on rare occasions an acceptable method for calling attention to something: "It was dark. Storm clouds. Thunder." This technique is probably appropriate only to fiction or poetry (if there) or personal correspondence. Fragments are often signaled or emphasized in themselves by the addition of ellipses.

A final device for emphasizing is the use of *auxiliary* verbs: "I do believe this is important." This method borders on the mechanical devices listed above and should not be abused by overuse. Better to use variety of structure and word choice, attention to placement of key words or phrases, and the selective application of more radical and mechanical devices to make sure that your writing has force and makes its important points clear to your readers.

Ensure. See *assure*.

-er. When "er" is added to most *adjectives,* it creates their comparative degree: "The cat is fat, but the dog is fatter." See *comparison*.

-est. The particle or *suffix* "est" is added to *adjectives* to form their *superlative* degree of comparison: "All the

Himalayas are high, but Everest is the highest mountain of all.''

Et al. This partial *abbreviation* of the *Latin* words "et alia" means "and others" (usually people). Like most such Latinisms, it can be used in academic or very formal prose without much chance of reader incomprehension or distaste. But even in the "highest" *styles,* "et al." and similar Latinisms are best avoided and replaced by the equivalent English phrase or a clearer and more explicit statement of what is being abbreviated.

The proper place for "et al.," if anywhere, is in endnotes and footnotes rather than in text. In notes it indicates that other people were involved in the writing, editing, or production of a text: "Dalton, et al., *Style: A Handbook.*"

Although "et al." comes from the Latin, it is not treated as a foreign phrase and so appears in regular, or *Roman,* type rather than being underlined or put in *italics.* Be careful not to put a *period* after the "et," but always have one after the "al."

Etc. This *abbreviation* of the *Latin* words "et cetera" stands for "and so on." This is perhaps the most overused abbreviation, often being a written version of the hems, haws, and pauses that dot our speech. Such interruptions of your train of thought communicate little or nothing to your *audience* except the fact that you probably haven't given enough thought to what you want to say and are filling the gaps in your ideas with meaningless things like "etc."

Replacing "etc." with "and so on" gets you out of the

trap of overly formal style, but it doesn't add much to your weak statement. In short, see "etc." as a signal that you need to go back and rethink, revise, and amplify what you are saying.

Every day, everyday. The solidly spelled "everyday" is an *adjective* that suggests commonness, ordinariness, or mundaneness; the open *compound word* "every day" is an *adverb* and means day after day in unending succession: "Connie reads books every day but doesn't read everyday books."

Everyday. See *every day*.

Every one, everyone. The first *phrase*, the open *compound word* "every one," is usually used as an *adjective* to modify *nouns* and means "all": "Sarah ate every one of her beans." The second word is a singular *indefinite pronoun* and means all the people being talked about: "Everyone ate all of his or her beans." See also *modifier* and *pronoun*.

Everyone. See *every one*.

Everything. Distinguish between the *compound word* "every thing" (which means things one by one: "Sandy picked up every thing in the room no matter how heavy it was") and the *indefinite pronoun* "everything" (which means all things: "Sandy picked up everything in the room immediately").

Except. See *accept*.

Exclamation point. The exclamation point (!) is a *punctuation mark* that is used for emphasizing statements: "You're telling me!" The exclamation point can appear inside or outside *quotation marks,* depending on the role it plays in the sentence and what is being emphasized. The example sentence correctly puts the exclamation mark inside the quotes since a whole emphasized *sentence* is being quoted in full. If you are quoting speech that is not an exclamation but want to emphasize your feelings about the quoted statement, put the exclamation point outside the quotes: "How disgusting it is to hear words like 'damn'!"

When the exclamation point ends a quoted statement that is followed by a *phrase* that identifies the speaker, no *comma* should appear after the exclamation mark. WRONG: " 'Be gone!,' the artist said." RIGHT: " 'Be gone!' the artist said."

The exclamation point can appear inside or outside *parentheses:* "Don't dare use *expletives* here (like 'damn')! I said this (and by heaven, I meant it!) in the meeting." See *emphasis*.

Expletive. There are two things called "expletives" to think about as you write: strong language and bland introductory words.

Grammatical expletives are bland constructions too often used to introduce sentences. These expletives begin with "*it*" or "*there*" and are followed by forms of "*be*": "There are four of them." Although they represent a sort of *emphasis* because they change the most common *order of words* in a *sentence* (*subject, verb, object*), too many writers have used and overused this device. As a result, there is little emphasis to be gained from such sentences, which probably should be rewritten when you find them during *revision* or proofreading phases of your writing.

Words beyond the boundaries of good taste (however that is defined by you and the people who will read your writing) can add spice and emphasis to your writing. But such words must be used with the greatest care, as it is impossible to predict the effect they will have on your *audience* or who might be among your readers that you didn't expect to be there or to offend.

F

Fall, fell, fallen. An *irregular verb* in its main, *past tense*, and past *participle* forms.

Fallen. See *fall*.

Farther, further. The formal distinction between these two words is fading but should be observed in strictly standard statements. Use "farther" to refer to distance and "further" to refer to degree or time: "The farther we walked the more I realized this situation could go no further."

Feel, felt, felt. An *irregular verb* in its main, *past tense*, and past *participle* forms. See *linking verbs*.

Fell. See *fall*.

Felt. See *feel*.

Fewer, less. The difference between these two words is important but very commonly ignored. By preserving the distinction and using the words properly, you will add precision and *clarity* to your writing and demonstrate to your *audience* that you are an attentive writer fully in command of your language.

"Fewer" refers to things that are easily enumerated one

by one, such as pins, people, or penguins: "Fewer penguins were in the zoo than we expected to see."

"Less" is used with things that are not easily divisible or that you intend in your writing to be seen as a not easily enumerable mass: "There is less sand in my shoe than I expected. Fewer grains of sand fell out when I took it off than I thought would." In the first sentence in the example, sand is seen as indistinct mass, while in the second sentence emphasis is put on the number of distinct grains of sand by using "fewer."

Fight, fought, fought. An *irregular verb* in its main, *past tense*, and past *participle* forms.

Find, found, found. An *irregular verb* in its main, *past tense*, and past *participle* forms.

Firstly. There is no reason to add "ly" to this or other *ordinal numbers*, especially when they are used to *list* things.

Flew. See *fly*.

Flown. See *fly*.

Fly, flew, flown. An *irregular verb* in its main, *past tense*, and past *participle* forms.

For. *Preposition* governing the *objective case*: "There was a package at the post office for her."

Forget, forgot, forgotten. An *irregular verb* in its main, *past tense,* and past *participle* forms.

Forgot. See *forget*.

Forgotten. See *forget*.

Formal English. See *standard English*.

Fought. See *fight*.

Found. See *find*.

Fractions. When a *number* is divided by another number, the mathematical operation can be represented as a fraction, which is two numbers linked by a slash: "3/5," "22/143," "2/3." In most ordinary writing, simple fractions that represent proportions of things are spelled out rather than written in figures: "The first-graders' play will take up three-quarters of the program." But fractions of any kind that are attached to other numbers, that are in lists of numbers, or that represent scientific or technical quantities are usually presented as figures: "22 ½"; "The scores were 10, 9 ¾, and 6."

　Standard English requires a *hyphen* in any spelled-out fraction that is used as an *adjective* to modify a *noun*: "A two-thirds majority voted for the bill."

Fragments. Incomplete *sentences* of any kind are called "fragments." Generally they should be avoided except on the rare occasions when they can serve as a *rhetorical* or emphatic device: "This company needs energy. Drive. Imagination" (see *emphasis*).

Fragments are not always short bits of sentences. In fact, the most common error with fragments occurs when long *phrases* are linked together but a main *subject, verb,* or *object* is omitted: "In industrial democracies of the sort that have risen over years and through the efforts of imaginative entrepreneurs—the sorts of people who work endless hours and inspire and infuriate others by demanding that they do the same." This example is full of subjects, verbs, and objects, as well as several complete *clauses.* But there is no main clause with a subject, verb, or object; therefore, this long string of words is nothing more than that: a fragment.

Check all sentences to make sure they are complete even if they are long or complex collections of words. Use length and complexity of a group of words as a reminder that fragments often hide behind long phrases and clauses. Other clues include *colons, dashes,* and *parentheses,* which often are interjected into sentences before a subject has linked up with its verb or object. And since the phrases or clauses contained within the *punctuation* often do have subjects, verbs, and objects, the careless or distracted writer will sometimes lose sight of the fact that the main subject, verb, object connection has been left unmade. Another similar warning sign is a long introductory prepositional, adverbial, or dependent clause, which can also contain subjects, verbs, and objects galore and never lead to a full sentence. The example in the previous paragraph is of this type. See *clause, prepositional phrase,* and *interjection.*

Freeze, froze, frozen. An *irregular verb* in its main, *past tense,* and past *participle* forms.

French. French *names* of people, works, places, and so on may contain *articles* and special characters (*accents* and letters like a cedilla, "ç"): "<u>forêt</u>," "<u>français</u>," "<u>l'homme</u>." Be sure to represent such elements of French as accurately as possible. Consult a French *dictionary* or other source book to explore further details of French, such as *capitalization* and *punctuation.* See *Languages.*

From. *Preposition* governing the *objective case*: "The strongest objection came from us."

Froze. See *freeze.*

Frozen. See *freeze.*

Further. See *farther.*

Future tense. *Verbs* indicate the time of the action they represent by changing form to reflect *tense,* including action in the future: "This explanation will become clear in time." In most cases the future is signaled by the appearance of the *auxiliary* verbs "will" or "*shall*": "Shall we dance?" "Shall" is not very common in American usage except in questions like the example just given or in other cases when you want to add *emphasis* to your writing: "We shall overcome." "Will" is correct in all other instances for *standard English,* although *British English* preserves a distinction in using "shall" and "will" that should be explored in British *grammar* books by those who will be writing for strictly British *audiences*.

Adding other auxiliaries to simple future tenses creates other tenses. Adding *gerunds* ("ing" forms) to "will be" creates a tense called future progressive, used to depict action sustained or ongoing in the future: "I will be going to France." "I will be staying there six months." This tense suggests continuing future action or existence.

Combining past *participles* ("ed" forms) with "will have" produces the future perfect, representing actions conceived as completed in the future: "I will have lived in France for the whole summer."

Finally, gerunds and "will have been" go together to make the future perfect progressive, for actions that end in the future but have some ongoing sense to them: "I will have been traveling to France for four years." Again, there is a notion of continuation conveyed by this tense, as there is with future progressive.

Each of these combinations is a form of emphasis because it calls attention to a kind of action that has unusual conditions and verb forms attached to it. The names of these tenses are less important than recognizing the utility of the forms made from the future tense.

G

Gave. See *give*.

Gender. People, animals, and some objects have gender—they are male and female. Some grammatical elements reflect this natural fact, and others are oddly indifferent to it. Moreover, the pattern of assigning gender to living things and then to words that represent them has left odd traces in English, particularly when English words are somehow related to or derived from non-English ones. Add to this the troubling overidentification of some words with gender, and one arrives at one of the more tangled sides of our language (see *sexist language.*).

Despite the complexity of this aspect of English, the consequences for *grammar* and *usage* are relatively slight. Few, if any, English words have gender-specific forms, which means issues of gender *agreement* are few. *Pronouns* have clear genders: masculine and feminine "*he*" and "*she*," "*him*" and "*her*," "*his*" and "*hers*" (*nominative, objective case*, and *possessive*, respectively). And it is relatively easy to match up distinctly male and female beings with the corresponding pronoun: "The bull rams his horns." "The cow chews her cud." "The woman writes her novel." "The man irons his shirt." "The boy hugs his sister." But some words for animals or people don't match a gender. For animal words of this type we can turn to the neuter "*it*" and "*its*": "The dog chews its bone." Of course, if the gender of an animal or plant is known, a gender-specific pronoun can be selected to match: "The dog chewed his bone." See also *case*.

Words that depict human roles, occupations, and so on are trickier. It is clear that mothers are females and fathers are males. But doctors, lawyers, nurses, truck drivers, boxers, and presidents of companies and countries can be either male or female. Thus the sentence "The lawyer checked his notes while the secretary waited for her assignment" assumes gender identifications that might not be accurate and that are certainly stereotypical. Your writing should not assume such gender identifications but should find ways to indicate the possibility of either a female or a male performing the action or occupying the role you are writing about. Use "he or she," change singular to *plural*, or reconstruct the sentence to get out of the *phrase* that is causing the problem. Whatever solution you find to correct assumed and perhaps biased gender identification, make sure you pay attention to this problem and avoid it in your writing.

English words that have nothing to do with living things also have gender identifications that have persisted from older forms of our language or have been imported with words from other *languages* we now use as though they were English in origin: "The ship sailed at her full speed, but the plane had reduced her rate of descent." Since these distinctions have their roots in older forms of English or other languages, the genders of the objects tend to fade or become less distinct. Thus it is proper to refer to a ship or airplane as "it." Adjust your style to fit your *audience*'s requirements.

Genetive case. See *possessive*.

German. German has some special characters that need to be represented with care. Several German vowels can have double dots—an umlaut—over them, which distinguishes their pronounced sound: ä, ö, ü; and there is a joined double "s"—f. Umlauted letters are sometimes represented in English with an added "e" instead of the umlaut, and the doubled "s" is sometimes spelled "ss." It is better to use the *accents* and special character if you can.

   Note also that German capitalizes all *nouns* of any kind: "mein Vater, ihrer Mutter, ein Haus" (see capitalization). Check a German grammar, dictionary, or other source book for more details about German *usage, punctuation,* and so on. See *languages*.

Gerund. The *verb* form created by adding "ing" to the root of a verb is called a gerund or present *participle*. (See *conjugation* for the *spelling* and formation rules of gerunds.) It is used to form *tenses* and in a variety of *phrases* and *clauses,* and it can function as a *noun* or *adjective*: "Painting is relaxing."

   As nouns or adjectives, gerunds can play any of the parts that those words can in a *sentence,* including when they are combined into phrases or clauses. "The wilting flower, sitting in a vase on the peeling windowsill, represented declining vigor to the writer, who faced the rapid ebbing of his talent but was eyeing many cures for his ills." Here the gerund and present participle play many roles (too many for a single sentence!): Adjective ("wilting," "peeling," and "declining"), noun ("ebbing"), and verb form ("sitting" and "was eyeing").

So versatile a form has many uses, and it happily has few issues of *agreement* to be concerned with. One should, however, pay attention to how the "ing" form functions in a sentence in order to match it with the correct *pronoun* modifying it or related to it (*antecedent*). Since the gerund is a noun form, it requires a *possessive* pronoun to modify it: "The writer improved his typing." Here "typing" is a gerund and a noun possessed by a male *subject*. Hence the proper possessive pronoun is "*his*." See *modifier*.

Get, got, gotten. An *irregular verb* in its main, *past tense*, and past *participle* forms.

Give, gave, given. An *irregular verb* in its main, *past tense*, and past *participle* forms.

Given. See *give*.

Go, went, gone. An *irregular verb* in its main, *past tense*, and past *participle* forms.

Gone. See *go*.

Good, well. "Good" is an *adjective* that can only modify *nouns* or refer to them; "well" is an *adverb* that can modify or refer only to *verbs* (with one exception noted below). Be careful to modify only verbs with "well." WRONG: "The dog obeys good." RIGHT: "The dog obeys well." "*Better*" and "*best*" are both adjectives and adverbs, so they can be applied to either nouns or verbs: "Ferraris are better cars than Porsches, but Rolls Royces run best." See *modifier*.

The modest exception or unexpected *usage* here is when "well" denotes health and "good" appears after the *linking verb* "*feel*": "The child is well and feels good." In this example "well" is an adjective in the *predicate* and modifies "the child," and "good" plays the same grammatical role—*predicate adjective*. One can also say, "The leader does good" in the sense of performing good acts, but it is wrong to use "good" in this sentence if the meaning is does decently or adequately. In that case it is correct only to say, "The leader does well."

Got. See *get*.

Gotten. See *get*.

Grammar. Grammar records currently acceptable *usage* of all words and their forms in the combinations that make up *sentences* and longer statements. It is not immutable; and even though it sometimes seems impenetrable, it is only a way of describing the rules and variations that are in force in our language at whatever level grammar codifies. Most grammars are schoolbooks, and so the standards established are usually those for academic writing or some variant of "formal" *style* and usage. In business, in private life, in other kinds of writing than formal school prose, we might well apply different standards than are prescribed in academic or formal grammars. Indeed, some industries and organizations have strong views about what they believe correct English is, and they provide their employees or members with guidelines for "proper" writing. Such guidelines are variant grammars.

Which grammar should you follow? Which is right? None. Or at least none all of the time. At various moments, for various reasons, any grammar or set of rules for writing or speaking will be inappropriate, become outmoded, or simply not suit unanticipated needs. Rules written down are fixed, but circumstances change. Our speech and writing change with circumstances, "violating" grammatical rules whenever communication, art, science, or our lives demand a different, fresh, new way to express our thoughts. See *scientific language* and *audience*.

That said, it must be kept in mind that writing or speaking without any rules can be chaotic and may not meet with comprehension at any level. In that case speech or writing has lost its main purpose. And even minor violations of the rules can lead to the same mess and misunderstanding. Therefore, unless there is a compelling reason to break a rule or reshape it, follow it with care. It exists to help keep statements clear, concise, and comprehensible. Breaking it intentionally might help achieve the goals of speaking or writing; but breaking a rule through sloppiness, inattention, or lack of concern will surely not aid expression or understanding. More likely, careless errors will disrupt the delivery of your ideas and lead your audience to mistrust the source of such confusion. See *colloquial*, *dialect*, non-English *languages*, *clarity*, and *efficiency*.

Grew. See *grow*.

Grow, grew, grown. An *irregular verb* in its main, *past tense*, and past *participle* forms.

Grown. See *grow*.

H

Had. See *have*.

Hang, hung, hung. An *irregular verb* meaning to suspend something, in its main, *past tense*, and past *participle* forms. Note that "*hanged*" is the regular past tense and past participle of the verb "to hang" that means to execute by hanging.

Hanged, hung. Commonly confused *past tense* forms of the *verb* "hang," these words refer, respectively, to executions ("The traitor was hanged.") and any other form of hanging things or people ("The curator hung by a thread of suspense while the priceless painting was hung by the klutzy assistant.").

Have, had, had. An *irregular verb* in its main, *past tense*, and past *participle* forms.

Have, of. Do not use "*of*" to complete a compound *verb*. WRONG: "I could of come." RIGHT: "I could have come." Acceptable or undetectable in speech, the use of "*of*" with verbs is simply an obvious error in all writing but fiction or linguistic reporting.

He, him, his. The *personal pronoun* "he" has an *objective*

case form of "him" and a *possessive* case form of "his."
See also *case*.

Hear, heard, heard. An *irregular verb* in its main, *past tense*, and past *participle* forms.

Heard. See *hear*.

He'd. This *contraction* of "he had" and "he would" should not normally be used in *standard English* writing.

Helping verb. See *auxiliary*.

Her. See *she*.

Her/him. See *she/he*.

Hers. See *she*.

Herself. See *-self*.

He's. This *contraction* of "he is" and "he has" should rarely, if ever, be used in *standard English* writing.

He/she, him/her. Rewrite this awkward concession to *gender* equality into more easily digested forms like "he and she" or "they." See *sexist language*.

Hid. See *hide*.

Hidden. See *hide*.

Hide, hid, hidden. An *irregular verb* in its main, *past tense,* and past *participle* forms.

Him. See *he.*

Him/her. See *he/she.*

Himself. See *-self.*

His. See *he.*

Hit, hit, hit. An *irregular verb* in its main, *past tense,* and past *participle* forms.

Homonym. Homonyms are words that sound alike and therefore are easily confused with each other and hard to spell: "Write the rite right." The example is silly but makes the point that spelling mimics the sound patterns of English in different, sometimes strange and unpredictable, ways. The writer can only try to remember all the words that exist in homonym pairs or sets and check whether the correct one appears in any sentence. If you don't know that there are several words that sound like "rain," you might well choose the wrong one when you are talking about royalty or carriages. The only thing to do is look up "rain" in a *dictionary* and see if it is used for a monarch's "reign" or the "reins" that control horses. Obviously it isn't, and most dictionaries will list the homonyms.

The most commonly confused homonyms and similar words appear in entries throughout this book and are cross-referenced for all similar or homonymous forms. You can thus find "*their*," "there," and "they're."

Hopefully. It seems the struggle to help people use this word correctly has all but ended in defeat. The word is improperly used at the beginning of a sentence (or anywhere else) to mean "it is hoped." WRONG: "Hopefully, I will win the lottery and get rich." This sentence actually means, I, full of hope, will win the lottery and get rich. However, almost everyone makes the "wrong" sort of statement on the assumption that it means, I hope I will win. . . . "Hopefully" is used properly as follows: "The student looked hopefully to the professor as a font of wisdom."

Don't use "hopefully" in the wrong way in formal, school, or academic writing, even though it is now appearing even there without comment or censure.

However. "However," is used in many ways: as an *interjection* ("The experts don't, however, agree with you."); as an *indefinite* adverb ("However you do it is okay with me."); and as a *conjunctive adverb* ("Jan wants to go; however, Chris doesn't."). See also *adverb*.

Hr. Use the *abbreviation* for "hour" (hr.) only in tables, scientific writing, or other special circumstances. In most cases, hr. should be spelled out as "hour." See *scientific language*.

Hung. See *hang* and *hanged*.

Hyphen. The hyphen *punctuation* mark (-) is used to join words to some *prefixes,* to indicate where simple words were joined but are now divided at the end of a printed or typed line, or to link together *compound words.*

PREFIXES

In modern *usage* most *prefixes* are spelled solid (closed up) with words: "Antiwar protestors were arrested at the rally." But in some cases hyphens are mandatory: before capitalized words or before numerals: "Pre-Prohibition wines include the post-1918 vintages." When a prefix spelled solid with a word is confusing, a hyphen can be inserted to clarify and is sometimes required: "Re-creating recreational settings is refreshing." See *capitalization* and *numbers.*

LINE ENDS

When words don't fit onto the lines of paper, they are sometimes "broken" into pieces placed at the end of one line and the beginning of the next (as in many lines in this book). A hyphen is placed at the end of the last fragment of the word at the end of a line to indicate that the rest of the word is at the beginning of the next line. Words are broken only at the ends of *syllables* or where hyphens naturally occur in them. If possible, it is best to avoid introducing a line-ending hyphen into a word or string of words that already has one or more hyphens in it. One-syllable words are not divided over lines, nor are words with single-letter syllables at their beginning or end broken at those points (for example, don't break "wordy" and leave a hanging "y" at the beginning of a line).

Compounds

Although some *compound words* are formed without a hyphen, most include it: "That is a decision-making factor." Compounds with hyphens include fractions, spelled-out *numbers* from twenty-one to ninety-nine, and specially concocted strings of words: "One-seventh of the one hundred and thirty-five gurus believed in life-after-death manifestations."

I. The first-*person* singular *pronoun* is "I." Its *objective case* is "*me*": "It is I; give me the package." The *plural* form of "I" are "*we*" and "us": "It is we; give us the package." Obviously, the grammatically correct forms of "I" following *linking verbs* like "be" now seem somewhat stilted. Most people would say (and many would write in the most formal circumstances): "It is me/us." See also *case*.

Ibid. This *abbreviation* of the *Latin* word "ibidem" means "in the same place." It is used only in footnotes and endnotes in scholarly writing and should be avoided elsewhere. Even in notes or references to scholarly writing, the modern preference is for repetition of a shortened title or author's name instead of the somewhat opaque Latinism.

I'd. The *contraction* of "I had" or "I would," normally not used in formal *standard English* writing.

I.e. This *abbreviation* of the *Latin* words "id est" means "that is." This *interjection* is frequently useful as a device to draw attention to something, but it is best in most writing to use the English rather than the Latin form or abbreviation unless space is a very important consideration. WRONG: "The governor, i.e., R. J. Warren, signed the bill."

BETTER: "The governor, that is, R. J. Warren, signed the bill."

If. "If" is a *subordinating conjunction* suggesting conditionality.

Ill. The comparative forms of this *adjective/adverb* are irregular: ill, worse, worst. See *comparison*.

Illicit. See *elicit*.

Illusion. See *allusion*.

I'm. The *contraction* of "I am" is "I'm." It should not normally be used in standard, formal (particularly academic) writing. See *I, and,* and *standard English*.

Immigrate. See *emigrate*.

Impact. "Impact" does not mean to affect or to influence and should not be used in that sense. WRONG: "Poverty impacts the ability to learn and earn." RIGHT: "Poverty affects/diminishes the ability to learn and earn." "Impact" is properly used mainly as a *noun* meaning a blow or a collision. As a *verb* the word denotes pushing or packing together and is usually applied to teeth: "The teenager has impacted wisdom teeth."

Imperative. *Verbs* can be used to describe actions or states of being, but they also can be used to request or demand action of someone: "Read this carefully." When verbs command, they are said to be in the imperative *mood*.

Most verbs in the imperative take their main or root form. Commonly, imperative statements add an *exclamation point* to emphasize that they are commands, demands, or important requests: "Form a line!" Even with the addition of "please" to a sentence like the example, an exclamation point can be used to mark an imperative statement. However, mild, nonimperious imperatives need not have any exclamation attached to them but can appear with a period: "Consider this." This example would probably look a bit odd with an exclamation point.

The *subject* of an imperative statement is usually omitted and merely implied—you do this or that, with the *"you"* not stated. However, an explicit subject can appear. When it is "you," it is treated as any subject: "You get to work!" The appearance of "you" is an emphatic device in itself, and imperatives with explicit subjects often end in exclamation points. When there is a subject that is not "you," it is usually treated as being in apposition to the implied "you" and is therefore set off with a *comma*: "Soldiers, pick up your weapons!" Military commands of this sort usually have an exclamation point, by the way.

Two short imperatives in the same sentence constitute two independent *clauses* and therefore should be separated by a comma. However, since the subjects of the imperatives are the same by implication and do not appear in the sentence, such a comma is frequently omitted: "Rise and shine!" The longer the imperative statements or the more possible confusion of implied subjects, the more necessary a dividing comma becomes: "Consider the implications of all the statements we made and you reviewed, and then rewrite what was initially drafted by the others." This sentence benefits from adding the comma between clauses (although it could be omitted without much risk of confusing a reader) and certainly does not need an exclamation point.

More than two imperative clauses should be joined by commas: "Wake up, smell the flowers, and get on with life." See *appositive* and *emphasis*.

In. *Preposition* governing the *objective case*: "The anger was welling up in them."

In order. A *subordinating conjunction,* indicating a purpose.

Indefinite. *Pronouns* that do not refer to specific *persons* or numbers are said to be indefinite: "None of them is here." The indefinite pronouns are "all," "another," "*anybody,*" "anyone," "anything," "both," "*each,*" "either," "everyone," "*everything,*" "few," "most," "*neither,*" "*nobody,*" "*none,*" "no one," "*nothing,*" "*one,*" "other," "*some,*" "somebody," "someone," and "something."

Their use is fairly straightforward except for the complexity of deciding whether they are singular or *plural.* The example above treats "none" as a singular indefinite and suggests that the writer thinks of the group of "them" as individuals, not one of whom is present. It would be correct to write "None of them are here," suggesting that "them" is a group of more than one individual conceived of plurally. It can be argued that when "none" refers to a group of things that are readily divisible into individuals, it should agree with plural *verbs* (see *agreement*). This is a good rule of thumb to follow, particularly when there is some doubt in your mind—check the *antecedent* or thing referred to by the indefinite pronoun and choose singular or plural appropriately. But all the indefinites in the following list are unclear in their number and can be used as you see fit: "all," "any," "enough," "*more*," "most," "none," and "some."

The same *rule* and variation holds for pronouns that refer to indefinite pronouns: "Enough of the paint remains to use it on the barn." Here "enough" refers to a singular quantity of paint and therefore governs the subsequent singular pronoun "*it*." But: "Enough of the pigs remain to make them into many hams." Here "enough" is plural because it refers to pigs; it therefore requires a plural referent pronoun—"them."

You should take care not only with agreement and antecedents of indefinite pronouns but with their overuse. If you can put a *number* or quantity to something, don't say "some" or "a few." Obviously, there are times when things are not certain, and indefinites express the lack of counts or amounts. But the presence of many indefinites in your writing might signal a failure to find out how many whatevers are being talked about. And too many whatevers might leave your reader with too many doubts about what you are writing about.

Indefinite article. See *a*.

Independent clause. See *clause*.

Indicative mood. See *mood*.

Indirect object. Sentences in which *subjects* act on an *object* and convey that action in some manner to another thing or person are said to have "indirect objects" that receive the action or the object less directly than the object itself: "The mail carrier gave the letter to Chris." "Letter" is the direct object, and "Chris" is the indirect object in the example. Indirect objects are often preceded by "to" or a similar word, but not always: "The mail carrier gave me the letter." "Me" is the indirect object in this sentence. *Pronouns* are not always indirect objects, however: "The clerk directed me to the manager." Here "me" is the *direct object* and "manager" acts as the indirect object.

Note that pronouns in the *objective* (also called accusative) *case* change form (are inflected)—"me" is the inflected objective case form of "*I*," a *nominative* singular form considered uninflected. See *inflection*.

Indirect question. *Questions* that are reported rather than stated directly are called "indirect questions." They are not followed by *question marks* but by *periods*: "My roommate asked what I thought." But: "My roommate asked, 'What do you think?'" *Interrogative* pronouns like "what" often signal an indirect question and take the place of any *punctuation* that might mark a question. See also *pronouns*.

Indirect quotation. Like *indirect questions,* indirect *quotations* talk about someone's speech but don't record it directly: "The reporter said that the politician made a speech." No *quotation marks* set off words reported in indirect quotations. But: "The reporter said, 'The politician made a speech.' " The word "*that*" is the most common signal that speech is being reported indirectly rather than being quoted directly.

However, sentences that include "that" can report speech directly and thus use quotation marks in place of the more common *comma* that sets off direct quotes: "Tolstoy never said that 'war is hell.' It was Clausewitz who said, 'War is hell.' " Note that the second example—with a comma— requires *capitalization* of the first word of the quoted *sentence.* The first example quotes only a fragment of speech and introduces it with "that," which means that no capitalization is required.

Infinitive. The main or root form of a *verb* plus "*to*" constitutes the grammatical form of a verb called an infinitive.

Infinitives can be used in many ways, including as *adjective, adverb,* or *noun phrases*: "To err is human." They also often appear with *auxiliary* verbs: "It is going to rain."

When infinitive phrases appear as *objects* of verbs, the *subjects* of those *phrases* are in the *objective case*: "We asked the cab driver to move." Although the case of "cab driver" in the example is not apparent since most *nouns* do not change form in English objective *case,* putting a *pronoun* into the *sentence* reveals what has happened: "We asked her to move."

Another peculiarity of infinitives is their cohesiveness—

their need to stand together with their supporting "to" for *clarity*. This has led to a "rule" that bars "splitting" the infinitive with words falling between the "to" and the main verb. But the *rule* cannot be slavishly followed, as many unsplit infinitives sound awkward or pretentious: "I want quickly to reach our goal." The example is correct (as would be: "I want to reach our goal quickly," though slightly different in meaning and slightly less awkward). "I want to quickly reach our goal" is acceptable in most circumstances, although it probably shouldn't appear in school papers. If your sentence simply won't work without splitting an infinitive and you are worried that breaking the rule will bother your *audience,* you might revise your statement to avoid the infinitive altogether: "I want our goal reached quickly." See *split infinitive*.

When infinitive phrases begin a sentence and are not its subject, they are usually followed by a *comma*: "To reach our goal quickly, we need to work hard." As with all such phrases (*prepositional phrase,* adverbial phrase, and *interjections*), *usage* varies, allowing some shorter phrases that "fit" a sentence more closely to stand without a comma. However, the *inversion* that occurs when infinitive phrases lead a sentence rarely allows the comma to be dropped.

When using infinitives in *titles* or other emphasized material that is capitalized, do not capitalize the "to" unless it is the first word: "The article was called 'Working to Reach Goals.' " See *capitalization* and *emphasis*.

Inflection. Inflection is the change in word forms to reflect changed grammatical roles—for *case, number, tense, comparison,* or for any other reason. "Her" and "him" are inflected forms of "*she*" and "*he*"—the *objective case*—just as "*were*" is an inflected form of "to be"—the *past tense* plural or *subjunctive*.

Inside of. In formal writing there is no reason to add "*of*" to any *preposition* like "inside" or "outside."

Instead of. *Preposition* governing the *objective case*: "My assistant went instead of me."

Insure. See *assure*.

Intensifier. Words that are added to emphasize statements are sometimes called "intensifiers." More specifically, there are two main classes of intensifiers: *adverbs* and intensive *pronouns*. See *emphasis*.

Virtually any adverb modifying an *adjective* can be said to intensify it, but the term is usually reserved for such words as "very": "The apple is very red." Lesser and greater degrees of intensification are possible with words like "somewhat" or "extremely." See *modifier*.

Intensive pronouns work like intensifying adverbs, adding force to other pronouns or *nouns*: "The tiger itself ate the kill." Compounds of "self" are the commonest intensive pronouns, as in this example.

Interface. Except in discussions of computer technology, "interface" as *noun* or *verb* is probably best avoided as jargon or a *cliché*. WRONG: "We need to interface on this problem." RIGHT: "We need to meet on (talk about) this problem."

Interjection. Words that appear intrusively in a sentence and that carry some force or charge of feeling are called "interjections": "Oh my, what a nice day!"

Such words are usually set off in *commas* wherever they appear in the *sentence,* and the sentence that includes interjections can end in an *exclamation point* to further emphasize the statement: "We don't, of course, want that to happen!" This example could have ended with a *period.* It would be hard to justify omitting the commas from the example because the interjection is fairly forceful; but other sentences with milder interjections do so: "It is therefore clear what happened." "Therefore" in the example is an interjection that could have been enclosed in commas but is perfectly clear as shown. See *emphasis.*

Interrogative. Words that signal questioning in a sentence are called "interrogatives": "how," "what," "*when,*" "where," "which," "*who,*" "whose," "why," and the like. Interrogative *sentences* usually end in a *question mark*: "How are you feeling?"

Just as interrogative words can function in a sentence that is not a *question* ("I told how I felt and what I wanted."), so questions can be formed without interrogative words, by changing the *order of words,* adding question marks, and so on: "Are you feeling well?" The most common way to indicate a question besides the question mark is to invert the word order of a sentence, moving a *verb* to the initial position, as in the example (see *inversion*). Very often the verb moved to the front of a sentence to make a question is an *auxiliary* verb: "Did the pupils write well?"

But interrogative forms can also be produced more

crudely, without inversion or interrogative words: "Working hard?" The question signal here is the shortness and fragmentary nature of the sentence (see *fragment*), along with the question mark. Longer sentences that lack interrogatives or changed word order but are followed by question marks are not really questions, usually, but statements in which the writer has no confidence. Such superfluous questions should be avoided.

Into. *Preposition* governing the *objective case*: "The arrow whizzed into the target."

Intransitive. *Verbs* that indicate action taken on an *object* are said to be *transitive*: "My neighbor chopped wood." Verbs that do not suggest action transmitted to an object are said to be intransitive: "My neighbor spoke." In the latter example, the verb is intransitive because there is no object even though "speak" can function as a transitive verb with an object: "My neighbor spoke French." While many verbs can be either transitive or intransitive in a sentence, some are always intransitive: "My neighbor relented."

Inversion. To invert something means to turn it around or over. Grammatical inversion means turning around the *order of words* to create *emphasis* or a different meaning, such as a *question*, an order, or some other *rhetorical* effect (effect on the presentation and reception of words): "Is that so?" "Prove it!" "To demonstrate such a thing would be difficult."

Each of the sentences in this example is inverted from the "normal" order of *subject, verb,* and *object* to make a different meaning or to call attention to itself. The first sentence is a question, the second is an *imperative,* and the third is a rhetorical inversion meant to vary the pace or rhythm of writing or to draw attention to the words moved to the front or the end of the sentence. In the last sentence the writer emphasizes "demonstrate" as the first word and "difficult" as the last, perhaps calling attention to a higher standard of proof, such as scientific argument, and how hard it is. Or perhaps the intention was simply to avoid another bland "it is . . ." sentence—"It would be difficult to demonstrate such a thing"—in which the key concepts of proof and difficulty are lost in the middle of the statement. See also *expletive.*

With other purposes in mind, the last sentence in the example could be inverted in other ways: "Such a thing would be difficult to demonstrate." Here, the emphasis is on the thing that needs proof, which is unstated in the example but, according to the writer of this sentence, something to be reckoned with. Another variant: "Wouldn't it be difficult to demonstrate such a thing" could reasonably end with either a question mark or an exclamation point, depending on what the writer was trying to do—raise doubts about how hard the task would be (which could be done ironically to suggest that the person being addressed might find it difficult, or straightforwardly, to wonder about the degree of difficulty) or express warning or sympathy about the task proposed. See *irony.*

Inversion is a very powerful way to enliven and enrich your writing. Take care that sentence elements in a different order than expected work according to all the necessary *rules* and are still clear enough to be followed.

Irony. When a writer or speaker says one thing but suggests somehow that a different or opposite meaning is intended, the statement is said to be "ironic": "Life is short, but who would want it any other way?" Clearly some people want life to be longer, so that this *rhetorical* question could be said to be ironic. Irony is a useful device to draw attention to a point, but it often eludes some readers who treat statements literally.

Irregardless. Don't use this word, which is in fact a *double negative* that contradicts itself. The right word is "regardless."

Irregular verbs. The following list includes the most common irregular verbs. Only the forms listed below vary from the normal patterns of *conjugation*: these verbs all form their *future tenses*, for instance, in the same way others do—by adding "will" to the main form. Each verb has an entry of its own for further explanations, if necessary.

Since some of the commonest verbs, including many *linking verbs* and *auxiliary* verbs, are irregular, it is important to be aware of how these verbs work.

MAIN	PAST TENSE	PAST PARTICIPLE
be	was, were	been
beat	beat	beaten
become	became	become
begin	began	begun
bite	bit	bitten
blow	blew	blown

break	broke	broken
bring	brought	brought
build	built	built
burn	burned	burned
burst	burst	burst
buy	*bought*	*bought*
catch	caught	caught
choose	chose	chosen
come	came	come
cost	cost	cost
cut	cut	cut
dig	dug	dug
dive	dived	dived
do	did	done
draw	drew	drawn
drink	drank	drunk
drive	drove	driven
eat	ate	eaten
fall	fell	fallen
feel	felt	felt
fight	fought	fought
find	found	found
fly	flew	flown
forget	forgot	forgotten
freeze	froze	frozen
get	got	gotten
give	gave	given
go	went	gone
grow	grew	grown
hang	hung	hung
have	had	had
hear	heard	heard
hide	hid	hidden

hit	hit	hit
keep	kept	kept
know	knew	known
lay	laid	laid
lead	led	led
leave	left	left
lend	lent	lent
let	let	let
lie (down)	lay	lain
lose	*lost*	*lost*
make	made	made
mean	meant	meant
meet	met	met
pay	paid	paid
prove	proved	proved
put	put	put
read	read	read
ride	rode	ridden
ring	rang	rung
rise	rose	risen
run	ran	run
say	said	said
see	saw	seen
send	sent	sent
set	set	set
shake	shook	shaken
shine (light)	shone	shone
shoot	shot	shot
show	showed	shown
shrink	shrank	shrunk
sing	sang	sung
sink	sank	sunk
sit	sat	sat

sleep	slept	slept
speak	spoke	spoken
spend	spent	spent
spread	spread	spread
spring	sprang	sprung
stand	stood	stood
steal	stole	stolen
strike	struck	struck
swim	swam	swum
swing	swung	swung
take	took	taken
teach	taught	taught
tear	tore	torn
tell	told	told
think	thought	thought
throw	threw	thrown
wake	woke	woke (see entry)
wear	wore	worn
win	won	won
wind	wound	wound
write	wrote	written

Is. The third-*person* singular *present tense* of *be*: "He/she/it is important." Also see *agreement, auxiliary, conjugation, number,* and *tense*.

It. The *third-person* singular *pronoun* is "it" in both the subjective case and *objective case*. See *its*.

Italics. Slanted type is called "italic," as distinguished from the normal upright forms called "*Roman*": "Most printing is in Roman, but *some* words are italic." Italicized words are emphasized for various purposes: to indicate *titles* or names of various things, to distinguish non-English words from English ones, and to draw attention to the words for any other purpose: "The teacher was reading *War and Peace* out loud, but mispronounced the Russian word for 'war'—*voina*—and got *very* angry." The example is a bit forced, but it shows the title of a work of literature, a non-English word, and a word italicized for *emphasis* ("very"). The use of italics for the last kind of emphasis (or of underlining or *quotation* marks to do the same thing) is one of those overused devices that should be resorted to only occasionally if at all. Create force and point in your writing in other ways than through typographical enhancement.

When words, letters, or numbers need to be emphasized so that it is clear they are being talked about as words in the grammatical sense rather than being used directly in a sentence, underlining, quotation marks, or italics can be used: "Grammatical terms like *verb* or *noun* can be misunderstood." In this book, words that have entries explaining or defining them are set in italic type. See *names, titles,* and *typeface.*

It's. See *its.*

Its, it's. Don't confuse "its," the third-*person* singular *possessive* pronoun, with "it's," a *contraction* of "it is." the first term is used to indicate something that belongs to something ("That is its den."), while the second word only stands in place of "it is" ("It's very clear that we are not welcome here."). See *pronoun.*

J

Japanese. One of the main *Asian languages,* Japanese has a well-established system of transliteration into English. In most everyday writing, the *accents* that appear in some Japanese words are not used. Consult relevant reference works for details.

Jargon. A specialized *vocabulary* that is used mainly by a limited group of people in the same work or profession is called jargon. Since the meaning of jargon is known only to a restricted *audience*, its use limits the number of people who can understand what you are saying or writing. Such a limitation is not a problem if you are addressing only colleagues, professional associates, or peers; indeed, it can be a benefit since jargon is often shorthand that lets someone in the know quickly understand what you are trying to say. Jargon conveys information quickly about one's knowledge, status, and membership in groups. But for more general audiences or those who might not be among the initiated in special *usages* of words, stick to more commonly recognized terminology.

Jargon: "How many megabytes in your box?" Translated: "Does your computer have lots of memory?" Even the second, translated example might be too obscure for those who are not computer literate. A better, but longer, question for them might be: "Does your computer have a large additional storage device to permanently record files?"

Jargon need not be technical. Many people speak in special ways among friends, neighbors, or others with whom they can identify by some means or other. Such language is also called "argot," "lingo," or "*slang*." As it becomes more commonly recognized, it merges with *colloquial*, or everyday, speech and sometimes passes into accepted usage.

Jr. The *abbreviation* of "junior," used very often with a *comma* after appropriate names ("Adam Arkin, Jr."), but it's never acceptable as an independent element in a *sentence*.

K

Keep, kept, kept. An *irregular verb* in its main, *past tense,* and past *participle* forms.

Kept. See *keep*.

Kind. "Kind" is one of those words used in English too often because it takes the place of thought or extends what looks like a skimpy idea or *phrase* into something larger or longer. Most often it signals weak or sloppy thinking: "That kind of work is poor." This *sentence* is acceptable but communicates little to the reader. Better to specify what is hidden behind "kind": "Careless work is poor."

   "Kind of" is another flabby form for avoiding *clarity* of thought or expression: "It is kind of warm." This is not acceptable and can be improved, again, by getting rid of "kind of" and spelling out what you have in mind: "It is very (not very, a little) warm." Also see *sort*.

   It is also best to avoid "kind" in place of words like "variety": "That is a kind of banana." It is either a banana or not, or it is some variant form of a banana; but it tells your *audience* nothing worth knowing to say it is a "kind of" banana. Do you mean it is a form of banana you've never seen before? Or maybe you don't know what it is called? Then say so: "This looks like a banana, but I don't know what it's called." "I think it is related to bananas, but it might be something else altogether." If you do know that it is a variety ("sort" or "type") of something, "kind" can be used to indicate a relationship to a larger category: "I don't know the name for this, but this kind of banana grows here."

"Kind" is singular and is modified by singular *demonstrative* pronouns: "This kind of banana grows only here." WRONG: "These kind of bananas are tasty." RIGHT: "This kind of banana is green, but those kinds of oranges are yellow." See *modifier* and *pronoun*.

Do not use "*a*" after "kind of." WRONG: "There is some kind of a banana growing here." RIGHT: "Some kind of banana is growing here, but I don't know its name."

Knew. See *know*.

Know, knew, known. An *irregular verb* in its main, *past tense,* and past *participle* forms.

Known. See *know*.

L

Laid. This is the *past tense* and past *participle* form only of the *verb* "to *lay,*" meaning to put or place: "The lecturer laid the notepad aside and spoke." Don't use "laid" as a form of "*lie,*" which means being in a horizontal position and forms its past tense differently: "The child lay in bed asleep."

Lain. See *lie, lay, lain.*

Languages. Look under specific language names for guidance on *spelling, punctuation, accents,* and other matters related to major languages (e.g., *Arabic*).

Keep in mind that non-English words are usually marked by *italics* or underlining, but that many words from other languages are now used in English as native words and are unmarked in any way: "Pass the pasta and pesto, please."

Overuse of other languages in English documents can be irritating to those who don't know the language. Avoid this practice and use non-English words for occasional *emphasis* or when no genuine English equivalent will suffice: "We were discussing the Russian verb <u>perestroit</u>, which is the form from which <u>perestroika</u> comes."

Take care as well with the overly familiar use of non-English words or phrases, particularly when addressing those whose first language is not English. They might find quite offensive what strikes you as slangy or cute. Also, a word that entered English at some point as acceptable usage in another language might now have become objectionable or inappropriate: "Howdy, Comrade (Tovarishch) Yeltsin. Welcome to America." "Comrade" is an English word, but in Russian it has come to have connotations of a distasteful past and should not be used. Señor can have the same effect with some Spanish speakers, just as señorita might prove offensive for linguistic, political, or moral reasons. See entries for *Arabic, Asian languages, French, German, Japanese, Latin, Russian, Spanish,* and other languages.

Later, latter. "Later" is an *adverb* that refers to time: "My friend called later than I expected." "Latter" is an *adjective* that means second of two: "Of the two suits, I like the latter."

Latin. Many *abbreviations* used in scholarly and scientific writing come from Latin. Unless you are writing scholarly or scientific works, you probably shouldn't use such abbreviations (*e.g., ibid.,* and *i.e.*). Similarly, unless your *audience* is made up of Latin scholars, the use of full Latin phrases is not helpful to most readers. See *languages.*

Latter. See *later.*

Lay, lie. These two *verbs* have different meanings and irregular forms that are often confused. "Lay" means to put or place something (usually specified) and has the forms "*laid*" (*past tense*), "*laying*" (present *participle* or *gerund*), and "*laid*" (past participle). "*Lie*" means to be prone or not standing (and never has an *object* because it is *intransitive*), and it has the forms "lay" (past tense), "lying" (present participle or gerund), and "lain" (past participle). Note that "lie" has no "laid" form, which is often the root of confusion. See also *irregular verbs*.

lb. The common *abbreviation* for "pound" is "lb." It is used mainly in recipes, technical presentations, and the like. In ordinary or formal writing not intended for technical or cooking *audiences*, spell out "pound."

Lead, led, led. An *irregular verb* in its main, *past tense*, and past *participle* forms.

Least. See *little*.

Leave, left, left. An *irregular verb* in its main, *past tense*, and past *participle* forms.

Led. See *lead*.

Left. See *leave*.

Lend, lent, lent. An *irregular verb* in its main, *past tense* and past *participle* forms. This verb usually does not refer to money lending. Use "loan, loaned, loaned" for financial transactions.

Lent. See *lend*.

Less. See *fewer* and *little*.

Let, let, let. An *irregular verb* in its main, *past tense,* and past *participle* forms.

Let's. This *contraction* of "let us" is not normally used in *standard English* writing.

Lie, lay, lain. An *irregular verb* meaning lie down, in its main, *past tense,* and past *participle* forms. The verb that means to speak falsely has a regular *conjugation*: lie, lied, lied. See *lay.*

Like. "Like" has several functions and is commonly misused in many of them. Besides having once been a common *interjection* in a *style* considered out of the mainstream ("Like, wow, man, that is awesome and groovy!"), "like" is still resorted to when thought fails and some sound must be made or letters put on paper: "This painting is, like, sensational!" In informal speech this use of "like" is probably unavoidable, just as one is forced to mumble "ya know" or "ummm" sometimes while the brain catches up with the mouth. But "like" in these *usages* should never appear in formal, *standard English* documents unless it is accurately quoted as such.

Proper uses of the *preposition* "like" involve *comparisons*: "That tree looks like a scarecrow." Such a construction is called a "simile," calling attention to similarity between things. "Like" is used when comparing two or more *nouns* or nouns and their *modifiers* (*adjectives* or adjective *phrases*). It can be replaced by "such as" in many cases, but it can never be substituted for "*as,*" which links *verbs* or verb and adjective complement or *adverb* (or phrases): "I worked as a sailor." This example means held a job as a sailor. "I worked like a stevedore" means my work was hard, like a stevedore's work, not that I held the position of stevedore. WRONG: "I worked hard, like I should have." RIGHT: I worked hard, as I should have." "As" is correct because it links verbs or verb phrases, not nouns.

Linking verb. *Verbs* that join two or more *nouns* or nouns and *adjectives* more or less equally are called "linking verbs." The commonest linking verbs are "appear," "*be*," "*become*," "*feel*," "*grow*," "look," "*make*," "*prove*," "remain, "*seem*," "smell," and "sound."

Forms of "be" are probably used most often to link words: "He is a writer. He is good." In the first sentence in the example, a *pronoun* is joined to a noun, which is called a *predicate noun.* In the second example, "*is*" links a pronoun and *adjective,* called a *predicate adjective.* The names of these forms are not so important as the point that both the noun and the adjective remain in the same *nominative* case that is used for the sentence *subject.* The words that are linked to the subject are not its *object*—since there is no action transmitted from subject to object—but its *subject complement.* Remember that a pronoun subject complement does not change form: "It is I."

Note that many linking verbs can also function in different ways, as *transitive* verbs that do govern the *objective case* when their objects are expressed: "The musician sounded the trumpet." In its linking form "sound" is usually followed by an adjective (not an *adverb*): "The trumpet sounded rough." When a linking verb is followed by an adverb, the adverb does not express a quality of the subject but of the verb: "The child looked blankly at the television screen." "The child looked blank" is a sentence with "look" as a linking verb joining a person and a quality or condition of the person—blankness.

It is tempting to make living verbs agree with their subject complements rather than their subjects, particularly when the *emphasis* is on the complement rather than the subject or when the sentence is inverted: "My favorite animal is bears." This sounds somewhat awkward, but it is correct, since the subject is "animal" and the complement is "bears." "Bears are my favorite animal" is also correct and less awkward. "Is your favorite animal bears?" is also correct, as would be "Are bears your favorite animal?" You can choose whichever of these constructions sounds best to you or will best suit your *audience*. Some rewriting might help, too: "Are your favorite animals bears?" See *agreement* and *inversion*.

Lists. More than three things put together grammatically constitute a "list." Lists can be set off from the rest of a *sentence* by a *colon*: "Here are the parts: piston, ring, valve, spark plug, and hose." If the elements in a list are numbered, put the *numbers* or letters for each item into *parentheses*: "There are four parts: (1) pistons, (2) rings, (3) valves, and (4) hoses." The items can be divided by *commas* or, if they are to be kept more distinct or are more complex, *semicolons* (especially if the items include other punctuation): "There are three important factors: (a) items of value, including gold, silver, and platinum; (b) insurance. . . ." Lists can also be distinguished by putting each item in them on a separate line and starting each line with a number, letter, or other marker:

- nouns
- adjectives
- verbs

Such typographically emphasized lists can include *punctuation* marks at the end of each item or appear, as in the example, with only their spacing to mark them (see *emphasis*). If the items in such a list are sentences or *clauses,* it is probably clearer to end them in *periods, semicolons,* or *commas.* Adding "*and*" before the last item in lists on separate lines can be helpful, or it can prove tricky, especially when the punctuation is not suitable or the spacing leaves "and" dangling somewhere.

Within lists it is important to maintain *parallelism,* or equivalency among the items. Thus the list set on separate lines would be incorrect or harder to follow if we added another item like "writing sentences too long." The shift from simple nouns to a *gerund* phrase makes it hard to see the relationship among the parts of the list. If the list is made up of sentences or clauses, it is particularly important to keep similar structures so that your reader can follow what is being said.

Little. The comparative forms of "little" in the sense of quantity are irregular: little, less, least. "Little" in the sense of small size is compared regularly: "little, littler, littlest." See *comparison.*

'll. An *apostrophe* plus "ll" is commonly used to form *contractions* of *future tense* verbs and *nouns* or, more often, *pronouns*: "The dog'll eat the chicken bone, and it'll die." Neither contraction normally appears in *standard English* writing, but those with nouns are considered particularly substandard.

Loc. cit. This *abbreviation* of the *Latin* words "<u>locus citatus</u>," means "the place cited." The abbreviation is used only in footnotes or endnotes to scholarly or scientific writing and is growing less common even there. Current practice is to use a shortened title or author's name to repeat a citation.

Loose, lose. Commonly confused, these words have different meanings and are different *parts of speech*. "Loose" is most commonly an *adjective* that means not tight or scattered: "The seal on the window was loose, letting lots of loose sand blow in." (There is a *verb* "to loose," which means to release something or to make it loose; but the word is a bit archaic and not commonly used.) "Lose" is a verb that means to fail to keep track of or misplace: "You will lose your place if you don't pay attention." Its *conjugation* is irregular: lose, lost, lost. See *irregular verbs*.

Lose. See *loose*.

Lower case. Letters that are not capitalized (large and in special form) are said to be "lower case." Capitalized letters are called "*upper case*." See *capitalization*.

Ltd. This British *abbreviation* of the word "limited" refers to a kind of company and is like the U.S. abbreviations "*Co.*" or "Inc."

-ly. The *suffix* "ly" is added to words to make them *adverbs,* which modify *verbs*: "Merrily we roll along!" Some words that end in "ly" are not adverbs: "family." It is important to note this distinction when words that end in "ly" are joined to *participles* to form adjectival *phrases* that modify *nouns*. Adverbs and participles so linked are not hyphenated: "The merrily rolling wagon sped ahead." Words that are not adverbs in such constructions are linked to participles by *hyphens*: "Our family-gathering places include the kitchen table and the newly landscaped back-yard." Since "family" is a noun, it is linked by hyphen to its participle in this adjectival construction; but "newly" is an adverb that should not be hyphenated to a related participle. See *modifier* and *adjective*.

M

Made. See *make*.

Main clause. See *clause*.

Main form. Groups of words are built on a core of letters that represents the simplest element of meaning, known as the main form (also called a root). The main form "vid" carries the sense of seeing or sight into such forms as "video" and "evident." A variant of "vid" is "vis," which has the same main, or basic, core of meaning related to sight: "vision," "visible," "visually."

Recognizing a main form in words can often help us understand how *prefixes, suffixes,* or other modifications of the root word have changed or created meaning: "vis" can add the prefix "in-" (meaning not) and the suffix "-ible" (meaning capable or possible) to form "invisible" (meaning not possible to see). "Ject" (which means move or propel) can add the prefix "in-" (in the sense of direction) and the suffix "-ion" to produce "injection" (which means the process of moving or propelling something into something else).

With *verbs,* the main form, or root, of the verb plus the word "to" makes up the *infinitive*: "to sleep," "to wake," "to rise."

Make, made, made. An *irregular verb* in its main, past tense, and past *participle* forms.

Man, mankind. Do not use these words to refer to people in general, since there are women as well as men in humankind. Say either "woman and man," "women and men," "man and woman," "men and women," "people," or "human beings." "Humanity" or "humankind" is an adequate substitute for "mankind," as is "human population," or "human community." In anthropological writing, use "ancient peoples" or "*homo sapiens*." See *sexist language* for further guidelines.

Mankind. See *man*.

Many. The comparative forms of the *adjective* "many" are irregular: "many, more, most." See *comparison*.

May. See *can*.

May be, maybe. These two words have different functions and meanings. "May be" is a compound *verb* that means "could exist or happen": "Our neighbors may be coming to dinner." "Maybe" is an *adverb* that means perhaps: "Maybe our neighbors will come to dinner."

Maybe. See *may be*.

Me, myself. Don't use "myself" when "me" (the *objective case* of "*I*") is meant. WRONG: "The memo will come from Jones and myself." RIGHT: "The memo will come from Jones and me." See "*-self.*"

Mean, meant, meant. An *irregular verb* in its main, *past tense,* and past *participle* forms.

Meant. See *mean.*

Media. "Media" is the *plural* of "medium" (it retains a *Latin* plural form) in the sense of devices or modes: "The news media are out in force." Singular uses of "media" are becoming more common, but they are wrong in formal writing. "Medium" in the sense of one who mediates between realms, especially psychic worlds, has the plural "mediums": "The mediums all agreed that a great flood would come in five years."

Meet, met, met. An *irregular verb* in its main, *past tense,* and past *participle* forms.

Met. See *meet.*

Metaphor. A metaphor is a word or phrase that implies or indirectly expresses a comparison or identity. It often enlivens writing by adding an unexpected dimension to words: "The car, an arrow in flight, sped down the road." This stylistic device should be used with caution—many of the obvious comparisons have already appeared so often in writing that they have become trite, or clichéd: "The golden orb shed its warming rays on the sunbathers." See also *simile, style, cliché*.

Min. The common *abbreviation* for "minute" is "min." It is not used in formal, *standard English* writing, but it often appears in such special *styles* as scientific, sports, or cooking writing. In more technical writing, "min." can stand for "minimum" or various measurements ("minim"). Consult a *dictionary* for these more specialized usages of "min."

Misplaced modifier. One of the commonest ways of confusing your *audience* is to misplace *adjectives* or *adverbs*—single words or whole *phrases* or *clauses* used as *modifiers*—leaving readers or listeners in doubt about what you mean to say or write.

The answer to this sort of problem is to write and revise with care, noting all adjectives and adverbs of whatever length and complexity and making sure that they are close to the words they modify or are otherwise unambiguously linked to them. Particular care should be taken with inverted sentences, in which phrases or clauses are purposely put where they are less expected and often not very close to the words they modify. The examples that follow are marked "right" and "wrong," although in many cases it would be more accurate to say that meaning in one is clearer than in another or that meaning differs from one sentence to another.

WRONG: "Aiming carefully, the gazelles were shot by the hunter one after the other." RIGHT: "Aiming carefully, the hunter shot the gazelles one after the other." Here the first sentence is incorrect because gazelles don't use guns and don't aim them.

WRONG: "The tourist saw a painting in the museum of birds." RIGHT: "The tourist saw a painting of birds in the museum." The first sentence could be correct (there could be a museum devoted to birds); but if it is right, it is likely that the museum is called "The Museum of Birds," or it would be a better sentence if the correct name of the museum were given and capitalized so that readers would not have to wonder if the statement is about a painting of birds or a museum of birds.

WRONG: "I almost completed all my work." RIGHT: "I completed almost all my work." The first sentence could be correct, suggesting that you were near to finishing your work or intended to do so; but it leaves some doubt about what precisely you mean. The second sentence leaves no doubt that you did the larger part of your work.

WRONG: "We want to visit the library after our friends." RIGHT: "We want to visit the library after we visit our friends (or after our friends visit the library or to find our friends)." The incomplete first sentence does not make it clear whether he is visiting his friend first or if he is visiting the library after his friend does, or in order to look for his friend. Depending on what is intended, any of the second variants might be more accurate.

There are dozens of other ways to put modifiers where they don't belong or in places where your audience can't tell which word or idea they refer to. Check where you put modifiers so that you don't confuse more than you *clarify*. See *revision, inversion,* and *capitalization.*

Miss. See *Ms*.

Modifier. Words that qualify or explicate the condition or status or other words (or *phrase* or *clauses*) are called "modifiers." Modifiers of *nouns* (things or people) are called *adjectives*, while words that refer to *verbs* are called *adverbs*. Because they add so much to the nouns and verbs we use, modifiers are important *parts of speech* that do a great deal to enliven, enrich, and *clarify* our statements.

"Put the bleached flour in a deep pan warming on the stove. Stirring constantly, blend in the toasted almonds, then the vanilla taken from the beans that have soaked in brandy boiled down until its alcohol has completely evaporated." In this long passage, the following are modifiers of one sort or another:

> "Bleached": adjectival past *participle* modifying "flour"
>
> "Deep": adjective modifying "pan"
>
> "Warming on the stove": adjectival present participle phrase modifying "pan"
>
> "Stirring constantly": adverbial *gerund* phrase modifying "blend"
>
> "Constantly": adverb modifying "stirring"
>
> "Toasted": adjective or past participle modifying "almonds"
>
> "Taken from the beans . . .": adjectival past participial phrase modifying "vanilla"
>
> "That have soaked in brandy": adjectival *demonstrative* pronoun clause modifying "beans"

"boiled down . . .": adjectival past participial phrase modifying "brandy"

"Until its . . .": adverbial *prepositional phrase* modifying "boiled down"

"Completely": adverb modifying "has evaporated"

The simplest relationship between a word and its modifier is for them to be next to each other: "the red house" or "walking quickly." But groups of words can function as nouns or verbs and also as their modifiers in *sentences,* and long combinations of words can put modifiers fairly far away from the thing they qualify. Sometimes modifiers get in each other's way and are said to be misplaced or to *dangle* (see *misplaced modifier*). When this happens, your *audience* will not know what you mean or will have to pause and figure out what the most likely sense of your words is. They will then probably lose concentration, fail to pay attention to what follows the confusing passage, or simply give up on you as a clear or cogent speaker or writer.

To avoid such consequences, make sure your thoughts are in order and that the words you choose to express them match and convey that order (see *order of words*). Put modifiers as close to the words they refer to as possible, or find a way to make the link between word and modifier unambiguous. Read and reread your writing to listen for adjectives, adverbs, phrases, and clauses that might be heard differently by your audience than you intended. Put yourself in your audience's place whenever you intend to put a modifier into a sentence or whenever you find an adjective or adverb when you are proofreading or revising.

Does it belong where it is? Could it possibly be taken to modify more than one thing in the sentence? Is it in the right place to qualify just the word, phrase, or clause I want modified? Is there something in the sentence to which it refers? Is it the right thing?

Only by asking all these questions of every modifier will you be certain to avoid the ambiguities, stupidities, and irritations that misusing modifiers can cause. See *revision* and *editing*.

Mood. Besides *tense,* indicating time of action, and *voice,* indicating whether a *subject* is acting or being acted on, *verbs* have "mood," indicating feelings or attitudes toward the action. There are three moods: **indicative,** the "normal" mood for describing action or condition directly; **imperative,** the mood of command or request; and **subjunctive,** the mood of unreal conditions, desires, or needs.

The **indicative mood** is used for all statements, questions, and so on that aren't in the *imperative* or *subjunctive.* It is the "normal" or neutral mood in which a writer or speaker expresses what is believed to be fact or evident, inquires into aspects of reality, or reports what others have assumed to be ordinary or correct: "The bear hibernates in winter. Is the bear in its den? Scientists believe bears hibernate to survive the cold winters." Most sentences in most circumstances are *indicative,* a mood not marked in any way grammatically.

The **imperative mood** is used for commands or requests: "Go study bears in hibernation, but don't disturb them." Imperative statements are often marked by *inversion* or unusual word order, and they commonly are followed by *exclamation points* to further distinguish them.

The **subjunctive mood** is sometimes called "conditional." It is used to express things that are not real or not certainly matters of fact, to convey wishes, or to state requirements: "If I were to poke that bear, it might wake up, and it might attack me." Subjunctive verb forms are sometimes different ("*I were*"), and subjunctive sentences often include words like "*if*" or "*that*" to introduce *clauses*. In the last example, all the verbs have a conditional sense to them.

Sentences should not mix moods. WRONG: "Study hibernation, and you should be careful when you do." RIGHT: "Study hibernation, and be careful when you do."

Moral, morale. These two *nouns* are pronounced differently and have different meanings despite some similarity in their appearance and spelling. "Moral" means a story's sense, ethical lesson, rule for behavior: "The moral of the story is. . . ." The plural, "morals," means a person's ethical rules or behavior. "Moral" is also an *adjective* that means behaving ethically or in keeping with higher law: "The minister is a very moral person." "Morale" means spirit or sense of well-being: "Morale was high in the firm because sales results were good."

Morale. See *moral*.

More, most. These words are the irregular comparative forms for three *adjectives*: *many*, *much*, and *some*. See *comparison*.

Moreover. "Moreover" is a *conjunctive adverb* suggesting exception or addition.

Most. See *more*.

Mr. Men addressed formally, as in a business letter, are usually called "Mr." This *title* appears directly before their last names unless they are well known to you or the person you are addressing: "Dear Mr. Sirota: It was a pleasure to talk to you and Mr. Wolff about our products. Our company's representatives, Ms. Patel and Mr. Rachinsky, will call on you next week to continue our discussion." The title, or honorific, "Mr." is rarely spelled out as "Mister" unless special attention needs to be drawn to the title itself: "He sees himself as Mister Gish, but I just call him Jim." The intent of such usage is usually *ironic*.

Mrs. See *Ms*.

Ms., Miss, Mrs.. Recently, the designations given to women to indicate their marital status have undergone immense changes. In many instances "Miss" (the title traditionally applied to an unmarried woman or a girl) has become unacceptable and is felt to be derogatory. In the same way, the term "Mrs.," traditionally applied to married women, conveys a concern with marital status that is unnecessary and may be considered offensive.

For these reasons, the term "Ms." came into being as a kind of contraction of "Miss" and "Mrs." It is intended as a direct equivalent to "Mr." in brevity and age, class, and marital status neutrality. Its use has become widespread, and "Ms." should be considered the preferred term of address. When the woman in question has expressed a clear preference, it should be honored: "Jane Jones prefers to call herself 'Mrs. Jones.' " See *sexist language*.

Much. "Much" forms its comparatives irregularly: much, more, most. See *comparison*.

Myself. See *me* and *-self*.

N

Namely. The *conjunctive adverb* "namely" is used to specify relations between *clauses*.

Names. When things or people have words that identify them as specific individuals, those words are called "names": "Jan served on the battleship *North Carolina* sailing in the Pacific and spent leisure time reading *War and Peace*." Names of things and people are usually marked in some way to distinguish them from more general *nouns*—by *capitalization* or by *italics* (or both). There are several categories or types of names that are treated somewhat differently.

NAMES OF PEOPLE

Personal names are capitalized: "John and Mary are here." When *common nouns* are used as personal names, they are capitalized as well: "Father is here, but Mother is in Detroit." Common nouns that refer to relatives are not capitalized when they stand alone, but are capitalized when they have personal names added to them: "My uncle is dead, but Aunt Mary is still with us." Non-English names are sometimes not capitalized, particularly parts of last names: "Ludwig van Beethoven's symphonies were being played." Honorific titles are also capitalized when parts of names, but not *prepositions*, *conjunctions*, or *articles* in

them: "Prince Joseph of Holland and the Low Countries."
See *capitalization* and specific languages.

NAMES OF PLACES

Place names are capitalized, including common nouns that
are part of the names: "Mount Hood and Lake Zots are in
Oregon State. The state of Oregon has Hood and other
mountains, as well as Zots and other lakes." *Prepositions,
conjunctions,* and *articles* that are parts of place names are
not capitalized: "Lake of the Woods." Check non-English
words in *dictionaries* or other reference works to determine
which parts of them are capitalized in place names. See also
capitalization.

NAMES OF THINGS

Vessels and vehicles of various kinds, along with machines,
brand names or models or products, and the like, can have
names that follow the *capitalization* rules of personal and
place names: "I took my Toshiba on the Learjet and on the
train." Named ships, planes, and other vehicles and vessels
have capitalized and italicized names: "We sailed on the
Queen Mary, then flew on the *Spirit of Los Angeles,* a
DC-10." See also *italics.*

NAMES OF WORKS

Literary, artistic, architectural, engineering, and other products of human endeavor can have names. Such names and
titles are usually capitalized, and they are italicized if they

are the result of individual effort. "I was reading *Pride and Prejudice* in the shadow of the Boulder Dam." As in most names, *prepositions, conjunctions,* and *articles* are not capitalized in such names unless they are the first word of the name. In some *languages* names of works have only initial capitals unless they include other words that are capitalized in their own right (e.g., *Russian*). Check relevant reference books to be sure. See *italics* and *capitalization.*

NAMES OF INSTITUTIONS, ORGANIZATIONS, AND THE LIKE

Governments, companies, religions, associations, *languages,* and other things or groups of people can also be named specifically enough to warrant capitalization: "The bill on English as the national language went to Congress, sponsored by Republicans and the National Association of Scholars, as well as by the Baptist Synod of Arkansas."

Almost anything can be named, and almost all such names merit capitalization if not italicization.

N.B. This *abbreviation* of the *Latin* words "Nota bene" is "N.B." It means note well or pay attention. Neither the abbreviation nor the Latin phrase is welcome in most modern, standard writing.

Negatives. Words that convey some sense of "no" or "not" to a *sentence* are said to be "negatives." The sentences in which they occur are negative sentences: "I will not do it."

The most common negative words are "*no*," "*not*," "*never*," "*nothing*," "*nobody*," "*none*," and "*no one*." Their presence in a sentence usually signals that it is negative. Note that negatives are frequently contracted into other words, particularly verbs: "I won't do it." Even though the full word "not" is not visible in this sentence, the sentence is still negative. See *contractions*.

There are quite a few common mistakes that are made with negative words. The most common are misplacement of negatives (see *misplaced modifiers*) and *double negatives*.

MISPLACED NEGATIVES

Just as it is easy to allow *modifiers* to slide into positions in *sentences* in which it is less than clear what the modifiers refer to, so negatives (a kind of modifier) often pop up in the wrong or less than helpful places. WRONG: "The class reads never the books I'd want." The example is unclear about who reads or wants what and when. BETTER: "The class never reads the books I'd want them to read."

DOUBLE NEGATIVES

Only one negative word can occur in a *phrase* or *clause:* "to nobody"; "give it to nobody." When two negatives appear in the same phrase or clause, there is an error. WRONG: "I did not give it to nobody," "I never gave it to nobody," "Nobody never gave it to me." The variations (and the instances of their occurrence) are all but endless. Particularly in longer clauses or phrases, careless writers tend to forget that a negative appeared earlier and that another is out of place later. Just as common are the kinds of errors in the examples, evidently because writers forget that "nobody," "never," and "nothing" are negatives that can't be doubled in a clause or phrase.

To avoid this all too common mistake, proofread and revise with care, looking especially for the longer negatives in combination with each other or shorter negatives. When you find mistakes like those in the examples, change one of the words to positive form: "I did not give it to anybody," "I gave it to nobody," "I never gave it to anybody," "Nobody ever gave it to me." Sometimes, as with the last clause in the example, a positive rephrasing is not possible for one of the negatives: "nobody" can't become "anybody" or anything else and make sense with the rest of the clause. Larger rewrites are then necessary: "Nobody ever gave me anything," or something of the sort, depending on what you mean. See *revision*. Never use the negative contraction "*ain't*" in *standard English* statements.

Remember that some words can be made to have a negative sense without becoming negatives and thus are not subject to the rules of double negation. This happens when "negative" *prefixes* or *suffixes* are added to the beginnings or ends of words: "nonstarter." The example is a word that can appear with true negatives in phrases, clauses, or sentences because its "negative" sense is merely a connotation or suggestion of the particle added to it. It is not, in other words, strictly speaking a negative: "Nonstarters never get going." The example is correct. WRONG:

"Nonstarters never do nothing." RIGHT: "Nonstarters never do anything."

Neither, neither . . . nor. Remember that the negative *adjectives* and *conjunctions* "neither" and "neither . . . nor" cannot be used with a second *negative* in the same *sentence*. WRONG: "Neither one of them never arrived." RIGHT: "Neither one of them ever arrived."

Neither . . . nor. See *neither*.

Nevertheless. This *conjunctive adverb* suggests reservations in the relationship between *clauses*.

Nobody. "Nobody" is a singular *indefinite* pronoun: "Nobody is home." WRONG: "Nobody are responsible for quality." See *pronoun*.

Nominative. Words that function as the *subjects* or *subject complements* (*predicate nouns* or *adjectives*) of *sentences* are in the nominative *case*. Such words are not marked from their normal or main form, which is in fact the form that "names" (or "nominates") the basic form of the word from which others are made. The nominative is also called the subjective case, since its main function is to serve as subject or subject complement.

None, no one. Do not confuse these words, both of which are usually singular. "None" is an *indefinite* pronoun that means not one: "None of the executives travels often."

"No one" is an indefinite *pronoun* that means single person: "No one travels more than the chairperson."

Nonrestrictive clause. *Clauses* that appear to be added to *sentences* for supplementary, nonessential explanation are called "nonrestrictive."

They are set off in the sentence by *commas*: "The actor, who drove a Ferrari, was the star of a soap opera." Here the information about the car the soap opera star drives is considered ancillary, additional, and therefore nonrestrictive. The "*who*" clause is thus set off in commas. If the commas are omitted, the meaning of the sentence changes to suggest that more than one actor is being talked about, and the only way to distinguish which one is the soap opera star is to note who drives a Ferrari. This "who" clause is then a *restrictive clause* and is not set off in commas.

How can you tell if a clause is nonrestrictive or restrictive? There is no hard-and-fast *rule*. However, the essential question is whether the main action or condition of the sentence is understandable without the clause. In the example, the actor is a soap opera star (and we know it) whether or not we know what kind of car the actor drives. It might be interesting that it's a snappy sports car; but it does nothing to change our understanding of the main point being conveyed: the actor is a soap opera star. We might also learn in nonrestrictive clauses that the actor is tall, blond, and speaks fluent French. All those points would not change the basic fact of the actor's starring role.

When the commas are taken out of the sentence, the nature of the clause changes. Somehow we can grasp the identity of the soap opera star only by knowing what kind of car the star drives. Apparently other actors and stars drive other cars, and that is what sets them apart from the soap opera star. The information is essential to understanding the main point of the sentence and is therefore part of a restrictive clause.

Because *punctuation* varies with the type of clause, it is important to understand and master this abstract grammatical category. Without good comprehension of it, you are prone to make errors that might embarrass you.

Besides punctuation, you must also consider proper *pronouns* when writing clauses that might be restrictive or nonrestrictive. It is wrong to begin nonrestrictive adjectival clauses (modifying *nouns* or *noun phrases*) with "*that*." WRONG: "The building, that is standing in ruins, is old." RIGHT: "The building, which is standing in ruins, is old" or "The building that is standing in ruins is old." The examples show that nonrestrictive adjectival clauses must begin with "which" or some other *relative pronoun*. The choice of pronoun is an additional signal to the reader that the information in the clause is not as important as other statements in the sentence and is therefore nonrestrictive.

Nonrestrictive phrase. The same *punctuation* rules that apply to *nonrestrictive clauses* and *restrictive clauses* are in force for *prepositional phrases*, participial, and *infinitive* phrases: nonrestrictive *phrases* are set off with *commas,* while restrictive phrases are not.

Here are some examples of nonrestrictive and restrictive phrases: "The purpose of the work, to elucidate literature, was well served." The infinitive phrase "to elucidate literature" is set off in commas here because it does not contribute to the main point being made by the writer. One could equally well decide to use commas here because the phrase is a sort of *interjection* or aside to the reader, restating what is assumed to be known, the work's purpose. *Dashes* or *parentheses* might also have been used to set off this phrase, depending on the degree of *emphasis* one wanted to accord it.

"The dog, tied to the tree, could not chase the squirrel." The participial phrase "tied to the tree" can also be seen as a phrase in apposition, adding nonessential information to the main sense of the sentence. In either case, as appositional or nonrestrictive phrase, the point is that being tied to the tree is not the cause of the dog's being unable to chase the squirrel, or the writer has chosen not to emphasize that possible reason for the dog's inactivity. Removing the commas would suggest either that being tied to the tree kept the dog from chasing or, more grammatically, that other dogs not tied to the tree also couldn't chase the squirrel, just as the one tied to the tree can't. See *appositive*.

"Rover, along with the rest of the dogs, ran off." Here the nonrestrictive phrase is prepositional. The choice of this sentence structure leads the reader to assume that the writer wants to call attention to Rover and thus has put Rover in the first position in the sentence. One could have made the same statement with slightly different emphasis by saying, "Along with the rest of the dogs, Rover ran off." The nonrestrictive phrase is still marked by a comma, which would also be necessary because the prepositional phrase now starts the sentence. In either case, it is essential only to understand that Rover ran off, and it is only of tangential interest that the rest of the dogs did so.

No one. See *none*.

Not, not only . . . but. See *negative* and *correlative conjunction*.

Nothing. Negative *relative pronoun*. "Nothing" is singular in most *usages* and cannot appear in a *sentence* that is already negated. WRONG: "Nothing never happens." RIGHT: "Nothing ever happens." See *negative* and *double negative*.

Not only . . . but. See *not*.

Noun. Words that name things or people, in the very broadest sense, are called "nouns": "dog," "house," "nurse," "flower," "egret."

Nouns can function in dozens of ways in sentences, as *subjects*, as *objects*, and in many other categories. Nouns have *number*—they can be singular when referring to one thing or person, or they can be *plural* when naming more than one. In the plural most nouns change form, adding "*s*." Nouns also have *gender*, indicating whether the person or thing they refer to is male or female in biological fact or analogical imagining. Finally, nouns also have *case*, which names the role they play in a sentence: *nominative* for subjects or *subject complements* (*predicate nouns*); *objective case* for objects of *verbs*, *prepositions*, and so on; *possessive* for ownership forms, usually marked with an *apostrophe* and "*s*" or just an apostrophe.

Nouns that are used as *names* of individual things or people are called "*proper nouns*" and are usually capitalized to indicate their special function: "John," "Mary," "Ivan," "*Titanic,*" "Blue," and "Smith." See *capitalization.*

Nouns agree with verbs, pronouns, *adjectives,* and other words when they need to—when plurals must match plurals, masculines must refer to masculines, feminines must refer to feminines, and so on. See *agreement.* The *gerund* ("ing" form) of verbs can function as nouns: "Swimming is relaxing."

Noun clause. When *nouns, verbs,* and other words are combined into *clauses,* they can play any role in a sentence that a noun can play: "What you are looking for is right there." The noun clause "what you are looking for" is the *subject* in this sentence, though it could just as easily be an *object* of an active verb ("I see what you are looking for"), an object for a *preposition* ("I attribute that to what you are looking for"), or a *predicate noun* (*subject complement*): "This is what you are looking for."

Noun clauses are usually begun with one of the *relative pronouns:* "*that,*" "what," "whatever," "which," "whichever," "*who,*" "whoever," "whom," "whom-ever," or "whose." Such words as "how," "*when,*" "*where,*" "whether," or "why" can also start noun clauses: "I don't see how you can do that." In this example "how you can do that" is the object of the verb "*see.*"

Noun phrase. Nouns plus any words that modify them are noun phrases: "the sleeping yellow lion." Like *noun clauses,* noun phrases can play any role in a *sentence* that a *noun* can—*subject, object,* or *predicate noun*: "The sleep-ing yellow lion rolled over." "The hunter shot the sleeping yellow lion." "The zookeeper offered meat to the sleeping yellow lion." "Where is the sleeping yellow lion?" In the examples, the noun phrase "sleeping yellow lion" operates, in turn, as subject, object, object of *preposition*, and *subject complement* (*predicate noun*). See also *modifier*. All other functions of nouns are possible for noun phrases, from apposition to verbalization.

n't. These letters and their *apostrophe* are often used to form *contractions* of *negative* verbs (combined with a shortened "not"): "isn't," "hadn't," "couldn't." Like all such contractions, these forms normally do not appear in *standard English* writing.

Number. Words are said to have "number" because they indicate whether one or more than one thing or person is doing something. When one person or thing is involved, the number is singular; more than one person or thing is *plural*. Both *nouns* and *verbs* show number by changing form (see *declension* and *conjugation*), usually by adding or dropping "*s*": "One dog lies in the shade of one tree." "Many dogs lie in the shade of many trees." Nouns must agree with verbs in number—singular *subjects* require singular verbs (see *agreement*). WRONG: "One dog lie . . . many dogs lies." *Pronouns* also should agree with nouns in number: "Many dogs pant, and I hear them." WRONG: "Many dogs pant, and I hear it."

Numbers. Numbers exist in two different forms and *styles*, from a grammatical point of view. They are spelled-out words ("twenty-one") or figures ("21"), and they are *cardinal* (essentially *nouns* like the first example given) or *ordinal* (*adjectival* forms like "twenty-first" or "21st").

Ordinals suggest ranking or ordering of things, while cardinals denote quantity or count in itself: "Twenty-one is the twenty-first number." " 'A' is one letter of twenty-six; it is the first in the alphabet." Ordinals are formed, in most cases, from cardinals by adding "th": "In the survey the schools ranked fourth, ninth, sixteenth, and thirty-seventh." The smaller numbers have special ordinal forms by themselves and in combination with numbers over twenty: "First, second, and third prizes go to those holding the fifty-first, one hundred and second, and thirteenth tickets. Those are the ticket holders for prizes one, two, and three." Note that compound numbers change only their last element into an ordinal form: "The one-hundredth and one hundred and first people to call get $5." WRONG: "I served in the One Hundredth and First Regiment."

Cardinals function like all other nouns except that they are all *plural*—except "one" and "zero." When numbers are treated as words in themselves, however, they can be singular or plural: "The mathematician put a 'one' in the first column of the table and three 'twos' in the next area." Here the numbers stand for countable written forms or marks on a page, and therefore they can have *number*.

SPELLING OUT VERSUS FIGURES

In most formal English writing, numbers under 100 are spelled out. This is particularly true of *ordinal numbers*, which are usually spelled out no matter how long they are. However, formal business, economic, scientific, and other *styles* permit (even encourage) showing most *cardinal numbers* in figures.

Ordinals vary depending on preferences; but generally there is more tolerance for terms like "101st" in scientific, military and some other styles than in other writing, where such figures are seen as errors. Newspapers and some other space-constrained publications favor figures because they are shorter, more visible, and more easily skimmed. Almost all styles encourage the use of "one," however, instead of or along with "1," which can be confused with the letter "el": "Please send me 1 (one) copy of the album."

Whatever style you adopt, be sure to be consistent within any *sentence* or *paragraph,* using all figures or all spelled-out numbers so that readers do not have to shift expectations. RIGHT: "I saw four birds and one hundred and six insects." WRONG: "There are ninety-six chapters and 102 verses."

Note that spelled-out cardinal numbers include *hyphens* for all numbers over twenty and below one hundred that are compounds of two or more numbers: "Twenty-one bears and ninety-six cougars gathered by the pond." Ordinals are hyphenated only when they modify a noun: "That is twenty first; it is the twenty-first time you have used that example." Longer ordinal compounds are also hyphenated in their last element only when used as *adjectives* with a *noun* present: "I see the one hundred twenty-first flag; it is one hundred twenty-first in line."

When numbers begin sentences, they should always be spelled out: "Nineteen sixty-five was a strange year." Although some newspapers and other publications concerned with space violate this *rule,* most styles observe it since initial figures in a sentence are hard to place—are they subjects, *list* numbers, *dates,* note numbers, or something else? Spelled-out numbers reduce this ambiguity and *clarify* writing. Another way to clarify such a sentence is to revise it, moving the number from the initial position: "What a strange year 1965 was!" See *revision.*

Figures are mandatory in certain circumstances, however: dates ("November 23, 1963"), addresses ("32 Barrow St., Apt. 8B, New York, NY 10014-4927"), phone numbers ("212-699-9999"), and times ("6 *A.M.*," but note that spelled-out numbers are fine without "*A.M.*" or "*P.M.*" or with "o'clock": "It was four in the afternoon." "I had an appointment for four o'clock this afternoon"). Figures are also required with larger or very exact amounts of money ("$6.82 million," "£3,475"), decimals and *fractions* ("6.9387," "3¾"), percentages ("36.9%," "42 percent"), sports or competitive scores ("Bears win 21–10!" "The pupil scored 97 on the test"), and parts of plays and books ("chapter 14," "page 22," "Act 3," "scene 2").

O

O, Oh. Distinguish carefully between "O" and "oh." The first is used mainly when directly addressing a revered or worshipped figure: "O Great One, grant your blessings and favors on us, your humble villagers." It acts as an *adjective* in that it stands directly before the word or words it *modifies* or evokes, but it is normally *capitalized* wherever it appears in a sentence to indicate reverence or solemnity, and it is not followed by any *punctuation*: "Hear us, O judge."

The *interjection* "oh" can appear anywhere in a sentence to indicate surprise or exclamation: "Oh, it's raining!" "It's raining, but, oh, I wanted to eat outside!" Since "oh" is an interjected part of a sentence, it is usually set off by *commas*, as in the examples. It is not normally capitalized unless it appears as the first word of a sentence or stands alone: "Oh! A mouse!"

Object. In sentences with *transitive verbs* in the *active voice*, the *subject* of the sentence performs some action on a thing or person. That thing or person is said to be the "object" of the verb and to be in the *objective case* (also called accusative case).

There is no special form for the objective case for *nouns*, but *pronouns* change form (see *declension*): "The soldier shot the prisoner; the bullet hit him." In the example both "prisoner" and "him" are objects of the active, transitive verbs "*shot*" and "*hit*." While "prisoner" is in the objective case, it is indistinguishable from the normal, ordinary, or *nominative* case of the word. "Him," however, is an inflected, or changed, form of "he" used for the objective case of this pronoun. See *inflection* and *case*.

Objects in sentences can be of any *gender, number,* or construction—that is, they can be *compound words, phrases, clauses,* or any combinations of them: "The artist painted vast swirls of color, leaping and falling, twisting vortices of emblems and their effigies." Everything in the example after the word "painted" is its object.

Although there is no limit on the complexity or content of any sentence's object, remember to make sure that all the pronouns in it are of the correct gender, number, and case to refer clearly and accurately to the subject or object they modify or relate to. See *antecedent* and *modifier*.

Prepositions also govern objects in the objective case: "The cow looked at her, and she glanced toward the farmer." The prepositions "at" and "toward" are followed by the objects "her" and "the farmer." Again, noun objects are not distinguishable by form but only by function, while most pronoun objects appear in a different form.

Remember also that *linking verbs* like "*is*" are not followed by objects but by predicate *nominatives* (also called *subject complements*) that are not in the objective case but in the nominative: "Who is he?" See also *predicate*.

Objective case. Words that function as *objects* (*direct object* or *indirect object* or objects of *prepositions*) in *sentences* are in the objective (also called accusative) *case*. This case is not distinguishable from the *nominative* or normal form of *nouns* but is marked (or inflected) in *pronouns*: "I, me"; "we, us"; "he, him"; "she, her"; and "they, them" (the nominative and objective cases, respectively, of the *personal pronouns*). See *inflection*.

Of. *Preposition* governing the *objective case*: "That is not characteristic of him." Do not add this *preposition* to other prepositions that don't need it and can stand on their own (*outside, inside, off*). Do not use "of" to stand for "*have*" in compound *verbs* like "could have."

Off. *Preposition* governing the *objective case*: "We helped take the heavy costume off her."

On, upon. *Preposition* governing the *objective case*: "The blame fell on us." Use "on" except in the few cases when fairy-tale language is the proper style: "Once upon a time." Otherwise, "upon" is an old-fashioned word that has lost its usefulness.

Once. See *adverb* and *conjunctive adverb*.

One. "One" is not only a *cardinal number* but an *indefinite* pronoun always used in the singular: "Shadow was one of my dogs, the one that remains my favorite." See also *number* and *pronoun*.

One another. See *reciprocal pronoun*.

Oneself. See *reflexive pronoun* and *-self*.

Onto. *Preposition* governing the *objective case*: "The burden of work shifted onto us."

Op. cit. This *abbreviation* of the *Latin* words "opere citato" ("in the work cited") is used only in footnotes and endnotes to scholarly works, and even there it is losing favor and being replaced by shortened titles or authors' names.

Or. See *correlative conjunction*.

Order of words. The simplest, "normal" order of words in a sentence is *subject, verb*, and *object* (or *subject complement*): "Flemming hit the target; Flemming is an archer." The example is a *compound sentence* made up of two independent *clauses* each of which displays the simple, normal word order on which all variants are made. And the variant word orders are endless, as shown in entries *emphasis, question, imperative, inversion*, and so on.

Subjects can come after verbs or stand in their "normal" place: "Hit the ball, Reid! The ball, Reid, is the thing to hit." Similarly, verbs and objects can move around in the basic sentence structure or in any of the many altered structures that are possible for sentences: "The ball, hit by Reid, soared toward a fence being painted by Johnson and being watched through a telescope by Potter."

One way to make your writing more lively or informative is to vary the order and structure of words in sentences within *paragraphs* and from paragraph to paragraph. Not only can you play with the order of the basic pattern of words but you can vary the length of *sentences,* shifting between long, complex ones and simple, short ones. Long sentences need not be complex; they can be made up of simple *lists* of subjects and objects: "Books, pamphlets, bulletins, newsletters, and software are created, compiled, edited, produced, and published by organizations, associations, government offices, military establishments, businesses, and publishing houses." The example simply combines compound subjects, verbs, and objects in the "normal" subject, verb, object pattern. In similar fashion, short sentences can be made complex by inversion or other devices: "To whom is it given?"

Voice, mood, and *tense* can also vary to modify word order and invigorate writing. While it is a generally correct practice to avoid many *passive* constructions, the occasional passive voice sentence can create emphasis or shift *tone* in interesting ways. Imperatives can also provide variety and point, as can careful shifting of the time in which an action or condition is cast.

Sentences need not all begin with subjects. *Prepositional phrases,* dependent clauses, verbal *phrases, interjections,* and other elements are sometimes welcome changes from subject, verb, object consistency: "Speaking of word order, try moving things around, and you will see an immediate change in your statements. Maybe even an improvement!"

Nor do sentences have to end with objects. Again, all sorts of phrases and clauses can appear at the end (or in the middle) of any sentence and help it make its point:

"Jumbled together at the end of sentences, words influence sense in a manner that is hard to judge, difficult to evaluate, and sometimes painful to experience."

In rearranging words from the simple sentence pattern into other forms, keep in mind the need to maintain *agreement* among all the sentence elements.

Ordinal number. *Numbers* that express sequence or order are called "ordinals": "The Porsche was first, and the Mazda was twenty-third." Simple numbers are called "*cardinal numbers.*" See also *number.*

Otherwise. See *conjunctive adverb.*

Our. See *are.*

Ourselves. See *reflexive pronoun.*

Out. *Preposition* governing the *objective case.*

Outside of. In formal writing there is no reason to add "of" to *prepositions* like "outside" or "*inside.*"

Over. *Preposition* governing the *objective case*: "The curse hung over us as we explored the tomb."

P

Paid. See *pay*.

Paragraph. A collection of *sentences* that is more or less fully focused on one subject, theme, or idea is called a "paragraph."

Paragraphs are usually distinguished by some form of spacing: The first lines of paragraphs are often "indented" or moved in from the left margin a bit, as in this book. Typewritten or computer-written documents often show a space between paragraphs, particularly when their first lines are not indented.

Most *grammar* and *style* books call for cohesion or focus of paragraphs in a fairly strict way. Paragraphs should begin with "topic sentences" that state their subject or theme, followed by some prescribed number of sentences expanding on the theme. They should end with a summary or transitional sentence that somehow introduces the next paragraph or logical passage.

Such *rules* should be followed in general; they can prove useful. But paragraphs that observe such guidelines too closely become blandly alike and boring. Variants of paragraph structure and intent abound and can help you avoid too much or stultifying consistency of paragraph size or shape. When to follow the "rules" and when to deviate from them are matters of style and choice. There are, in fact, no rules for paragraphs, only suggestions. Just make

sure that the sentences you gather into paragraphs are there
for a reason that will be clear to your reader.

Consult style books and guides to writing for more details
on variant paragraph structures, ways to build cohesive and
sensible paragraphs, and other aspects of style.

Parallelism. Although there is no grammatical *rule* that
demands balancing of elements in sentences—and, indeed,
there are circumstances that call for imbalance (see
emphasis)—writing is generally more intelligible and comfortable for readers when *sentence* and *paragraph* structures
are parallel. This means you need to consider whether each
element in your sentences roughly matches the others in
weight, length, *tone,* and so on.

All these categories, as well as parallelism itself, are
subjective and cannot be guided by definite rules. Rather,
the use, abuse, and avoidance of parallelism are techniques
that come with practice to those who write a great deal and
that escape the sometimes writer too often. These factors of
writing are parts of *style,* something we don't all have or
exercise in all circumstances.

But when style as well as substance comes into play,
parallelism can be effective as a technique. Its basic
requirement is that parts of sentences, paragraphs, or whole
documents be more or less equivalent. So a sentence made
up of three *clauses* will probably benefit by having all three
clauses be of roughly the same length, in the same *voice,
tense,* and *mood,* and made up of words that are similar in
tone: ''The soldiers marched into camp, the artillery set up
their cannons, and the cavalry tethered their horses.''

The following version of this sentence is not wrong, but it shifts so much in the basic categories of parallelism that readers might lose track of what is happening or how they are supposed to perceive the action: "The soldiers march into camp, cannons were set up by the artillery, and the horses of the cavalry were rounded up and then hobbled and tied together in a loose group so that they wouldn't run away or stampede." Shifts in tone can have the same disorienting effect as changes in length, tense, or voice of clauses: "The soldiers toddled into camp, the artillery puzzled over their outdated and dilapidated cannons, and the cavalry looked to their horsies."

Here are some general examples and points to watch for when you consider the level of parallelism in your writing:

1. Don't overdo it. Parallelism is not required and can get tiresome and artificial if imposed too stringently. If your writing seems bland, it might be overly parallel and lacking in emphasis. Try an abrupt shift of length or mood to liven things up.

2. Effective parallelism does not mean that every sentence follows the subject, verb, object (*subject complement*) model. The most boring writing is often a string of such simple sentences in which the reader is left to guess how the unconnected thoughts might go together or which is more important than the others. Variety of structure within the general guidelines of parallelism can provide readers with important information about the relative weight of ideas, words, and so on. See *order of words* and related entries.

3. The use of devices like *lists, numbers* introducing paragraphs and separate ideas, and similar methods of drawing attention to a series inherently calls for some attention to parallelism. The things listed, numbered, or otherwise highlighted in this way should be more or less equal in importance. They might also be parallel in grammatical structure, word order, and so on to add force to your thoughts: "I saw dogs, cats, and rabbits." It would not be wrong to write, "I saw dogs, felines, and little furry hopping animals with puffball tails and long ears," but a reader might wonder whether you just don't know the common names of the little furry animals or are being cute in naming or describing them. But do not perform contortions to make things too parallel: "I saw dogs, cats, and bandicoots." This example of a series is not parallel, even though each animal has a one-word name given to it, because most readers won't know what a bandicoot is. Better to say something like: "I saw dogs and cats. Another animal was the bandicoot, which is. . . ."

4. *Agreement* of subject, verb, *adjective, adverb,* and so on is a stricter, more mandatory form of parallelism. Although sentences don't have to agree across *phrases,* clauses, paragraphs, or beyond them in voice, mood, tense, and so on, you certainly should consider whether they would be more effective if such "agreement" were imposed.

5. One of the commonest violations of parallelism comes with unequal lengths of elements. The problem is that readers are often surprised or disconcerted to find long things following short ones or vice versa. The first phrase, clause, or paragraph tends to set expectations about length in particular. The combination of a short lead phrase or

clause with longer following ones violates those expectations and can disrupt the comprehension and attentiveness of your reader.

Similarly, a lead paragraph that contains short, simple sentences should probably be followed by more paragraphs of about the same length and containing sentences of approximately the same size and type. Building across several paragraphs to longer (or shorter) sentences will certainly work, as will signaling a change by adding a subheading or some other device to alert readers to an impending shift in length. But unless you prepare readers for a length imbalance or are striving for emphatic effect by abruptly imbalancing lengths, your writing will probably profit from having elements of roughly the same length perform roughly the same function.

6. The principles outlined in guideline five—of preparing for or signaling changes in parallelism in length—can be applied to all other alterations in roughly equivalent structures, tones, and so on. Let your reader know you are moving from something set in the *past tense* to *future tense* action; make it clear that what follows is no longer *active voice* description but *imperative* mood suggestion or command; or raise a flag that what follows is *subjunctive* because it is speculative while what came before was *passive* because it was scientific and impersonal. Subheadings, explanatory sentences, section numbers, and many other devices can be used to make your intentions clear and give your readers a better chance to assimilate your new direction and tone.

7. Use your imagination. Parallelism is a device for

writing well. It can be accomplished or played against in many ways. Think up a new trick your *audience* hasn't seen before.

Parentheses. One set of *punctuation* marks commonly used to set off *interjections* or supplemental materials is parentheses: "The dogs (a Doberman, a beagle, and a boxer) bounded into the show ring."

Parentheses are a rather strong way of separating elements of a sentence. Less forceful are *commas,* while *dashes* are as emphatic or more so than parentheses. All three could have been used in the example, with slightly different meanings resulting. In general, parentheses suggest the information they enclose is supplementary and not particularly germane to the overall sense being conveyed.

Parenthetical expressions work differently with punctuation, depending in part on the independence of the thought they enclose. If a full sentence is within parentheses, all its punctuation is also within the parentheses, including—and especially—the end punctuation, whether *period, question mark,* or any other ending mark: "(You better believe that!)"

When parentheses enclose *phrases, clauses,* or even whole *sentences* within other sentences, the parenthetical expressions are treated as words in themselves that end with the last parenthesis. All punctuation required by the sentence outside the parentheses falls just there—outside the parentheses: "The train (the 7:42 from Trenton, which is always late), slowly approaching the platform, made its way into the station." In the example a comma follows the last parenthesis because it is needed to set off the following *nonrestrictive phrase*. Had the example required a *semicolon* to mark the end of an independent clause, say, or a *colon* to introduce a *list*, or a period to mark the end of the sentence, all these marks would have fallen properly outside the parentheses.

The same rule applies to any *quotation marks* if the parenthetical expression is being quoted. If the quote ends before or begins after the matter enclosed in parentheses, then the quotes would not enclose the parenthetical matter: " 'Hi (sort of),' he said ironically." But: " 'Hi,' he said (ironically I thought)." In the first example the parenthetical phrase is part of the quoted speech and is within the parentheses. In the second example the parenthetical clause is within the double quotation marks of the example itself but not part of quoted speech and therefore outside the single quotes that mark it.

Parenthetical expressions within sentences may have any internal punctuation needed to make them grammatical and understandable. Thus the example about the train could have read: "The train (the 7:42 from Trenton, which is always late!), slowly approached. . . ." Similarly, the enclosed matter can include quotation marks independent of or related to what is being quoted in the main sentence: " 'Hi,' he said ('irony?' I wondered)." Here the parenthetical phrase includes an internal quotation and question mark. If this sort of sentence leads to a pileup of punctuation around a parenthesis, it is best to revise rather than expect a reader to figure it all out: " 'Hi (or should it be "Howdy?")," he wondered." The example can be followed, but why ask that much of a reader? See *revision*.

Capitalization rules also vary with the extent of material enclosed in parentheses: full sentences fully set off by parentheses begin with capital letters, but full sentences within other sentences and inside parentheses normally do not capitalize the first word: "She spoke so naturally (and she spoke with care and point!), so calmly, that I felt relieved. (False comfort, it later proved!)" Although there is an end punctuation mark shown for the sentence that is in parentheses but not capitalized, no end punctuation need be shown for such sentences set off within a sentence. The second sentence, fully enclosed in parentheses and not within a larger sentence, must have end punctuation within the parentheses and must be capitalized.

Parentheses need not come in pairs. They can be used singly to set off *numbers* in a *list* when the numbers begin a new line: "Here are the main points:

    1) . . .
    2) . . ."

If a numbered list is wholly within text and lines don't begin with numbers, it is better to use both parentheses: "Here are the main points: (1) . . . , (2). . . ." Numbered lists like the first example are better without the first parenthesis because the number is more visible.

Should it become necessary to set off material within a parenthetical aside or addition to a sentence, do so in *brackets*: "The substance (a carbonic compound [C-N] is volatile." Another level of enclosure within brackets returns to parentheses. Unless you are writing high science, it is usually best to revise a sentence that gets so complex, moving main sentence and parenthetical additions to it into two or more *subordinated* statements without parentheses-brackets-parentheses alternations that become hard to follow.

Participle. *Verbs* have two forms called participles, past and present. *Past participles* are made by adding "ed" to most main verbs: "paint, painted"; "walk, walked"; and "kick, kicked." There are, however, many *irregular verbs* whose past participles are not predictable from the main form and need to be checked in a reference source: "be, been"; "do, done"; and "write, written."

Present participles are formed by adding "ing" to the main form: "be, being"; "walk, walking"; "do, doing." See *conjugation* for more details on forming participles. Participles have a multitude of functions: *adjectives*, parts of other verb forms, and so on.

PARTICIPLE ADJECTIVES

By themselves participles can modify *nouns:* "I saw a painted barn and a walking horse." Here "painted" and "walking" are, respectively, past and present participial adjectives. In this adjectival function, participles work just as do other *adjectives,* requiring *adverbs* to modify them, linking together in compounds, and so on: "Standing on a hill surrounded by softly billowing clouds, I looked at a cheerfully painted, extravagantly decorated, and oddly structured barn." See *modifier* and *compound words.*

PARTICIPLES IN VERB FORMS

Several *tenses* are formed by adding *auxiliary* or helping *verbs* to participles: "I was painting the barn after I had walked a mile." See the entry on tenses and the related entries on specific tenses for more information on the formation, names, and functions of tenses made from participles; see also *conjugation*.

Parts of speech. The parts of speech—the grammatical elements that go into sentences—are listed below. Each one has its own entry explaining what it is, what rules are associated with it, and how it is properly and improperly used. The entries also include examples of good and bad *usage*, discussions of how to improve writing by using specific parts of speech or using them better, and references to other entries that are related to each part of speech.

ADJECTIVES

Modifiers of nouns are called "*adjectives*." They are words or groups of words that add qualities to *nouns* of all kinds, including *noun phrases*. Adjectives commonly come just before the nouns they refer to, but they can also appear removed from the noun, particularly when they stand in the *predicate* of a sentence with a *linking verb*: "The red barn is large." Both "red" and "large" are adjectives modifying or related to "barn."

ADVERBS

Modifiers of *verbs* and *adjectives* are called "*adverbs*." They are words or groups of words that add qualities to adjectives, adjectival *phrases,* verbs, and verb phrases of all kinds. They appear most often near the word they affect but can be located almost anywhere in a *sentence.* Many adverbs end in "*-ly,*" but not all do: "I am very glad to hear that you almost finished the job today." Both "very" and "almost" are adverbs, the first modifying an adjective ("glad"), and the second qualifying a verb ("finished").

CONJUNCTIONS

Linking words or groups of words are called "*conjunctions.*" They stand between or introduce elements of *sentences* in various ways. There are four different kinds of conjunctions (*conjunctive adverbs* and *subordinating conjunctions, coordinating conjunctions,* and *correlative conjunctions*), each with a somewhat different function.

INTERJECTIONS

Words or groups of words introduced into a sentence without such introductory or linking words as *conjunctions, prepositions, pronouns,* and the like are called "*interjections.*" Because such statements have no supporting words to join them to the rest of the *sentence,* they are often set off by *punctuation* of some sort to indicate their separateness from the rest of the sentence: "Indeed, the boat (always known to be leaky) was sinking." Both "indeed" and the phrase in *parentheses* have been interjected into the example.

Nouns

Words that name things or living things in a general way are called "*nouns*." The word "noun" is a noun itself, as is "word" in this sentence (and "sentence" too). Nouns that name specific individual things or living beings are called "*proper nouns*" and are usually capitalized to distinguish them from *common nouns*: "Fritters was a cat, and Chris is sad that the pet died." The proper nouns in the example are "Fritters" and "Chris," while the common nouns are "cat" and "pet." See *capitalization*.

Prepositions

Another type of word that links other words together in relationships is called a "*preposition*." In the preceding *sentence*, "*of*" and "*in*" are prepositions that "govern" nouns. Prepositions can also link *pronouns, phrases, clauses,* and other sets or kinds of words: "I found three errors in what you said." The *object* of the preposition "in" in the example is the clause that follows it. Pronouns that are the object of prepositions often change form to show that they are in the *objective case*: "The librarian handed the book to her."

Pronouns

Words that stand in place of nouns are called "*pronouns*." There are eight kinds of pronouns, explained in further detail in the entries on pronouns and each individual variety of them: *demonstrative, indefinite, intensifier, interrogative, personal pronoun, reciprocal pronoun, reflexive pronoun,* and *relative pronoun.*

VERBS

Words or groups of words that express actions, conditions, or the like are called *verbs.* In the previous sentence there are two verbs: "express" and "*are.*" By changing their form, verbs indicate the *number* and *person* of *subjects* acting or existing—how many people or things are involved, and whether they are you, me, or them. Verbs also show the time when things happened (*tense*), whether the action was or could be extended to an *object* (*voice*), and the speaker's attitude, intent, or purpose (*mood*). Please see the various entries on all these aspects of verbs for more details and examples.

Passive. There are two *voices* in English, active and passive. The *active voice* defines sentences in which action is transmitted directly or implicitly to another thing or person, an *object*: "The artist paints pictures. The artist paints." Both *verbs* are active, though with the second no object is stated directly.

When the sentence *subject* is the recipient of the action, and an agent of the action is stated directly in a *prepositional phrase* (or implied), the sentence is said to be in the passive voice: "The picture was painted by the artist. The picture was slashed." Both verbs in these examples are passive.

A universal rule of *usage* and *grammar* books is that the passive should not be overused or should be avoided altogether. The thinking behind this *rule* is that passives are less forceful because action is indirect, because subject and agent are not as closely and clearly connected as in the "normal" sentence pattern (active: subject, verb, object), and because many passive sentences together create an impression of inaction or blandness. Such thinking is justified to some degree, although the "rule" itself should not be overused any more than passive voice should. There are places and moments for passive constructions—for *emphasis*, variety of word order, and intentional removal or obscuring of a sentence's agent or subject.

EMPHASIS

Although passive is seen as less forceful inherently, the appearance of a passive *sentence* or group of passive sentences in an otherwise quite actively voiced document can call attention to the shift in *voice* and thereby to the message or point of the sentences constructed in the passive. Not much can be made of such *emphasis*, since the device used to stress something naturally is weak, less clear, and, in a word, passive.

WORD ORDER

Changing word order and gaining variety through occasional use of the passive can help a document full of simple, direct, active statements. Again, the change is not particularly forceful by nature, but it is there as a device. See *order of words*.

OBSCURING SENTENCE AGENT

When it is not important to make clear who is acting or if there is a good reason to obscure the active agent in a sentence, the passive works well. That is why so much government documentation, political *rhetoric*, and advertising is couched in the passive. If no active party is evident, no one can be blamed, held to promises, or made accountable for claims. Advertising sometimes takes the simpler path of omitting the subject: "Improved!"

If any of these considerations lead you to use the passive, make sure during your *editing, revision,* and proofreading cycles to avoid too much passive voice. Also take care to observe all the *rules* and requirements of *agreement* and consistency. Longer passive constructions naturally make *subject, verb,* and agent somewhat remote from one another, thereby enhancing the possibility that you will lose sight of the *number* or *person* with which the verb must agree. This is particularly true if the verb and prepositional agent phrase are close together while the subject is fairly far away. Then writers tend to make the verb agree with the number and person of the agent rather than the true subject of the sentence. WRONG: "The apple, fallen from a tree that stood for eons in the farmer's yard, were eaten by the hogs." RIGHT: "The apple . . . was eaten by. . . ."

Consistency should be maintained by making all *clauses* in a sentence either *active* or passive but not mixing *voices* in the same sentence. This is particularly true when a series of more than two clauses is joined together. WRONG: "The dog barks loudly, the cow stumbles toward the meadow, and the pig is herded toward the pen by the farmhand." RIGHT: "The dog . . . and the farmhand herds the pig toward the pen."

Past tense. *Verbs* indicate the time of the actions or conditions they depict by changing forms. Actions or conditions that took place before now or in the time the speaker or writer assumes to be now are said to be in the past and are depicted by the past tense. Most verbs form their past tenses by adding "d" or "ed" to their main forms: "walk, walked"; "type, typed"; "cook, cooked." But there are many verbs that change shape in the past and other forms irregularly. See the entry on *irregular verbs* and the individual entries for those verbs, which provide more details on how they are formed and used. Also see the entry on *tenses* for the more elaborately formed and less commonly used variants on the simple past tense.

Pay, paid, paid. An *irregular verb* in its main, *past tense*, and past *participle* forms.

Percent. The word "percent" can also be represented by the *symbol %*. In most *standard English* writing that is not highly mathematical, scientific, or commercial, the word is spelled out instead of using the symbol. In tables and other places where space is limited, the symbol can appear rather than the word.

Period. The *punctuation* mark that ends most sentences is the period (.). *Question marks* and *exclamation points* can also end sentences, and any ending punctuation can be enclosed in quotes, *parentheses,* or *brackets*: "Here is an example." The example could have been enclosed in parentheses or brackets as well as quotes, and (at least in theory) the *sentence* could have been construed as a *question* or command ending appropriately.

Periods are also used to mark the ends of most *abbreviations*: "The philosopher received the Ph.D. degree with honors." Some styles reduce or eliminate periods after abbreviations: "The stockbroker arrived at 6 am, and went home at 7 pm."

Ellipses are strings of periods used to indicate that words have been dropped from a statement, particularly a quoted passage: "The chairperson stated, 'The budget must be examined . . . and profits must rise." Three ellipses points indicate words dropped within a sentence, and four appear at the end of a sentence to show continuation (unless the shortened passage ends with other punctuation: "What are the consequences of using the active voice, the passive voice, and . . . ?").

Periods never fall outside quotation marks as the final punctuation of a sentence. WRONG: "Here is an example". Such punctuation is used only in *British English* and is not the right way to indicate that a quoted passage ends with other punctuation in the source even though you have chosen to end the statement at the point shown. If such specificity is necessary, you can indicate source ending punctuation with ellipses and brackets, still followed by period and quotes: "Kennedy said, 'Ask not what you can do for your country [. . .].' " If the ellipses and brackets were not used in this sentence, it would properly end as: ". . . your country.' " The period is inside all quotes.

Periods can come outside brackets (as shown in the preceding examples) or parentheses when a full sentence is not set off parenthetically: "The poet wrote an ode (I can't remember the title)." Even though the parenthetical expression is a whole sentence, it does not end in a period, while the full sentence ends after the parenthetical expression and therefore does show a period. Full sentences within parentheses and not contained within other sentences end with periods inside the parentheses: "(The ode is called 'To a Sparrow.')" Note that the period in this case is inside the single quote mark as well.

Person. Person is a grammatical category that indicates whether a *noun* or *pronoun* defines the stance of "*I*," "*you*," or "the other." That is, **first-person** words refer to the self as a *subject, object,* or in other grammatical roles: "I speak clearly." "It is given to me." "She handed the book to me." "We like it." "It pleases him." The pronouns "I, me," and "me, us" in these examples are all first person, singular and *plural*. **Second person** is always indicated by "you" in all *numbers* and *cases*. All the other pronouns are the person of the other, **third person:** "It, it"; "he, him"; "she, her"; and "they, them."

Verbs and other pronouns must agree in number and person with the pronouns they modify, refer to, or portray action for. First-person plural subjects take first-person plural verbs, which may have different forms than, say, first-person singular or third-person plural verbs. See *agreement, conjugation, irregular verbs,* and *number.*

Consistency of person from *clause* to clause in a sentence helps a reader follow your thinking, while changes of person can confuse. WRONG: "We play in the fields, and I enjoy it." The sentence is potentially confusing because the reader does not know how the others feel about play or the field, or why they were brought into the sentence in the first place if the point is "I's" feelings. Better to write: "I played in the field with them, and I enjoyed it." This sentence is still somewhat misleading in that the reader doesn't know how "they" felt about things, but it seems clearer that the statement is focused on "I" and not "they." Therefore the absence of information on "they's" feelings is not so striking.

Personal pronoun. The following words are called personal pronouns because they indicate people: *I, you, he, she, it, we,* and *they*. Each of them has a separate entry that explains the rules and nuances of their use, gives examples of poor and good *usage*, and refers to other entries with important information. See also *pronouns, case, number,* and *agreement*.

Ph.D. The *abbreviation* for the academic doctoral degree is "Ph.D." When names include the abbreviation (which follows the name and is set off by commas), they do not need any other honorific (such as Dr., Mr., Ms., etc.): "They honored Sally Fay, Ph.D., and her achievements in executive education. Ms. Fay could not accept the award in person."

Phrase. Phrases are groups of words that do not have *subjects, verbs,* or *objects* or *subject complements* but stand in place of or add meaning to those elements of sentences.

Phrases can function as various *parts of speech*: *adjectives, adverbs, nouns,* and verbs. In those functions phrases obey all the *rules* that apply to the *parts of speech,* though they may not change form or act in precisely the same way as one-word or simple parts of speech. That is, a verb may change form to agree in *number* or *person* with its subject, while a verbal phrase might not alter in any way or in the same way: "He is here, and they are here." The verb changes (is conjugated) to reflect subjects different in person and number. But: "The photographer sees the sleeping gorilla and six sleeping cheetahs." The verbal phrases "sleeping gorilla" and "six sleeping cheetahs" show no alteration in the adjectival form for singular or *plural.* See *agreement* and *conjugation.*

Phrases equal the noun, verb, *preposition, participle,* or other part of speech at their core plus any *modifiers, auxiliaries,* or supplemental words that are part of them: "To reach the farmer, the apparent victim, the car had driven to the red barn standing on the sloping hill above the house in the hollow." The phrases (and their types and functions) in this artificially complex example are the following:

"To reach the farmer" (*infinitive* phrase adverbially
    modifying the verb phrase "had driven")
"the apparent victim" (*noun phrase* standing in *appo-
    sition* to "the farmer")
"had driven" (verb phrase as *predicate*)
"to the red barn" (*prepositional phrase* adverbially
    modifying the verb and containing the noun phrase
    "red barn")

"standing on" (verbal/present participial phrase adjectivally modifying "barn")

"on the sloping hill" (prepositional phrase adverbially modifying the verbal phrase "standing")

"sloping" (verbal/present participial phrase adjectivally modifying "hill" and making up part of the noun phrase "sloping hill")

"above the house" (prepositional phrase adjectivally modifying "hill")

"in the hollow" (prepositional phrase adjectivally modifying "house")

The position and function of phrases in sentences dictate their *punctuation: Appositives* are set off with *commas*; longer introductory phrases of any kind are followed by commas before the main clauses of sentences; *nonrestrictive phrases* are set off with commas.

The entries for each part of speech contain more information on how they work and the rules that apply to them and equally to phrases.

Plural. *Nouns* that represent more than one thing or person are said to be plural, as are the *verbs* and *pronouns* that agree with them: "Dogs chew their bones" (see *agreement*). All the words in the example are plural. From the example it is clear that nouns form their plurals by adding "*s*," while verbs drop "s" in their third-person *present tense* forms: ("the dog chews," but "the dogs chew"). Plural pronouns (like "their" in the example) usually have distinct forms for plurals. See *collective pronouns, number, irregular verbs,* and *possessives.*

P.M. The *abbreviation* "P.M." stands for the *Latin* words "post meridiem" and means the time from noon to midnight: "I'll meet you at 8 P.M." The abbreviation is normally *capitalized* or appears as small capital letters where this is typographically possible. When you use "P.M.," do not add "o'clock" or such phrases as "in the afternoon." See also *A.M.*

Possessive. The inflected form of a *noun* or *pronoun* that indicates possession or ownership of something is called the "possessive": "This is my house and Spot's playground." "My" and "Spot's" are in the possessive (*case*). See *inflection*.

Pronouns form possessives in special ways. *Indefinite* pronouns follow the *rules* below, adding " 's" in most cases. *Personal pronouns* have unique possessive forms. See the entries for individual pronouns for more details.

Most singular nouns add an *apostrophe* (') and "s" to form a possessive: "The bird's beak is long." In the *plural*, nouns that end in "s" add only an apostrophe: "The birds' beaks are long." Plural nouns or *collective nouns* that do not end in "s" add both the apostrophe and "s": "The children's outing was Tuesday." Singular nouns or *names* that end in "s" also add apostrophe and "s" to form the possessive: "Sophocles's plays were of little interest in Jesus's time." Some styles form possessives for important or traditional names that end in "s" with just an apostrophe. Unless you are compelled to follow such a style, add " 's."

When more than two things or people possess something, you need to determine whether each one has an equal and separate share or whether the ownership is combined or joint. In the first instance, show individual ownership by more than one person or thing by making each word possessive: "Joan's and John's book is spellbinding." For the latter instance, show joint or combined ownership by making only the last person or thing possessive: "Nixon and Agnew's morals were suspect."

If you are unsure how shared or distinct contributions to or ownership of something is, then it is probably better to assume separate possessives will be more accurate and not offend anyone by slighting his or her role. This is particularly true for husbands and wives, male-female teams, and parent-child ownerships. It is considered offensive to subsume the wife's, female's, or child's role or ownership under that of the male or elder by putting only one name into the possessive. Be quite sure of your facts if you do write something like "Mr. and Mrs. Smith's business." It might well turn out that the Smiths would have preferred to see "Jane Smith's and John Smith's business," which gives them equal billing. See *sexist language*.

Precede, proceed. Commonly confused, these similar words differ in meaning. "Precede" means come before; "proceed" means to continue or move in procession.

Predicate. Everything in a sentence that is not the *subject* is the "predicate": *verb, object, predicate adjective* or *noun* (*subject complement*), and related words. "The door is open to the balcony, which overlooks the shining bay of Naples and the scattered islands that ring the harbor."

In the example all the words from "*is*" to the end are parts of the predicate. With *inversion* or other *orders of words* possible and common in English, predicates don't always follow subjects: "Is it true that time is up?" The predicate in the main sentence in this example equals everything but "*it*"; in the subordinate *clause* beginning with "that," the predicate equals "is up."

Besides the simple *agreement* requirements between subject and predicate—that verbs, predicate adjectives and *pronouns*, and subject complements match the subject in *number* and *person*—it is important that subject and predicate match in a more general way. They need to refer to the same thing or same order of thing. WRONG: "The reason I woke up is John made noise." A reason and a person are not really equivalent or of the same order. BETTER: "The reason I woke up is that John made noise." A reason can be a *clause* explaining something, as in the example.

Mismatches between sentence elements happen most often with forms of "*be*," the *linking verb* and a common weak spot in sentences. Combining "be" with "*when*," "where," or "*because*" is another weak writing move and often the sign of a predicate mismatch. WRONG: "Sleep is when it is quiet." Not really; sleep doesn't equal a time or condition of silence, though it might happen then. BETTER: "I sleep when it is quiet." "Sleep comes to me when it is quiet." "Sleep is best at times of quiet." There are many more variants that are clearer than the "wrong" example.

Look for linking verbs and other signals in all your *sentences*, and revise with care to ensure that subject and predicate agree and match grammatically and in terms of general sense. See also *phrases* for more explanation of the *parts of speech* that go into subjects and predicates and *revision* and *editing*.

Predicate adjective. *Adjectives* that fall in *predicates* are called "predicate adjectives": "The barn is red." "Red" is an adjective modifying or referring to "the barn." Such words are also called "*subject complements*."

Predicate noun. *Nouns* and *pronouns* that appear in *predicates* and are the simple equivalent of the *subject* are called "predicate nouns": "Jan is a student." "Student" is a predicate noun in this example. Such words are also called *subject complements*.

There is no limit to the length or complexity of *noun phrases* or pronoun *phrases* that can constitute predicate nouns. However, they must agree grammatically and in general with their subjects, sharing *number* and *person* in most cases. Longer and more complex phrases should be checked to make sure that *agreement* has not been lost sight of.

Prefix. Sets of letters that are added to the beginnings of words to modify their meaning are called "prefixes." The list that follows includes the most common prefixes and gives a sense of how their addition to a word changes its meaning. Note, however, that the same prefix can have different results with different words. For instance, "re" at the start of a word can indicate something is done again or once more ("revise") or that the action is directed back to its source or origin ("reveal" or "return").

Prefixes are usually spelled solid with the word to which they are attached: "recreate." But when distinctions are possible between meanings of prefixed words that are otherwise spelled the same, a *hyphen* may be inserted:

"recreation means leisure" but "re-creation means creating again." Similarly, when prefixes are attached to capitalized or *compound words*, hyphens are used: "pre-civil War." See *capitalization*.

a or **an**	without or negative: "apolitical"
ante	before: "antemeridian"
anti	against: "antiwar"
bi	two, dual; "bisexual"
bio	life: "biography"
circum	around: "circumspect"
co	with: "covalent"; also spelled **col, com, con,** and **cor** in some words: "collective," "communicate," "contract," "correlate"
contra	against or reverse: "contradict"
de	from or away: "detach"
dis	apart: "dislocate"
ex	from, out of; sometimes spelled **e**: "exhale, evade"
hyper	more than, over: "hypertext"
hypo	less than, under: "hypoallergenic"
inter	among, between: "interact"
il	not: "illegitimate"; also spelled **im, in,** and **ir** in some words: "impatient," "incontinent," "irrelevant"
mal	wrong, badly: "maladroit"
mega	large, million: "megabits"
micro	small: "microcomputer"
milli	thousand: "millipede"
mis	wrong, bad: "misnomer"
mono	one, single: "monofilament"

neo	new: "neoconservative"
non	not: "nonstarter"
omni	all, total: "omnivorous"
post	after: "postwar"
pre	before: "premarital"
pro	before, forward: "propound"
re	again, back: "retell"
self	oneself or itself (usually used with a hyphen): "self-centered"
semi	half: "semilegal"
sub	under: "submicroscopic"
super	above: "superconductor"
syn	simultaneously: "synchronic"; also spelled **sym**: "symphony"
trans	across: "translate"
tri	three, triple: "trilateral"
un	not: "unattractive"
uni	one, single: "unilateral"

Preposition. Prepositions are words that indicate a relationship between two or more things and/or people but not an action. They specify direction, scope, timing, and other aspects of action or condition by linking a noun to another *noun, verb,* or *adverb.*

The most common prepositions are the following: *about, above, across, after, against, along, among,* around, *as, at, below, before, behind, beneath, beside,* between, *beyond, by, down, during,* except, *for, from, in,* inside, *into, like,* near, *of, off, on, onto, out,* outside, over, past, *since, through, toward, under,* until, *up, with, without.*

Prepositions and the nouns and other words that they

"govern" make *prepositional phrases* that function as *adjectives* or adverbs. In the following artificial example, the many prepositional phrases play various roles that are explained after the example: "Toward evening, the elephant walked into the clearing and trumpeted to the skies above us its disapproval of our presence in its realm."

> "Toward evening" is an adverbial prepositional phrase modifying "walked." Although it comes before "elephant," it does not modify it, since living beings cannot have the kind of time relationship indicated by the phrase except through some action. Therefore the phrase modifies the action despite the sentence's word order (see *modifier* and *order of words*)
>
> "into the clearing" is another adverbial phrase that deals with "walked" and indicates direction rather than time
>
> "to the skies" is another adverb use of a prepositional phrase, here modifying "trumpeted"
>
> "above us" modifies the noun "skies" in the *phrase* before it, and even though that phrase is adverbial, this one is adjectival (since a noun is the thing qualified)
>
> "of our presence" is adjectival in function, modifying "disapproval"
>
> "in its realm" is also adjectival, here relating to the noun in the preceding prepositional phrase, "presence."

Note that prepositions govern the *objective case*, which means that *pronouns* that are the *objects* of prepositions change form to reflect their *case*: "I gave it to them." The function of the prepositional phrase in the sentence does not change this *rule*—all objects of prepositions are in the objective case.

Prepositional phrases placed at the beginning of *sentences* can be set off with *commas* in the following circumstances: if they are *nonrestrictive phrases* (contribute less than essential information to the sentence like "Toward evening" in the example); if they are long (though just what is long is a matter of judgment); or if not setting them off would confuse the reader (often true when the prepositional phrases are fairly far away from what they modify). Putting prepositional phrases at the beginning of sentences is a useful way to emphasize something or vary *style* to sustain reader interest (see *emphasis*).

Like all sentence elements with varying roles and flexible positioning within a sentence, prepositional phrases can be put in the wrong place or in a place that confuses the reader. If, in the example, the phrase "toward evening" appeared as the last words in the sentence, it would be hard to know what was happening at that time or what was being modified by the phrases "our presence" or "its realm" (presuming the elephant had a daytime realm). Check all sentences that have prepositional phrases to see that they are placed and worded so that it is clear what they are referring to (see *clarity*).

When prepositions appear in *names* or *titles* that are capitalized, the prepositions should not be capitalized whatever their length or function, unless they are the first word in the title (*On Golden Pond*) or are the subject themselves of the title in some way ("The Grammar of 'To' "). See *capitalization*.

Prepositional phrase. All the *nouns* or *pronouns* and the words modifying them that are "governed by" a *preposition* (follow it as its *objects*) constitute the prepositional phrase: "That meeting <u>of executives</u> was boring. The idea <u>of them making decisions</u> is ludicrous." All the underlined words are the prepositional phrases in these examples.

The prepositional phrase can function adjectivally or adverbially, following the *rules* for each such role as if it were a single word *adverb* or *adjective*. See the entry on *prepositions* for more information on *punctuation, order of words,* and other aspects of using prepositions and the words they govern; see also *modifier*.

Present tense. *Verbs* change their forms to indicate the time of the actions or conditions they depict. Actions or conditions that take place now or are perceived by the writer or speaker to be happening now are in the "present tense."

Verbs form their present tenses from the main form itself (in the first and second person) and the main form plus "*s*" or "*es*" (in the third person) in most cases: "walk, walks"; "type, types"; "echo, echoes." See *tenses* for more elaborately formed and commonly used forms of the present tense.

Principal, principle. Do not confuse these words that sound alike (*homonyms*). "Principal" means mean or primary as either an *adjective* or *noun*: " 'The principal means of attaining success is hard work,' said the school principal [main official]." In financial terms, "principal" is the main body of money in an investment. "Principle" means rule or belief: "The main principles of Buddhism are not commonly known in this country."

Principle. See *principal*.

Proceed. See *precede*.

Pronoun. Words that "stand for" more specific *nouns* are called "pronouns." The common pronouns come in many types: *personal pronouns, demonstrative, intensifiers, interrogative, reciprocal pronouns, reflexive pronouns,* and *relative pronouns*. There are entries for each of the important pronouns and for each of these types. Please consult those specific entries as well as the brief description of their functioning given below along with a list of the most common pronouns in each group.

PERSONAL. Personal pronouns are used in place of specific things or people. *I, you, he, she, it, we,* and they are all the personal pronouns.

DEMONSTRATIVE. These pronouns that indicate specific things or people and suggest their relationship to the speaker: this, these and *that*, those are the singulars and *plurals* of the demonstratives that suggest, respectively, closeness or immediacy versus remoteness.

INTENSIVE. Pronouns that add "*-self*" ("selves" in plural) can be used to emphasize the nouns they precede ("I myself saw that."). These forms are also reflexive pronouns. See *emphasis*.

INTERROGATIVE. These pronouns indicate questioning: what, which, and *who*.

RECIPROCAL. These pronouns, "each other" and "one another," are used with plural *antecedents* to indicate separate actions or conditions of the antecedent: "I saw the monkeys groom each other."

REFLEXIVE. Reflexives are formed like the intensive pronouns by adding "self" or "selves" (plural). These words stand alone (unlike the intensive) and indicate actions or conditions that go back to the sentence or clause *subject*: "The monkey groomed itself and its mate."

RELATIVE. These pronouns ("*that*," "what," "whatever," "which," "whichever," "who," and "whoever") link dependent *clauses* to the main parts of *sentences* and indicate the relationship between such clauses and the sentence's main thrust: "I saw the monkey that was grooming its partner, who was sitting nearby." See also *restrictive clauses* and *nonrestrictive clauses*.

Proper noun. In *grammar* terms, *names* are "proper nouns": "Bill told Marie that the *Titanic* had sunk with his copy of Tolstoy's novel." All the capitalized words in the example are proper nouns, or names of things or people (see *capitalization*). Proper nouns are almost always capitalized.

Prove, proved, proved. An *irregular verb* in its main, *past tense,* and past *participle* forms.

Proved. See *prove.*

Punctuation. The marks in sentences that are not letters are "punctuation." Punctuation marks tell how various parts of the sentence are related to one another and to other sentences. Each of the punctuation marks listed and briefly described here has an entry of its own giving further details about it and examples of how to use it.

ACCENTS. These marks appear above or below letters to indicate their pronunciation or other aspects of their function within a word. English has no *accents* in words that originated in the language itself, but it shows accents carried over from other languages: "The employee wrote a résumé." "Résumé" is an English word now, and it usually carries the accents that it had in its French origins.

APOSTROPHE. *Apostrophes* (') mark *possessives* and *contractions:* "The player's dog doesn't bite."

ASTERISK. The *asterisk* (*) is more a typographical device to emphasize parts of *lists,* notes to a page, and the like rather than a punctuation mark strictly speaking: "Here are the important points:

  ∗punctuality
  ∗neatness . . .''

COLON. The *colon* (:) stands before and sharply sets off lists and dependent or independent *phrases* or *clauses*. It appears in this book frequently before examples: "The important parts are as follows: punctuality, neatness, . . ." The colon also appears in time figures to separate hours and minutes: "See you at 2:45."

COMMA. The *comma* (,) separates elements without much abruptness or distance; put another way, commas link things as much as they separate them and mark borders between things: "The photojournalist photographed lions, cheetahs, and elephants. The photographer took the photos in Africa, and developed them in Indiana, where the studio is." The commas in the example link and mark borders between items in a list and then between two independent clauses, one of which has within it nouns in *apposition* (rephrased versions of the *nouns* next to which they stand) to the *object* of a *preposition*. Many other grammatical entities are similarly linked and delimited by commas.

  Commas also appear in *numbers* greater than 999 that aren't dates ("4,367"), in *dates* between days and years ("November 23, 1963"), and to set off honorific *titles* and direct *quotations* ("Jan Smith, Ph.D., said, 'That's right.' ").

DASH. The *dash* (—) is an abrupt or sharp divider of ideas or words that usually sets off something added or interjected into a sentence: "Everyone there—Bill, Mary, Inga—agreed." See *interjection*.

ELLIPSIS. This punctuation mark (. . .) indicates the omission of some words (three periods) or *sentences* (four periods) from quoted speech or from any incomplete statement whether attributed to someone or not: "The speaker said, 'The points to consider are sixteen in number: first. . . .' " "I decided that enough was enough. . . ."

EXCLAMATION POINT. The *exclamation point* marks an emphatic, loud, or important statement: "You better believe it!" See *emphasis*.

HYPHEN. The *hyphen* (-) joins two words together to form a *compound word*: "The decision-making process took too long." The hyphen also indicates that a word fragment at the end of a line should be joined to the rest of the word that appears at the beginning of the next line:

> "Here is the example that
> will show a hyphen appearing ran-
> domly at the end of one line."

PARENTHESES. Interjected words in a sentence can be marked in several ways, including by enclosure in *parentheses:* "Everyone there (Chris, Jan, Sandy) agreed." Commas or dashes can often be used for the same purpose.

PERIOD. The period (.) marks the end of sentences that don't end with question marks or exclamation points: "That is so.'' Periods also indicate the ends of *abbreviations*: ''Mr. Jones is here.''

QUESTION MARK. This punctuation ends a *question*: ''Isn't that so?''

QUOTATION MARKS. This punctuation surrounds a direct quote: ''King said, 'I have a dream.' '' Single quotes appear to mark direct quotes within quoted speech, as in the example. *Quotation marks* around single words or phrases are also used to indicate that they are somehow in question or are being considered as entities or grammatical categories in themselves: '' 'Dream' is a noun.''

SEMICOLON. The *semicolon* (;) functions somewhat like the comma, but it is used to mark clearer distinctions between or among things or when the phrases or clauses it separates already contain commas: ''We saw lions, tigers, and rhinos; and then we left the zoo and went to the movies.''

Put, put, put. An *irregular verb* in its main, *past tense*, and past *participle* forms.

Q

Qualifier. See *modifier, adjective,* and *adverb.*

Question. Sentences or sentence *fragments* can ask questions either directly or indirectly. *Punctuation* and *order of words* vary, depending on the type of question.

DIRECT QUESTION

Sentences that are wholly devoted to questioning or asking something are called "direct questions": "What is that?" "Is it the thing you said you would bring?" "Is it as heavy as it looked when we first considered buying it and bringing it here?" "Expensive?" Each of these questions is a direct question, even the last sentence *fragment* and the longer sentences that convey information as well as asking for more. The writer has indicated the directness of the questions in several ways typical of such sentences.

First, like all direct questions, the example sentences end in *question marks* (?). Second, like many direct questions, some of these sentences invert word order. Commonly the *inversion* puts an *auxiliary* verb at the beginning of the sentence ("*is*," "*do*," and the like) and follows it with a *pronoun* of some sort ("*it*" in the examples, though many others are used). The next word is often a *noun*, which can be seen as a shifted *subject* or a *subject complement* more or less normally placed. Other words that frequently start such sentences are *interrogative* pronouns ("what," "which," and "who"), as in the first example sentence.

Word order can be more elaborately changed, and other words can start questions ("how," "why," and so on). But the main features are clear: inversion, questioning word to start, and question mark to end. As with all inversions, those used for questions should be checked carefully to ensure *agreement* among all grammatical elements— movement of elements for question order can put subjects far from *verbs, objects,* or subject complements. Make sure all is in order.

The most common agreement errors occur with the interrogative pronoun "who" as the first word in a question: Should it be "who" (*nominative* case) or "whom" (*objective case*) when it hangs out there at the start? How can one tell? The simplest test of *case* in such sentences is to answer the question with a pronoun that changes form in its objective case: "Who is to be asked? She is to be asked." "Her" is obviously wrong here since it is not an object but the subject of a *passive* construction. "Whom did you see? I saw him." Clearly you see something or someone in an *active* sentence as its object, and therefore the objective "whom" is correct.

Besides their obvious function of asking for information, questions can play an emphasizing role by varying sentence structure and thus calling attention to something. In this function questions are often used rhetorically, to make a statement rather than request enlightenment: "Is our cause not just?" The writer has no desire to hear a response to this "question." *Rhetorical questions* thus often lead *para-*

graphs or longer portions of a document in order to establish a topic or idea in an emphatic way: "Isn't it curious how the caterpillar lives?" Again, no answer is expected, but our attention is focused on caterpillars and their evidently unusual patterns of life. See *emphasis*.

The device of rhetorical questioning to open a statement, *paragraph,* or whatever is somewhat clichéd—a bit tired and overused. Thus its emphatic force has been lost to some degree, and it is often seen as an obvious, mechanical, or awkward way to launch a subject. Certainly rhetorical questions, like all emphatic devices, should not be repeated frequently in the same document, paragraph, or statement. Remember that the question you did not intend anyone to answer might be responded to: "No, caterpillars aren't curious in the least." The reader or listener has now been lost. See *cliché*.

INDIRECT QUESTION

When questions are restated or reported within other *sentences,* they are "indirect questions": "The interviewer asked what interests you." These questions do not end in question marks and usually do not vary or invert word order since they are not emphasizing anything or marking themselves as questions. Indirect questions usually include *verbs* that suggest they are reporting a question: "ask," "question," "inquire," and so on. Indirect questions are identical to other sentences in all other respects. See *emphasis* and *order of words*.

Indirect questions can strike readers as weak because they

don't precisely record what has been asked. "The interviewer asked if you are happy" is not quite as accurate or certain a version of several possible questions that might have been asked: "The interviewer asked, 'Are you happy? Is he/she happy? Is Kim happy? Is anyone here happy?''

Question mark. The *punctuation* mark that indicates a direct *question* is called a "question mark" (?). The question mark is used straightforwardly and most often to end a direct question: "How are you?" Complications arise when question marks appear with other punctuation, especially *parentheses* and *quotation marks*.

Depending on what is being set off by the parentheses, question marks can appear inside or outside them. If the parentheses enclose a complete sentence (or more than one), any direct questions within them end with question marks that appear within the parentheses: "It was cold. (But why did the water stay liquid? Why were the ducks on the pond?) Was winter here?"

But if the parentheses set off a *phrase, clause,* or even a whole *sentence* within a direct question, the whole direct question ends with a question mark outside the parentheses: "How cold was it (ducks were on the pond, the water was still liquid)?" No *period* ends the sentences within the parentheses, by the way, though a question mark could have appeared within them as well if one of the parenthetical sentences was a direct question: "How cold was it (were there ducks on the pond? was it still liquid?)?" The example cries out for *revision* to eliminate the logjam of punctuation at its end and to give the reader a chance to follow what is going on. It would have been better to write several separate sentences as questions than to have knitted them together in this forced way.

With quotation marks the question mark can, again, appear either within them or outside them. If a direct question is being quoted (and not being restated as an indirect question), then it ends with a question mark followed by quotation marks: ''is that so?'' Or: ''The guest asked, 'Is that so?' '' (The indirect question ''The guest asked if that was so'' does not end in a question mark inside or outside the quotes.)

But if quoted material appears within a direct question and does not constitute the whole question, then the question mark appears at the end of the sentence and is not followed by quotes: ''Was the teacher talking about the 'decline of the West'?'' The question mark is outside the single quote that marks only words being set off for some other reason than questioning them. The question mark is within the double quotes only because that is how examples in this book are set off.

Note that a quoted direct question followed by a statement about who is asking the question ends with a quotation mark inside the quotes and no additional punctuation until the end of the whole sentence: '' 'Is that so?' the companion asked.'' No *comma* follows the quoted question, although one would have been necessary if the example were not a question: '' 'That is so,' the companion said.''

Quotation. Like *questions,* quotations come in two basic kinds—direct and indirect statements attributed to someone: '' 'That's right,' I said.'' ''Indeed, I said that it was exemplary.'' The first example is a direct quotation, and the second is indirect. Note the differences in their *punctuation* and *order of words* and selection.

Direct quotations are surrounded by *quotation marks* and contain within the quotation marks ending punctuation to indicate whether the quoted statement is a *demonstrative, interrogative, imperative,* or other kind of sentence: " 'Make it so!' the boss ordered." " 'Why must I?' the employee inquired." " 'Because I said so,' the boss responded." In this exchange the first quoted sentence is an imperative that ends with an *exclamation point;* the next is a direct question that ends with a *question mark* inside the quotes; and the last quoted statement is a simple demonstrative sentence, which ends with a *comma* inside the quotes when a statement follows about who is making the quoted statement. If a demonstrative sentence is quoted and ends a quoted passage, it ends with a *period* inside the quotation marks: "The employee said, 'I agree.' "

Indirect quotations restate or report statements rather than reproducing them directly: "He said that he was happy." Indirect quotations are not set off in quotation marks (except here as an example), do not include punctuation to indicate the nature of the quoted sentence, and usually include words like "said that," "stated that," or something similar to mark the reporting of speech indirectly.

Like indirect questions, indirect quotations expose the writer to some suspicion from readers. What exactly did someone say as opposed to what is reported? A few indirect quotations will not arouse such suspicion, but repeated indirect quotations from the same source can create doubts about accuracy of reporting.

Quotation mark. The *punctuation* marks used to set off quoted speech are called "quotes" or "'quotation marks'": " 'Yes,' Bloom said."

Simple direct quotations are surrounded by double quotes ("), while further quotes within double-quote–marked sentences use single quotes ('), as in the example. Further quotes within quotes within quotes would logically be set off by double quotes, but sentences of such complexity should rarely be imposed on readers.

Quotes are also used to mark single words, *phrases,* or *clauses* for *emphasis*—when they are being signaled as somehow suspect ("You call that a 'dog'?"); when they are being treated as grammatical categories or words in themselves (" 'That' is a pronoun."); or for other emphatic purposes.

Note that other punctuation is placed before or after quote marks differently, depending on whether quotes surround fully quoted speech or emphasized words. A fully quoted *sentence* or *fragment* has all its punctuation inside the quote marks, including any ending punctuation: "Did you call the dog?" "Call the dog!" "I called the dog." Similarly, fully quoted sentences or fragments that don't end a sentence have all punctuation inside quotes: " 'Are you sure?' the judge asked." Here the whole sentence ends with a *period* inside the double quotes as expected, and the sentence quoted ends with a *question mark* inside the single quotes that set it off. When a sentence is quoted and falls before and after the identification of the speaker, the first part ends with a *comma* inside the quotes, and the rest ends with whatever punctuation is appropriate: " 'Your fence,' the neighbor shouted, 'is too high!' " Similarly, if two sentences from the same speaker are quoted before and after the identification, all punctuation for the quoted sentences is within the quotes: " 'Come on in!' the host directed, 'Get comfortable!' "

When quotes are used to mark words for any other purpose than as a direct quotation, then end-of-sentence question marks and *exclamation points* do not fall within them: "Is this supposed to be an example of 'good writing'?" The question mark is inside the double quotes that set off the whole example but outside the single quotes that here suggest doubts or *irony* about the words "good writing." Had the example ended with a period, however, it would have been inside both sets of quotation marks: "This is supposed to be 'good writing.' "

Q.v. This *abbreviation* of the *Latin* words "quod vide" means "which see." It is better in modern writing to simply say, "Please see" or "See."

R

Raise, rise. Often confused, these *verbs* have different meanings. "Raise" means to elevate, pick up, or (of children) see through development. "*Rise*" means to go up or ascend; as an *intransitive* verb it has no *object*, while "raise" usually does. Their main forms are "raise, raised, raised" and "rise, rose, risen."

Ran. See *run*.

Rang. See *ring*.

Read, read, read. An *irregular verb* in its main, *past tense*, and past *participle* forms.

Real, really. A common error occurs when the *adjective* "real" is used for the *adverb* "really" or to mean "very." WRONG: "That color is right bright." BETTER: "That color is very/really bright."

"Really" and "real" are often overused when an argument or point isn't very clear or understandable. They then take the place of logic or sense and become crutches for weak thought and expression: "I really think you should join the army." The example means: I can't think of any persuasive reasons why you should join, but I'll try to make my point stronger by inserting a meaningless "really" in the sentence.

In short, the presence of "real" and "really" in your statements is a signal to you and your *audience* that your thoughts or words bear further attention and probably can't be trusted or accepted at face value. Avoid "real" and "really" in most cases.

Really. See *real*.

Reciprocal pronoun. "Each other" and "one another" are reciprocals that single out parts or individuals from a group: "The rats began to attack one another/each other."

Redundancy. A common weakness of writing is repetition of ideas or words, which is called redundancy. WEAK: "Please be sure to check the results and see that they are correct." BETTER: "Please be sure to check that the results are correct." There is no need to repeat the idea of checking in this sentence. If emphasis is wanted, better to change the words, the *order of words*, or some other aspect of the sentence than just to say the same thing in a slightly different way: "You better be sure you check the accuracy of the results!"

Removing redundancy from writing not only makes your message more direct and clear, it also removes unneeded words and makes it more likely that your *audience* will follow your thoughts and respond accordingly.

Referent. See *antecedent*.

Reflexive pronoun. Reflexive pronouns direct action back to the sentence *subject*. They end in "*-self*" in the singular and "-selves" in the *plural*: "herself," "himself," "it-self," "myself," "oneself" (or "one's self"), "our-selves," "themselves," "yourself," and "yourselves."

Note that the reflexives are formed from the *objective case* of the *personal pronouns* because they always are the *object* of action reflected back on the subject: "He shot himself." Thus such constructions as "hisself" or "theyself/ves" are in the wrong *case* and shouldn't be used (they actually don't exist except as *colloquial* or *dialect* forms).

Too often reflexives are used when simple objective cases of personal pronouns are enough, particularly when the choice is between "*me*" and "myself." Evidently, people think it is less egotistical or more grammatically correct to use "myself" instead of "me." Or perhaps they are avoiding distinguishing between "*I*" and "me." At any rate, such sentences as "She gave it to myself" are grammatically incorrect and should be avoided. "She gave it to me" is just fine.

It is even worse to use "myself" as a subject: "John and myself went to the movies." Why not "John and I"? Does the "I" sound too assertive? Are people worried that they should be using "me" (wrong because it is not used for sentence subjects)? Whatever the reason, it is simpler, more direct, and clearer just to use the *nominative* (subjective) case for subjects.

Regardless. Use this word and not "*irregardless*," which adds a negating *prefix* to a word that already carries the sense of negation in its ending. In fact, "irregardless" is not a word.

Regular verb. *Verbs* that follow the normal pattern of *conjugation* are called "regular." See also *irregular verbs*.

Relative pronoun. The *pronouns* "that," "what," "whatever," "which," "whichever," "*who*," and "whoever" link dependent *clauses* to *sentences* and suggest a relationship between the clause and the main statement.

Relative pronouns operate quite straightforwardly in sentences and clauses: "The lion is the biggest cat that lives in Africa." "Smithers is the hunter who shot a lion." "Kunga is a lion who eats whomever it can find." The relative pronouns change *case* (and sometimes form), depending on how they are used in their clauses. Thus "who" is the *subject* twice in the example sentences, while "whomever" is the *object* of "finds."

Agreement of relative pronoun subjects and their *verbs* or other pronouns that refer to them also follows expected *rules* and patterns. However, take care with the combination of "one" and "who." It is sometimes tricky to tell whether the "who" following a "one" refers to a singular or plural *antecedent*. The verb that follows "who" needs to be in the correct *number* in these instances, of course, so the antecedent must be checked: "Appleton is the one who baked the bread." "Who" is *singular* because Appleton is only one person. But "Appleton is one of those who bake bread." Here "who" refers to "those"—the many people who bake bread—and therefore the verb is *plural*. Many sentences are not so obvious as these examples, and errors in agreement between "who" and a verb are common.

Repetition. One device of persuasion or *emphasis* is repetition—using the same word, *phrase, clause, order of words,* sentence structure, *voice, mood,* or other feature of writing more than once to make a point or call attention to something.

If you choose to employ repetition in your writing, take care to maintain some degree of consistency or *parallelism* among repeated elements so that your *audience* can easily recognize them. However, repeating a simple sentence structure like a *noun* followed by a *verb* or *adjective* can dispel all the *rhetorical* force built up by repetition.

Restrictive clause. *Clauses* that add vital information to *sentences* are called "restrictive." They appear wherever the writer chooses in a sentence and are not set off by *commas,* as are *nonrestrictive clauses,* which are so marked to indicate that the information they contribute to a sentence is less critical.

Restrictive clauses are most commonly introduced by *relative pronouns* and *demonstrative* pronouns: "Sally is the person who is in charge. She has the plan that will be put into effect." In the example sentences, "who" and "that" introduce the restrictive clauses. It is clear that they are restrictive because the sentences would not be complete or convey the same idea without them. Compare: "Sally, who works in development, is in charge. She has a plan, which will be put into effect, that calls for automation." "Who" again introduces the same clause, but it is now nonrestrictive—if it is removed from the sentence, we still will get the main point: Sally is in charge. In the second example sentence "which" is now used to introduce the "will be put into effect" clause because it is now nonrestrictive—the point is about automation, not that the plan will be activated. Note that the nonrestrictive clauses created in the latter two examples are set off by commas.

Errors common with these two kinds of clauses include adding commas before restrictive clauses, using "which" for "*that,*" and not setting off nonrestrictive clauses with commas.

Restrictive phrase. Like *restrictive clauses,* restrictive *phrases* have some *rules* associated with them. They are not set off by *commas,* and they need to be clearly associated with the thing or person to which they refer—their *antecedent.* See the entry for *nonrestrictive phrases* for more information, examples, and *rules.*

Use the same method to determine if a phrase is restrictive or nonrestrictive as was suggested for restrictive and non-restrictive clauses: consider whether the sentence without the phrase is complete and means the same as with it. If the sentence makes it main point without the phrase, then the phrase is nonrestrictive. If the sentence needs the phrase to convey its message, then the phrase is restrictive. Restrictive: "The hiker saw the mountain goat standing on the hill." The sentence intends to identify the mountain goat as specifically the one on the hill, not any other. Nonrestrictive: "Standing on the hill, the hiker saw the mountain goat." The sentence is about seeing the mountain goat, and the information about where the hiker is standing is less important.

If a comma appeared in the first example before "standing,'' one of the most common grammatical errors would be apparent—a *misplaced modifier*. That is, the comma would have made it unclear whether the hiker or the mountain goat was standing on the hill. The second example cannot be misconstrued—it is the hiker on the hill. These examples show, in a modest way, that it is important to punctuate sentences with phrases with care so that the relationship between the phrase and the word it refers to is quite clear. Another way to ensure *clarity* of connection between phrase and antecedent is to position the phrase so that there can be no misunderstanding about what it refers to and whether it is restrictive or nonrestrictive.

Revision. The vital process of reviewing and rewriting to eliminate errors, unclear passages, inefficient communication, and poorly chosen *phrases* or vocabulary is called revision. The previous long sentence could probably use some revision. See *editing*.

Rhetoric. In the most basic sense, rhetoric is the art of persuasion. During the long history of the practice of this art, certain kinds of *sentences, phrases, clauses, paragraphs*, and other grammatical elements were identified as more effective persuaders or conveyers of information than other forms, at least in certain circumstances. Rhetoric, then, is the art of making choices among words, sentences, structures, and so on in order to communicate or express oneself most effectively.

While *grammar* has rather hard-and-fast *rules* to follow, rhetoric has accumulated experience to suggest devices, methods, and patterns of writing or speaking to good effect.

Put another way, grammar tells us how to write or speak correctly and clearly, while rhetoric helps us do so forcefully, persuasively, and effectively. There is not space or reason to recite the points of rhetorical practice here, except to say that rhetoric—the strength and efficacy of communicating—merits careful thought and attention, along with the accuracy and correctness of speech or writing (grammar). See the entries on *style, variety, parallelism, repetition,* and the like.

Rhetorical question. *Questions* to which a writer or speaker does not expect answers are called "rhetorical": "Isn't that the worst thing you ever saw?" This "question" is asked not to find out what anyone thinks about the "thing" but to make the point that the speaker or writer believes it to be quite bad.

Rhetorical questions are a tried-and-true stylistic device, tried so often that they have become somewhat clichéd. Don't use too many of them, and try not to use them if there is any chance that a negative response will follow and leave you without an *audience*. See *cliché* and *style*.

Ridden. See *ride*.

Ride, rode, ridden. An *irregular verb* in its main, *past tense,* and past *participle* forms.

Ring, rang, rung. An *irregular verb* in its main, *past tense,* and past *participle* forms.

Rise, rose, risen. An *irregular verb* in its main, *past tense*, and past *participle* forms. See also *raise*.

Risen. See *rise*.

Rode. See *ride*.

Roman. Type that appears in the form most commonly seen in printed matter is called "Roman" for historical reasons. Type that appears slanted is called *italic*, as in the word before the *comma*.

Root. See *main form*.

Rose. See *rise*.

Rules. *Grammar* sets and records the rules that govern how words are put together for maximum *clarity* and correctness of expression. Like all rules, grammar rules can be broken for a reason; today, grammar rules are more often violated for good and bad reasons than ever before. Rule breaking can be exhilarating in itself, which is probably reason enough to do it sometimes. But since communicating serves not only the self but others in an *audience* meant to comprehend what is said, too much of a fun thing can subvert one's communicative intent. Too much or arbitrary rule breaking can sever the tenuous bond between audience and writer or speaker, leading to confusion.

If you know the rules of grammar and apply them in most of what you say or write, then judicious violations of rules can be used successfully to emphasize points, to paint vivid pictures in or of *colloquial* or *dialect* language or speakers, or to draw energy into language by playing against the rigidity of rules. But this must be done with care, and it happens most profitably when the rule breaker knows well what rules are being violated and why. In short, the careful, conscious, conscientious writer will be heard better than the sloppy, thoughtless person who thinks grammar rules are unimportant. See *emphasis*.

Run, ran, run. An *irregular verb* in its main, *past tense*, and past *participle* forms.

Rung. See *ring*.

Run-ons. *Sentences* that include too many *clauses* or *phrases* are said to run on: "The chauffeur parked the limousine, and the passenger went into the restaurant, while a waiter talked to the host, who was standing next to the door that still showed scars from the fire that happened over the last weekend before Christmas." The example makes obvious the fault of such sentences and the ordeal they represent for readers or listeners.

The answer to most run-ons is to break them up into smaller pieces, tying together with *conjunctions* or through other constructions only those things that are fairly closely related to one another: "The chauffeur parked the limousine, and the passenger went into the restaurant. Meanwhile, the waiter talked to the host. She was standing next to the door, which still showed scars from the fire that happened over the last weekend before Christmas." Other divisions of the initial example are possible, of course, depending on the point being made. And it is likely that many of the words and ideas in the example could be dropped without loosing the main thrust of the sentences. Run-ons usually pile too much together and signal failure to think out what needs to be said, how to say it, and whether the way it has been said needs *revision* or rethinking.

Don't burden readers or listeners with your failure to decide what you want to say or how to say it.

Russian. The most widespread of the Slavic languages (which include Ukrainian, Polish, Czech, Slovak, and Croatian), Russian uses a different alphabet than English. Therefore, it can be represented in various ways in English. Which system of transliteration you choose will depend on your *audience* and the standards applied where and when you write. You should consult a Russian *grammar*, *dictionary*, or *style* book for further guidance on *capitalization*, *punctuation*, and other aspects of the language and its transliterated versions. See *languages*.

S

s. The letter "s" is added to words to change their *number, case,* or *person.* For instance, adding "s" to many *nouns* makes them *plural*: "The executive owns one dog but takes care of two dogs."

Similarly, *verbs* add "s" in the *present tense* to form the third-person singular: "I eat, you eat, he/she/it eats, we eat, they eat."

Finally, nouns add "s" preceded by an *apostrophe* to form singular *possessives*: "Spike is the executive's dog." Verb *contractions* do the same: "it is—it's"; "he has—he's."

Said. See *say.*

Salutation. In letters, the line that directly addresses the person to whom the letter is going is called the "salutation": "Dear Dr. Hesse:." The example ends with a *colon,* which is the typical *punctuation* in business or more formal letters. More personal letters or informal communications may use a *comma* in the salutation: "Dear Chris,."

In multiple-name salutations that include men and women or people with different ranks or titles, be sure to be consistent and parallel, giving each person her or his due: "Dear Professor Smith and Professor Jones:." This is better than "Dear Professors Smith and Jones," particularly if Smith is a man and Jones a woman or Smith a senior type

and Jones a junior. Avoid "Dear Dr. Jones and Bob."
Better: "Dear Dr. Jones and Mr. Smith" to indicate your
equal respect and regard for the people addressed. See *sexist
language* and *parallelism*.

Sang. See *sing*.

Sank. See *sink*.

Sat. See *sit*.

Saw. See *see*.

Say, said, said. An *irregular verb* in its main, *past tense*,
and past *participle* forms.

Scientific language. The ideology and rigors of science
have created a specific writing *style* for science that includes
some variants of "normal" grammar *rules* and *usage*.

Science writing tends to be cast in the *passive voice*, to
avoid the first-person singular, and to be laced with Latinisms and jargon. Each of these features is believed by
scientists and scientific writers to enhance the "objectivity"
and "neutrality" of the observations and conclusions they
report and analyze. Specificity comes, in this stylistic
vision, from precise naming of things and concepts, which
makes them repeatable and verifiable. See *person* and
Latin.

The stylistic strictures of scientific language have no
doubt contributed significantly to the blossoming and
achievements of science in our day. And it is certainly true

that many scientists are as aware of and committed to the colloquialization of their language as anyone else (see *colloquial*). Many scientists write and speak clearly and engagingly.

Still, the ways of scientific language are elaborate, mysterious, and sometimes baffling. Consult the many guides, handbooks, and rule books for instruction in this type of language.

Sec. This is the *abbreviation* of the word "second," the time measurement. Except in technical writing, where space is at a premium, and similar *styles,* the whole word should be used rather than the abbreviation. "Sec." is also the abbreviation for several other technical terms.

Secondly. There is no reason to add "ly" to this or other *ordinal numbers,* especially when they are used to *list* things.

See, saw, seen. An *irregular verb* in its main, *past tense,* and past *participle* forms.

Seem. A *linking verb* that takes a *predicate* nominative (*subject complement*) rather than a *direct object.* See *nominative.*

Seen. See *see.*

-self. This *suffix* is added to *pronouns* to make them *reflexive pronouns,* which refer back to themselves: "The committee berated itself in frustration." "-Self" forms are also used as *intensifiers*: "I myself will lead the parade." But "-self" forms should never be used when simple *cases* of pronouns will suffice. WRONG: "Fran will accompany herself and myself on the trip." RIGHT: "Fran will travel with her and me." The use of "myself" in these situations is probably attributable to a desire to avoid figuring out the correct *objective case* form of "*I*"—easier to say "myself" than to guess whether it should be "I" or "*me.*"

Semicolon. The *punctuation* mark called "semicolon" (;) indicates a stronger or more definite break in a *sentence* than a *comma.*

When two or more independent *clauses* are put together to form a sentence, they can be joined by *conjunctions* (words like "*and*") or simply stuck to one another without words of explanation. Such unexplained junctures require punctuation, which is usually the semicolon: "The writer likes sports; the programmer likes books." These two clauses could have been linked by a comma and "'and" or "*but.*" However, the choice of no conjunction and the semicolon makes the contrast between the writer's preferences and the programmer's a little more forceful or stark. Put another way, the semicolon here plays a *rhetorical* role in the sentence or its *style*; it adds *emphasis.*

If a sentence is built from two or more clauses or *phrases* that include other punctuation, particularly commas, then a semicolon is the best choice to separate the sentence elements and to make clear what belongs where: "The programmer likes books like *Northanger Abbey, Anna Karenina,* and *Rabbit Redux*; the writer likes sports like swimming, baseball, and biking; but the kids like music, and they play CDs morning, noon, and night.'' Without the semicolons dividing the independent clauses in this rambling example, readers would be hard pressed to figure out where the *lists* that go with each person end and the next person's preferences start. Phrases can present the same problem: ''Starting with a cup of flour, add two teaspoons of salt; one cup of smoked, peeled, and grated chiles; and three tablespoons each of chopped onions, peppers, and garlic.'' Again, the lists would jumble together without semicolons marking the segments that belong together.

Each of the example sentences in the previous paragraph could be revised into less *run-on* form. The writer and programmer might appear in one shorter sentence with their likes, whereas the kids could be given a sentence of their own, especially since the structure of the sentence changes somewhat to focus on timing of action rather than list of specifics. Similarly, the recipe could be broken up into a more readable form—each ingredient on a separate line, figures used instead of spelled out *numbers,* and so on. In short, use semicolons as a signal that sentences might be running on too long and be in need of rewriting or *revision*.

When two or more independent clauses are part of a single sentence and one or more of them includes dependent clauses that require commas to set them off within the independent clause, then a semicolon is used to join the independent clauses even if a conjunction appears: ''Having painted the ceiling, Michelangelo moved on to the walls; and all the while he made plans for decorating the floors.''

Even long and rambly sentences need not have semicolons if the elements are clearly distinguished and not listed or joined with commas. In fact, it is a common error to put in semicolons before dependent clauses or to mark the beginning of lists. Like all punctuation, the semicolon should not be overused or misused in these ways. Semicolons usually appear outside *quotation marks*: "We don't use words like 'damn'; we are above such vulgarity."

Send, sent, sent. An *irregular verb* in its main, *past tense,* and past *participle* forms.

Sent. See *send.*

Sentence. A sentence is one or more words that express action, condition, or thought, among many other things. Sentences normally include a *subject*—a thing or person at the focus of the sentence—and a *verb*—an expression of the action or condition of the subject. Often sentences have a third element as well that receives the action of the verb or characterizes the condition—an *object* or *subject complement.*

The three basic elements of the sentence can be stated in many words or just one: "Unite!" the single-word example is a complete sentence because the *imperative* mood allows unstated or implied subjects. Restated, the example could read: "You people should unite," which makes the subject more visible. However, not all single words followed by an *exclamation point* are sentences: "Termites!" This lone *noun* is a sentence *fragment.* While it has its use for *emphasis,* it does not have the verb or other components necessary to make it a sentence. And therefore it is not subject to the same *rules,* patterns, and possibilities as a complete sentence. See also *mood.*

Distinguishing sentences from fragments is important, especially beyond the limits of single-word constructs, because fragments are usually deficient, unclear statements that need to become full sentences to be understood. And once you do add whatever elements are missing from the sentence, be sure that such statements follow the rules of *agreement* and are revised in light of all stylistic potentials to make them effective communications. See *revision* and *style*.

Beyond the simplest sentence structure of subject, verb, object lies the territory of more complex statements. *Phrases, clauses,* and word combinations of all sorts can be added to any part of a sentence to emphasize or clarify its meaning. Similarly, any part of a sentence can move to vary the *order of words* for whatever *rhetorical,* stylistic, or other purpose.

Series. Another name for a *list* is a "series"—more than one somewhat equivalent thing or person presented together: "I saw Chris, Kim, and Jan." Things or people in series are joined and delimited by *punctuation* and *conjunctions*. In the example, the punctuation is *commas* and the conjunction is "*and*." In more elaborate lists or series that include commas in the listed items, *semicolons* set off the serial elements: "I saw Chris, who was watching television; Kim, who was reading a book; and Jan, who was listening to a record." More elaborate series can be introduced by a *colon,* especially if *phrases* like "the following" are used to lead into them: "The package contains the following items: one carburetor, . . ."

Set, set, set. An *irregular verb* in its main, *past tense*, and past *participle* forms. Do not confuse "'set" (meaning to place or position) with "*sit*" (to take a seat). "Set" usually has an object, while "sit" is *intransitive* and never has an object.

Several. A plural *indefinite* pronoun. "Several" means more than a couple but not many. See *pronoun* and *plural*.

Sexist language. Some features of common *usage* and *grammar* mirror and reinforce discrimination against both sexes. These aspects tend to minimize or exclude women through inaccurate grammatical constructions and restricted word choice and assign stereotypical traits to both women and men that unfairly circumscribe the objectives and attributes of both sexes. The language of our multicultural world is changing to reject the inappropriate limitations of a patriarchal society.

By using "*he*" generically, for example, language subsumes women's identities into men's and makes imprecise and outdated assumptions about today's world: "The mechanic entered the garage, and then he opened the hood of the car." Not all mechanics are men, and the *pronoun* connected to this or any other profession or position should always allow for both sexes to be represented.

GENDER-NEUTRAL WORD CHOICES

Words that end in "ess," "ette," "ine," or "trix" should be avoided. These *suffixes* have traditionally placed women in restricted roles or positions. This usage is easily revised to a gender-neutral construction or another term: "waitress" to "table attendant" or "server"; "suffragette" to "suffragist"; "heroine" to "protagonist" or "champion"; "executrix" to "executor" or "administrator."

The change from gender-marked words should be applied to words formed with "man" as a suffix: "fireman." Word pairs like "fireman, firewoman" should be eliminated whenever possible, and gender-neutral words like "fire fighter" should be substituted for both women and men: "policeman" becomes "police officer." Along the same lines, words that include "man" to represent humanity collectively ("mankind," "manpower"), words that imply males only when females are also included ("founding fathers," "freshmen"), and gender-specific words that convey myths and attitudes that are often construed to be pejorative or outdated ("Lady Luck," "old wives' tales"), should be avoided.

Choose words and *order of words* and construct words so that they will not contribute to the perpetuation of prejudice. Since it is impossible to know whether the "vice president" or "lieutenant" or "senator" is a woman or a man, make sure the form of address includes both possibilities and doesn't alienate one or the other to the detriment of what is stated. Alternatives to sexist, outdated terms include the following:

OUTDATED TERM	USE INSTEAD
Alderman	Aldermember, ward representative
Anchorman/woman	Anchor, news anchor
Authoress	Author
Aviatrix	Aviator

Bachelor's degree	Undergraduate degree
Black tie gala	Semiformal
Brotherhood of man	Human community
Businessman/woman	Businessperson
Chairman/woman	Chair, head, presider
City fathers	City leaders
Cleaning woman	Housecleaner, office cleaner
Clergyman	Cleric, member of the clergy
Committeeman/ woman	Committee member
Common man	Average person
Congressman/woman	Congressional representative, member of Congress
Councilman/woman	Councilmember
Craftsman	Artisan, crafter
Craftsmanship	Artisanship, craftship
Draftsman	Designer, drafter
Family of man	Civilization, human race
Fireman	Fire fighter
Fisherman	Angler, fisher
Forefathers/ mothers	Ancestors, forebears
Foreman	Superintendent, supervisor
Founding fathers	Colonists, founders

Freshman	First-year student, newcomer
Gentlemen's agreement	Honorable agreement, informal agreement
Goodwill to men	Goodwill to all, to people
Governess	Child-care attendant, instructor
Handyman	Odd-job worker
Heiress	Heir
Hostess	Host
Housewife	Homemaker
Journeyman	Certified crafter, or specify: carpenter, metalworker, etc.
Lady luck	Luck
Landlord/lady	Owner
Laundress	Laundry worker
Layman	Layperson, nonprofessional
Lineman	Line installer, line worker
Longshoreman	Stevedore
Maid	Housekeeper, house worker
Maiden name	Birth name
Maiden voyage	First voyage, premier voyage
Mailman	Mail carrier

Maintenance man	Maintenance worker
Man and wife	Husband and wife, married couple, wife and husband, spouses
Male nurse	Nurse
Manhole	Conduit, drain hole, sewer
Man-hours	Work hours
Man in the street	Average person, ordinary person
Mankind	Humanity, humankind
Manmade	Artificial, manufactured, synthetic
Manned space flight	Piloted, staffed, with crew
Manpower	Human resources, staff, work force
Man's achievement	Human achievement
Man-size	Big, large, sizable
Man the phones	Operate, staff
Master bedroom	Largest bedroom
Master's degree	Graduate degree
Meter maid	Traffic officer
Modern man	Modern humanity
Newsboy	Newspaper carrier, newspaper vendor
Newsman/woman	Newscaster, reporter
Old wives' tale	Superstitious folklore

Penmanship	Script, handwriting
Policeman/woman	Police officer
Proprietor/ proprietress	Owner
Repairman	Repairer
Salesman/woman	Sales representative, salesperson
Sculptress	Sculptor
Seamstress	Sewer, tailor
Spokesman/woman	Speaker, spokesperson
Sportsmanship	Fair play, sportship
Stewardess	Flight attendant
Tomboy	Active child
TV cameraman	Camera operator
Watchman	Guard
Weatherman	Meteorologist, reporter, weather-caster
Woman's intuition	Hunch, intuition, premonition
Working man/woman	Average wage earner, average worker
Workmanlike	Skillful, well executed
Workmen	Workers
Unmanned space flight	Mission controlled, unpiloted, unstaffed, without crew
Usherette	Usher

Ways to Avoid Use of the Exclusive Pronoun "He"

Use the *plural* if possible: Change "A policeman should be helpful and wear his uniform with pride" to "Police officers should be helpful and wear their uniforms with pride." If the plural won't work, try to find another way to say the same thing without using any pronoun or *gender*-marked word: "The stage makes heavy demands on each performer." Note how this example uses the gender-neutral term "performer." The example could be extended to a *pronoun* usage: "The stage makes heavy demands on performers, requiring each to contribute everything possible." Here "*each*" replaces the restrictive "him." The less preferable "his/her" construction can also be used: "Every carpenter should bring his or her own tools." "*One*" is also a useful word to facilitate such choices: "One needs to give one's all to the stage."

Other devices focus less on *noun* forms and more on *verb* constructs to avoid possibly biased language. The *passive voice* can eliminate an *object* of a sentence that would otherwise have to be gender marked: "Uniforms should be worn with pride, and helpfulness should be made top priority." Of course, the inherent weaknesses of the passive voice are evident in such examples. Still, the potential for sexist bias has been eliminated.

Imperative and *reflexive* constructions also can help: "Wear your uniform with pride and be helpful." But this commanding tone may not always be appropriate. One might try: "Officers should be helpful at all times and should wear their uniforms with pride." Here a gender-neutral word (''officers'') in the plural is combined with the reflexive ''themselves'' to avoid talking about ''policemen,'' ''policewomen,'' ''policepersons,'' or any less-than-general pronoun.

TITLES

The same care should be applied to the use of *titles* or honorifics: ''Drs. Smith and Jones'' might include one man and one woman, and the woman might be offended if she is Jones and is subsumed in Smith's title. Better to say ''Dr. Smith and Dr. Jones.'' Similarly, it is inappropriate to address ''Mr. Jones and his wife''; the woman who married Mr. Jones deserves her own honorific, be it *Ms.* or Mrs. (Ms. rather than Mrs. is generally preferred).

When works or achievements are attributed to more than one person, it is important to take care that all titles are equivalent and fully stated so that recognition is equally distributed. WRONG: ''An article was published by Dr. Jones and Milly Smith.'' Unless you know Milly Smith, and she has specifically requested that she be referred to in precisely this way, write: ''An article was published by Dr. Jones and Ms. Smith.'' Unless you can supply Dr. Jones with a first name or initial, don't do so for Ms. Smith either.

Shake, shook, shaken. An *irregular verb* in its main, *past tense*, and past *participle* forms.

Shaken. See *shake*.

Shall, will. The two forms of the *future tense* of *be*. Modern American usage rarely requires "shall" unless a polite inquiry or invitation is being made: "Shall we have a drink?" "Shall" is more common in *British English* than in American writing, and appears almost exclusively with first-*person* constructions.

She, her, hers. The third-*person* singular *personal pronoun* "she" has an *objective case* form of "her" and a *possessive* case form of "hers." See *case*.

She'd. This *contraction* of "she had" and "she would" is not normally used in *standard English* writing.

She/he, her/him. Rewrite this awkward concession to *gender* equality into more easily digested forms like "she and he" or they. See *sexist language*.

She's. This *contraction* of "she is" or "she was" is not normally used in *standard English* writing.

Shine, shone, shone. An *irregular verb* meaning to put light on or give off light, in its main, *past tense,* and past *participle* forms. the verb meaning to polish has a regular *conjugation*: "shine, shined, shined."

Shone. See *shine*.

Shook. See *shake*.

Shoot, shot, shot. An *irregular verb* in its main, *past tense,* and past *participle* forms.

Shot. See *shoot.*

Should. See *auxiliary* and *verb.*

Show, showed, showed (shown). An *irregular verb* in its main, *past tense,* and past *participle* forms.

Showed. See *show.*

Shown. See *show.*

Shrunk. See *shrink.*

Shrink, shrank, shrunk. An *irregular verb* in its main, *past tense,* and past *participle* forms.

Similarly. See *conjunctive adverb.*

Simile. *Comparisons* of things to other things often enliven writing by adding an unexpected dimension to words: "Like a dropped football, the stock market bounced up, down, and every which way." When such direct comparisons use the words "like" or "as," they are called "similes."

  This stylistic device should be used with caution since many of the obvious comparisons have already been thought of by other writers, and have appeared so often in writing that they have become trite, or clichéd: "The champagne flowed like water." See also *metaphor, style, cliché*.

Since. A *preposition* governing the *objective case*: "No one has done as well since her." Also a *subordinating conjunction* of time and causality.

Sing, sang, sung. An *irregular verb* in its main, *past tense*, and past *participle* forms.

Sink, sank, sunk. An *irregular verb* in its main, *past tense*, and past *participle* forms.

sit, sat, sat. An *irregular verb* in its main, *past tense*, and past *participle* forms. See *set*.

Situation. The word "situation" is badly overused today. Too many times writers and speakers say things like "a recession situation," "a snow situation," or something similar. It is much clearer and more direct to take "situation" out of these *phrases*, where it functions as a kind of "ummm" or "you know," filling space or time while the writer or speaker thinks up something else to say.

Slang. Words that do not conform to current standards of acceptability are often called "slang." There are slangs associated with the military, teenagers, scientists, computer enthusiasts, yuppies, preppies, and so on.

Since the words that some people find to be slang are usually those they don't understand, and since by nature slang is the language of an in-group rather than the population at large, using slang means limiting your *audience* to those who understand or accept it. And since one purpose of grammatically correct, *standard English* is to make statements that are as widely and effectively understandable as possible, using slang is usually incorrect.

Of course, a few slang words eventually pass into the vocabularies of virtually all English speakers, while others gain at least momentary and broad acceptance. And it may be that a specific audience will be attuned to some slang and tolerant of it in any circumstance. Moreover, the very unacceptability and limitedness of slang can make it an attention-getter that you can use for *emphasis,* or you can use it for *rhetorical,* humorous, or other effect.

The point is to make sure that any words or *phrases* that could hinder communication or even offend an audience or part of it are chosen consciously and with recognition that a risk of incomprehension or rejection is being run. In this regard, slang should be treated with the same care as *colloquial* words, *expletives, dialect,* jargon, foreign terms, and other language that might not be understood or approved. Be cautious, sure of your audience, and willing to be misunderstood. Or don't use slang.

The line between the various categories of words or phrases with special or limited use or currency blurs and is of little consequence outside the *grammar* classroom. The point is that all these vocabularies have purpose and pitfalls that must be attended to in writing, checking, revising, and rewriting. See *revision* and *editing.*

Slavic languages. See *Russian.*

Sleep, slept, slept. An *irregular verb* in its main, *past tense,* and past *participle* forms.

Slept. See *sleep.*

Smell. See *linking verbs.*

So, so that. These are *subordinating conjunctions.* "So" is also an *interjection*: "So, Schwartz, how is O'Keefe?"

Some. The *indefinite* pronoun "some" can be either singular or *plural,* depending on the *number* of its *antecedent*: "The child spilled salt, some of which is still on the tabletop." "The parent swept up the grains off the floor, but some of them are still visible." See *pronoun.*

Some body, somebody. "Somebody" is a singular *indefinite* pronoun that means one person or another. "Some body" is a *compound word* that refers to some physical presence or other: "The zookeeper saw some body beneath the feeding lions but couldn't tell what the prey had been." See *pronoun.*

Somebody. See *somebody.*

Some one, someone. "Someone" is a singular *indefinite* pronoun. "Some one" is a compound *adjective* that intensifies meaning: "Select some one career, and then get on with it." See *intensifier* and *pronoun.*

Someone. See *some one.*

Some thing, something. "Something" is a singular *indefinite* pronoun. The *compound word* "some thing" means one thing or another. See *pronoun*.

Something. See *some thing*.

Some time, sometime, sometimes. "Sometime" is an *indefinite* adverb that means at one time or another ("I'll call you sometime."). "Some time" is a *compound word* meaning an indistinct amount of time ("I spent some time in Paris."). "Sometimes" is another indefinite *adverb*, this time meaning at various times: "Sometimes I feel so blue."

Sometime. See *some time*.

Sometimes. See *some time*.

Sort, sort of. A singular *noun*, "sort" should agree with singular *adjectives* and *pronouns*, though in bad *usage* it often doesn't. WRONG: "These sort of books are boring." BETTER: "This sort of book is boring." The second example is only "better" and not "right" because "sort," like "*kind*," is a flabby word that is best avoided. RIGHT: "I find this book boring" or "Books like this are boring." "Sort of" as an *adverb* is even more imprecise and should not be used: "It is sort of boring." Either it is boring, very boring, or not very boring—say what you mean and don't hedge.

Sort of. See *sort*.

So that. See *so*.

Sound. See *linking verb*.

Spanish. When using Spanish words in writing or when referring to Spanish-named people, places, or things, take care to include all relevant *accents*: "Señor Rodriguez."

Speak, spoke, spoken. An *irregular verb* in its main, *past tense,* and past *participle* forms.

Spelling. English is not an easy language to spell. There are many words that sound alike but are spelled differently, many combinations of letters that can be pronounced different ways ("ough" in "through," "bough," "slough," etc.), and many other oddities that cannot be summarized in simple lists or *rules*.

The only way to be sure of correct spelling is to check a *dictionary,* whether a book or contained in a *computer* program. In either case, be wary of words that are spelled correctly but altogether incorrectly used: "They're are in miss take on thus sun tints, butt eye canned fined id." All these words are in the dictionary and won't be caught by a computer spell checker, but there is indeed an error or two in the sentence.

Spend, spent, spent. An *irregular verb* in its main, *past tense,* and past *participle* forms.

Spent. See *spend*.

Split infinitive. When a word (usually an *adverb*) appears between "*to*" and the *verb* form that follows and makes up the *infinitive*, the infinitive is said to be "split": "To boldly go where no person has gone."

The highest formal standard of English bans split infinitives. However, in our more *colloquial* and informal age, "unsplitting" some split infinitives can lead to awkward or pretentious sentences: "It's important to quickly pick up your room" sounds better than "It's important to pick up your room quickly." That such a sentence in either form should not appear in a college composition or high-school lesson is not the point. Rather, the issue is deciding which *audience* will tolerate or be better served by a split infinitive and its informal directness or by an unsplit infinitive and its correctness. See *standard English*.

More and more, writers, editors, and even grammarians recognize the efficacy of allowing split infinitives at times. If it is unclear when that can happen, revise or rewrite to eliminate the problem: "You should quickly pick up your room. It's important." And if a split infinitive does seem acceptable, make sure it is also comprehensible. Don't allow the intruding adverb or adverbial phrase to so separate "to" and the verb that the link of comprehension is broken. WRONG: "To boldly, unequivocally, and as rationally as possible in the circumstances go where no person has gone." RIGHT: "To go boldly, unequivocally, ..." See *clarity, editing,* and *revision*.

Spoke. See *speak*.

Spoken. See *speak*.

Sprang. See *spring*.

Spread, spread, spread. An *irregular verb* in its main, *past tense,* and past *participle* form.

Spring, sprang, sprung. An *irregular verb* in its main, *past tense,* and past *participle* forms.

Sprung. See *spring.*

St. The *abbreviation* "St." is not normally used in *standard English* writing when it refers to a street (except in letter addresses). But when "St." is used for a saint's name, it is more commonly admissible: "What a beautiful painting of St. Jerome!"

Stand, stood, stood. An *irregular verb* in its main, *past tense,* and past *participle* forms.

Standard English. The generally accepted norms of *grammar* and *usage* are called "standard English." Although it is true that standards change over time and from place to place, and although the standards of some people are not those of others at any time or place, there is still some solid core of practices and *rules* that must be observed if a statement is to be considered grammatically correct, acceptable, and understandable. That core equals standard English. It includes *agreement* between *subject* and *verb,* between *antecedent* and *modifier,* and between referent and *pronoun.* Only in the most unusual circumstances can these rules be broken or ignored and the result be considered allowable (usually in fiction, entertainment, journalism, and the like). Even in such circumstances, rule violations are commonly still seen as violations, even if their purpose is condoned or appreciated.

Standard English extends beyond the core of inviolable rules to less-certain strictures that deal with language at a moment of change or dispute. Closest to the core and therefore least bendable are rules of *spelling, conjugation,* and *declension*—there are rather clear practices in these areas, and violations are more likely than not to attract unwanted attention. That said, it is clear that perfectly reputable, acceptable writers, publishers, teachers, and others differ on the tolerability of spellings like "centre," "travelled," "decision-making," and many other quite common words. Most likely, attention to *audience,* locally accepted guidebooks or *style* manuals, and consultation with others can resolve these disputes quickly for the writer or speaker making immediate choices about the applicable standard. But standards are somewhat fragmented nonetheless.

The forms of verbs and *nouns* or pronouns in different *cases* are, like spellings, not very volatile. But, for example, there is a movement toward wide acceptance of "*who*" in all circumstances or more than would have been permissible until recently. Almost everyone says, "It's me," and many people now write it and are not corrected or seen to be in error. Similarly, contracted *negatives* and other verb forms are far more common in the most rigorously checked and examined prose than they used to be (see *contraction*). Other examples abound of *colloquial, dialect,* and *slang* conjugations and declensions entering the language so pervasively that they have become standard or close to it in many respects.

Once one moves beyond the fundamental patterns of shape changing in words, one enters the realm of *order of words, sentence* structure, style, *rhetoric,* and similar categories in which grammar provides far less direct or clear guidance. All these categories are, after all, matters of choice, areas for writers to select the means and devices best suited to what they want to say and how they want to say it. Grammar and usage can only point to common errors, weak or overused methods, and general strictures about *clarity, efficacy,* directness, and the like. It is up to the writer or speaker to match expression to idea and purpose, to audience and prevailing standards, and to the moment.

Yet for all the deviations from standards, the mission of making statements—to convey one's message most effectively, clearly, and efficiently—remains and must be observed.

Stationary, stationery. Do not confuse the *adjective* "stationary" meaning to stand still and the *noun* "stationery," paper.

Steal, stole, stolen. An *irregular verb* in its main, *past tense,* and past *participle* forms.

Stole. See *steal.*

Stolen. See *steal.*

Stood. See *stand.*

Stricken. See *strike*.

Strike, struck, struck (stricken). An *irregular verb* in its main, *past tense,* and past *participle* forms.

Struck. See *strike*.

Style. The choices writers and speakers make in selecting words, applying grammar *rules,* arranging words in a particular order, using or playing against devices or conventions, and so on—all these choices result in a way of writing or speaking that can be called "style."

There are no real "rules" of style, just as no one can dictate choices of life, work, and other patterns freely accessible to writers and speakers. But there are some aspects of communicating to keep in mind when a style is chosen. First, some degree of consistency or *parallelism* in a broad sense will be appreciated by *audiences*. Shifts from one style to another can be disorienting, but if managed well, they can be useful ways to add *emphasis* and to make points.

Just as there are no style rules, so there are few, if any, useful definitions of style. What for one writer or speaker would be quite informal might strike another (or some audience) as quite the opposite. Everyone has experienced statements made with all good intentions of being ordinary and *colloquial* but that are in fact laden with jargon, stilted academic or bureaucratic constructions, or otherwise far less accessible or open than the speaker or writer had intended. Similarly, it is all too common to find *dialect,* for instance, in statements that should adhere rigorously to the highest standard of formal English. Not that any single style is inherently wrong or inappropriate. The point is to be sure to find the right style for the right moment.

The safest, most certainly communicative style is usually formal *standard English,* especially when it is unclear who the audience for a statement will be. Standard English is more or less universally understood and accepted in this country, and therefore it is unlikely to seem very out of place under any ordinary circumstances. See *order of words* and *grammar.*

Subject. The word or words that designate the thing or person in a *sentence* that performs an action or is in a condition is the "subject" of the sentence: "Connie dances the polka." "Connie" is the subject of the example sentence.

Subjects can be single or multiple *nouns, pronouns, phrases,* or *clauses.* More than one subject in a sentence is called a "compound" subject. All noun and pronoun subjects are in the *nominative* case, not marked or changed from the basic or main form of the word (uninflected). See *case.*

Whatever structure or shape of subject is chosen for a sentence, it must agree with its *verb*(s) and any pronouns that are linked to it in an *antecedent* relationship (see *agreement*). Consistency and *parallelism* of subjects should also be observed—more or less equivalent subjects should be joined in compounds.

In some sentences, particularly *imperative* mood commands or requests, the subject is only suggested: "Shape up!" The subject of the example is the suggested or implied "*you*," which does not normally appear in imperative constructions. See *mood*.

NOUN SUBJECTS. Any *common noun* or *proper noun* and its *modifiers* (of whatever length or complexity) can serve as a sentence subject. The underlined words in the following examples are all noun subjects (and their modifiers); note that not all fall at the beginning of the sentences. "Herb and Gladys, the couple from Buffalo, spent the night at our house." "Our house, standing on the banks of the river, holds guests comfortably." "Throughout the winter, there stands the house, guarding us from the weather, standing sentinel over the water, and giving us and our guests peace of mind." Take care that long, complex subjects like some of those in the examples have verbs to complete the sentence and not leave it a *fragment*.

PRONOUN SUBJECTS. Here are some examples. The underlined words are the pronoun subjects. "He is mowing the lawn." "She was supposed to mow the lawn, but she is too tired." "She washed the cars last night when he was tired." "It is a busy time for them, but they keep themselves calm." "We help them out as much as we can."

PHRASE SUBJECTS. The underlined words are phrase subjects. "To err is human" (*infinitive* phrase). "Standing calmly is the best defense against charging rhinos" (*gerund* phrase). In these functions such phrases are said to be "*noun phrases.*"

CLAUSE SUBJECTS. The underlined words are a clause subject. "<u>What you are looking for</u> is fool's gold." The whole clause, including its own subject, verb, and object, is the subject of the verb "*is.*" Like noun phrases, "*noun clauses*" may contain many other words that do not function as nouns within the subject phrase or clause.

Subject complement. *Linking verbs* ("*be,*" "*appear,*" "*become,*" "*feel,*" "*grow,*" "*look,*" "*make,*" "*prove,*" "*remain,*" "*seem,*" "*smell,*" and "*sound*") are sometimes followed by *nouns* or *adjectives* that are called "subject complements": "The dog is big; it is a hunter." The words after "*is*" in each *clause* of the example sentence are subject complements (also called "*predicate nominatives*").

Subject complements can be as long or complex as necessary to make a point. As long as it remains clear what they refer or are linked to, they can fall virtually anywhere in a *sentence.* But whatever their length, complexity, or position, they are always in the same *case* as the subject— the *nominative*: "It is I." "*I*" is the nominative or subject form or case of the *pronoun* that properly appears in the example sentence. Current *usage* permits (even encourages) violation of this grammatical *rule,* so that most people say (and some write), "It is me." Despite the widespread use of "*me*" in such sentences, "I" is correct.

A singular subject can be followed by a *plural* subject

complement, and just the reverse: "We are a team; the team has ten members." Both examples are correct. Make sure the subject agrees with the verb, not the subject complement (see *agreement*).

Subjunctive. The conditional or "subjunctive *mood*" is a *verb* form that indicates nonexistent, possible, potential, or desired circumstances: "Would that Chris were here!" Note that "*were*" (the past subjunctive of "*be*" in the third-person singular) is not in the same form as the simple *present tense* or *past tense* of the verb. Verbs form the present subjunctive from the main or uninflected root: "The boss asked that I be there, and I demanded that my department head request that in writing." "Be" and "'request" are present subjunctives that differ from the present indicative first- and third-*person* singular forms one might expect to see here: "am" and "requests."

In the past tense, subjunctive forms are the same as the indicative past except for "be," which uses "were" in all circumstances, as in the first example.

The oddity of the subjunctive forms has led to their virtual disappearance from spoken language and has contributed to their fading use in writing. But they are correct and clear and should be used in all situations calling for formal *standard English* or when standards are unclear and one tries to err on the side of caution.

The typical situations in which subjunctive should appear are *clauses* that are introduced by "*if*," "as if," and "as though": "If I were there, my friend could visit me"; clauses that convey requests, requirements, demands, or suggestions and start with "*that*" (as in the initial example);

and clauses that convey a wish: "The other driver wished that I be responsible, but I hoped that I would not be held accountable."

Subordinating conjunction. Subordinating conjunctions link dependent and independent *clauses* in some distinctive way. The most commonly used subordinating conjunctions are *"after," "although," "as," "*as if,*" "because," "before," "*even though,*" "if," "*in order that," "once," "since," "*so that,*" "than," "*that," "though," "*un-less,*" "until," "*when," "*where,*" and "*while."

Subordination. *Clauses* or *phrases* that depend on a main clause and modify its meaning or add to it are called "subordinate" (or "dependent"). They are usually introduced by *subordinating conjunctions* or *relative pronouns* that indicate some relationship of time, location, causation, or the like: "When the mail carrier came, the dog was there."

Subordinate expressions cannot stand on their own, no matter how long or complex they are: They must be joined to a main or independent clause so that their relationship to a main idea can be clear. One of the commonest errors is to leave elaborate subordinate clauses or phrases without an independent clause, creating an indecipherable sentence *fragment*. WRONG: "If the ball bounced fair and never reached the outfield wall, which was covered in a protective mat made from a synthetic fiber recently developed in the labs the university established to take advantage of commercial opportunities like this." For all its length and piled up *verbs* and *nouns* and more, the example is only a fragment, a dependent clause looking for a sentence to which it can be linked and thereby gain meaning. Be sure to check all long and complex clauses that begin with subordinating conjunctions or relative pronouns to make sure they are part of a full *sentence*, complete with independent clause.

Subordination is a particularly useful way to add *emphasis* to a point. Putting one idea in a dependent clause and another in a main clause can add considerable force to the unsubordinated statement. Of course, like any device of emphasis, subordination can be overused, become tedious and overly complex, and fail to enliven or enforce your writing. In long stretches of sentences that use subordinating constructions, emphasis often comes by an abrupt switch to simple declarative sentences of the subject, verb, object type.

Suffix. Groups of letters attached to the ends of words or parts of words to make new meanings, new grammatical forms, or new nuances of meaning are called "suffixes": "teach—teach<u>er</u>"; "tender—tender<u>ness</u>"; "clear—clar<u>ity</u>—clear<u>ing</u>"; "vision—vis<u>ibility</u>."

Suffixes may attach to the common *demonstrative* form or *case* of a word or to its *root*, the smallest cluster of letters that still conveys the word's fundamental meaning ("clear" and "clar-" as well as "vis-" in the examples). The roots that end with a *hyphen* are those that don't stand as words by themselves and must always have some ending attached to become independent words. From words or roots suffixes can make *nouns* of various kinds and meanings, *verbs*, *adjectives*, or *adverbs*. From the root "assum-," for instance, come the noun "assumption," the verb "assume," and the adjective "assumable." Roots or words can form more than one noun, verb, or adjective with different suffixes: "Real" can become the nouns "reality" or "realism," with quite different meanings.

The list below records the major suffixes and the meanings they usually add to a word or root.

able	potential: "capable"; also spelled **ible**: "convertible"
acy	state: "meritocracy"
al	act, relating to: "denial," "historical"
ance	state: "reliance"; also spelled **ence**: "reticence"
ate	cause: "renovate"
dom	place or state: "freedom"
en	cause: "open"
er	person who: "painter"; also spelled **or**: "editor"
ful	quality: "fearful"
ian	person: "historian"
ic	relating to: "historic"
ify	make: "ratify"
ish	quality: "youngish"
ism	doctrine, belief: "materialism"
ist	person who: "spiritualist"
ity	quality: "mendacity"
ive	nature: "evaluative"
ize	cause: "nationalize"
less	lacking: "pointless"
ment	condition: "development"

ness	state: "happiness"
ous	characteristic: "analogous"; also spelled **ious**: "obvious"
ship	position: "leadership"
tion	state: "motion"; also spelled **sion**: "tension"

Sung. See *sing*.

Sunk. See *sink*.

Superlative. In *comparison* the highest degree is called "superlative": "Superlative is the highest degree." In the example "highest" is a typical superlative, formed by adding "*-est*" to the simple form of the *adjective* "high." The same pattern applies to most one-*syllable* or short adjectives and *adverbs*. Longer adverbs and adjectives form the superlative by combining "most" and the simple form: "Superlative is not the most acceptable form of the adjective. One most commonly sees the simple form." Note that these compound *modifiers* are never hyphenated. Since the line between long and short modifiers is not very clear, it is necessary to check a *dictionary* or reference *grammar* to be sure that an "est" superlative form exists. See also *compound word* and *hyphen*.

There are many irregular adjectives and adverbs, the most common of which are listed here with their unpredictable superlative forms: "*bad* (badly), worst"; "*good, best*"; "*ill*, worst"; "*little*, least (not in sense of size; little, littlest)"; "*many*, most"; "*much*, most"; "*some*"; and "well, best." These words have unexpected comparative forms as well.

Superlatives can be used only when comparison extends beyond two things or people: "Superlative is the highest degree of the three levels of comparison." WRONG: "Johnson is the best of the two skaters." RIGHT: "Johnson is the better of the two skaters. Johnson is the best skater in the whole class." *Standard English* permits only this use of the superlative and comparative, while more *colloquial* usage allows superlative when *emphasis* is sought. In no circumstances should "most" be added to an adjective or adverb that has already taken the "est" superlative form. WRONG: "Johnson is the most fastest skater in the world." RIGHT: "Johnson is the fastest skater in the world."

Make sure that superlatives (especially when they appear as *subject complements* in *predicates* after *linking verbs*) have a clear link to the thing they are being compared to. WRONG: "Johnson is the fastest." Unless there is a good deal of surrounding text to make it clear in what way Johnson is the fastest what, this sentence would be better and more complete if it added something like "skater in the world." In everyday speech, "the greatest" and similar unconnected superlatives are tolerable as empty expressions of enthusiasm or agreement. But in more formal writing, it is unfair to leave the *audience* to guess what is being compared to what. See also *-er*.

Swam. See *swim*.

Swim, swam, swum. An *irregular verb* in its main, *past tense,* and past *participle* forms.

Swing, swung, swung. An *irregular verb* in its main, *past tense,* and past *participle* forms.

Swung. See *swing.*

Syllabification. See *syllable.*

Syllable, syllabification. Words fall into more or less natural segments that are called "syllables." It is important to know where syllables fall in order to add *hyphens* when words are divided between lines typographically:

> "Where should the hy-
> phen go in this sentence?"

In the example one word is hyphenated at the end of a syllable, but another word could have been broken across lines as well: "sen-tence." No other word in the example should be hyphenated at a line end because all the other words are single-syllable words, which should never be hyphenated.

Many patterns of syllabification do not follow the segmentation suggested by the sound of words. It is necessary to check a *dictionary* to be sure that all words divided over lines are broken correctly.

Some general *rules* exist to guide hyphenation choices, but they should be followed with caution and a dictionary consulted in most instances. If a *computer* program divides words for you, be careful that it is following the standard dictionaries and not applying rules that can fool you and it.

Symbol. typographical elements that appear in documents but that are not letters, *punctuation, numbers,* or the like are called "symbols": "You get 10% off on that purchase." The *percent* sign (%) is a symbol.

Other common symbols include @, #, $, &, *, +, =, and ¢. In formal nonscientific, noneconomic writing these symbols are usually spelled out rather than appearing as symbols. The major exception is the *dollar* sign ($), which is acceptable in any prose. As our lives become more pervaded by science, economics, business, and other kinds of writing and thinking that commonly use symbols, it becomes more acceptable not to spell them out in many circumstances. The percent sign is increasingly common in more formal writing. See *scientific language.*

The use of symbols rather than spelling them out can also be used for *emphasis*: "Communism = socialism + electrification!" This old slogan from the time of the Russian Revolution was first coined in a speech. But it was later written with symbols to suggest that communism was a mathematical and scientific certainty and not just a political system.

Consult any local or specific *style* manuals that guide writing for your *audience.*

Synonym. Words that mean more or less the same thing are called "synonyms": " 'Short' and 'shrimpy' are synonyms, although one is simply descriptive and the other is too *colloquial* to use in formal statements about people." Very often synonyms have similar definitions but quite different qualities, as in the example. For that reason, synonyms cannot simply be substituted for other words to vary or enliven your statements. You must pay attention not just to the basic meaning of a word but also to what it suggests—to its connotation, which can vary depending on the circumstances and the *audience*. So you should be cautious when you use a regular *dictionary* or a special dictionary of synonyms; choose synonyms not only for their similar senses but for the affect they will have on those who hear or read them.

T

Take, took, taken. An *irregular verb* in its main, *past tense,* and past *participle* forms.

Taken. See *take.*

Taught. See *teach.*

Teach, taught, taught. An *irregular verb* in its main, *past tense,* and past *participle* forms.

Tear, tore, torn. An *irregular verb* in its main, *past tense,* and past *participle* forms.

Tell, told, told. An *irregular verb* in its main, *past tense,* and past *participle* forms.

Tense. *Verbs* vary in form to indicate time of action or condition. The changed forms and time relationships they suggest are called "tenses."

There are twelve tenses, listed below with examples. It is useful to recognize the variety of tenses available and how they are used to convey nuances of time and other aspects of the actions or conditions that verbs can present.

PRESENT TENSE

Present tense is the normal, everyday tense that indicates things happening more or less now: "The dog snores, the owner complains, and the kids wake up." This *verb* form can also be used for continuing or persistent actions or conditions: "Life is long." In some circumstances, when other words are used to clarify an expected action in the future, the simple present performs a future function: "Tomorrow the traveler comes home."

FUTURE TENSE

Verbs that depict events or situations in the future are usually in the *future tense:* "The day's snoring will irritate the owner and will wake up the kids." Note in *present tense* (above) that enough qualifying words in a *sentence* that specify an action in the future can allow the use of the present tense for future actions or conditions.

PAST TENSE

Actions or conditions cast directly in and limited to the past use the *past tense*: "The dog snored, the owner complained, and the kids woke up."

PRESENT PERFECT TENSE

Formed with the *auxiliary* verb "*have*" (or "has") and the past tense form of a *verb,* the present perfect merges the two tenses to depict actions or conditions begun in the past but extending into the present or not completed at a specific time: "The dog has snored for years, and the kids have usually gotten up every night as a result."

FUTURE PERFECT TENSE

By joining the *past tense* form of *verbs* with "will have," the future perfect depicts things that will end at a definite moment in the future: "The dog will have snored for ten years by August, but the kids will have been bothered only for the last two years in the new house where the dog sleeps in the hall."

PAST PERFECT TENSE

Combining "had" with the *past tense* form of a *verb*, the past perfect conveys a sense of action or condition ended at a specific moment in the past, often before some other event in the past: "The dog had snored that night, but the kids did not wake up."

PRESENT PROGRESSIVE TENSE

This tense combines the present *participle* ("ing" form) with the present tense of "*be*" ("is" or "are") to indicate continuing actions or conditions: "The dog is snoring again tonight, and the kids are complaining to the owner." Unlike the present tense, the present progressive depicts an action that is actually occurring at the moment, while the present refers to repeated or habitual current activities or situations: "The dog is snoring right now, but the owner complains every night." Like the *present tense*, the present progressive can perform a future function if a *sentence* contains enough qualifying words to make clear the future setting of the event: "The dog is going to snore tomorrow night, the owner is sure."

FUTURE PROGRESSIVE TENSE

Actions or conditions that continue in the future use the future progressive tense, which combines "will be" with the present participle ("ing" form): "The dog will be snoring for years to come, and the kids will be getting used to it."

PAST PROGRESSIVE TENSE

By linking the past forms of "*be*" ("was" or "were") with the present *participle* "ing" form), the past progressive conveys things that continued to happen in the past but have ended: "The dog was snoring in the summer, but stopped in the fall."

PRESENT PERFECT PROGRESSIVE TENSE

To depict things that continue from the past into the present or beyond, the present perfect progressive is used. It combines the *auxiliaries* "has" or "have" and "been" (the past *participle* of "*be*") with the present participle ("ing" form): "the dog has been snoring for far too long."

FUTURE PERFECT PROGRESSIVE TENSE

Combining "will have been" with the present *participle* ("ing" form), the future perfect progressive suggests actions or conditions that will end at or by a definite moment in the future: "The dog will have been snoring for ten years in August."

PAST PERFECT PROGRESSIVE TENSE

The past perfect progressive tense joins "had been" with the present *participle* ("ing" form) to portray things that continue in the past and that start before some other specific time, event, or situation: "The dog had been snoring for ten years before it was cured of it."

Than, then. "Than" is a *conjunction* that links words or *phrases* being compared: "Smith is taller than Brown is." See *comparison*. Do not confuse "than" with "then," an *adverb* that modifies *verbs* and suggests actions or conditions following one after the other: "The nurse weighed the patient, then measured her height." See *modifier*.

That, which. "That" normally is the *relative pronoun* introducing a *restrictive* (or independent) *clause,* while "which" does the same for *nonrestrictive* (dependent) *clauses*. Restrictive *clauses* add considerable information to a sentence that is essential for its meaning and are not set off by *commas*. Nonrestrictive clauses add ancillary or less than essential ideas to a *sentence* and show this supplementary status by being surrounded by commas.

Their, there, they're. These three *homonyms* (words that sound alike but are spelled differently) are frequently confused and misused. They are quite different *parts of speech*, with very different meanings and functions.

THEIR. A *possessive* pronoun, "their" modifies *nouns* and indicates ownership of something: "The parrots take their time eating the fruit." See *modifier* and *pronoun*.

THERE. "There" is an *adverb* suggesting some degree of remoteness: "The boat is anchored over there." With *linking verbs* ("*be*") "there" forms the *expletive*: "There were nine boats anchored at the shore."

THEY'RE. This *contraction* joins "they" and "are": "They're going to crash into the pier!"

Theirselves. An incorrect or *colloquial* form of "themselves," the proper third-person *plural* of the *reflexive pronoun*. Never use "theirselves" outside fiction or reports on *dialect*.

Them. "Them" is the correct *objective case* form of "they": "The guard saw them." But it is not, and should never be used as, a *demonstrative* pronoun. WRONG: "I saw them things." RIGHT: "I saw those things." See *pronoun*.

There. See *their*.

Therefore. See *coordinating conjunction* and *interjection*.

They, them, their. "They" is the third-*person plural pronoun* and has an *objective case* form of "them" and a *possessive* case form of "their."

They're. See *their*.

Think, thought, thought. An *irregular verb* in its main, *past tense,* and past *participle* forms.

Thirdly. There is no reason to add "ly" to this or other *ordinal numbers,* especially when they are used to *list* things.

Though. See *subordinating conjunction* and *although* (as it is usually spelled).

Thought. See *think*.

Threw. See *throw*.

Through. *Preposition* governing the *objective case*: "The current jolted through him."

Throw, threw, thrown. An *irregular verb* in its main, *past tense,* and past *participle* forms.

Thrown. See *throw*.

Thus. See *subordinating conjunction*.

Title. A title is a name given to a person as a sign of distinction. Creative works can also bear titles.

PEOPLE'S TITLES

Designations of jobs, status, marital condition, inheritance or nobility, academic achievement, and so on constitute a whole range of personal titles: "Dr., senator, Mrs., count, Ph.D., officer." Depending on how they are used in *sentences* and with *names*, titles have different *punctuation* or *capitalization*.

Titles immediately associated with a name are usually capitalized and frequently abbreviated: "Rev. Jones sat next to Senator Bradley and across the table from Mrs. Schneider, Ph.D." When most of these titles appear without a specific name, they are usually not capitalized and never abbreviated: "The reverend sat next to the senator and across the table from my wife, who holds a doctorate." "Ph.D." is an exception to this rule, appearing sometimes by itself and capitalized: "Smith has a Ph.D." In some very formal styles this usage is considered unacceptable. Titles with last names only are usually spelled out in full, while those with more than a last name can be abbreviated: "We refer to Prof. Judith Ginsberg and Prof. Paul LeClaire." See *abbreviation*.

Titles that follow a name are set off from it and following words by *commas*: "let me introduce Chris Schneider, Ph.D."

Titles of Works

Creative works made by people have names that are treated differently depending on the length, longevity, seriousness, and type of work. All these criteria are somewhat subjective, but the *rules* that are outlined here can be applied consistently.

Italicized Titles

BOOKS. Titles of books are underlined (or in *italics*), and words in the titles are capitalized except for *conjunctions* and *prepositions* that don't begin the title: *War and Peace, A Tale of Two Cities, The Decline and Fall of the Roman Empire*. See *capitalization*.

BROADCAST PROGRAMS, DANCES, MOVIES, MUSICAL WORKS, PLAYS, POEMS, PAINTINGS, AND SCULPTURE. Longer dance, musical, and poetic works, along with these other artistic or entertainment categories, are treated like book titles: *The Simpsons, The Nutcracker Suite, Dances with Wolves, The Goldberg Variations, The Crucible,* the *Aeneid, View over Delft, Laocoon*.

JOURNALS, MAGAZINES, NEWSPAPERS, AND PAMPHLETS. All these things are treated like book titles: *Studies in Obscurity, Prevention,* the *New York Times*.

VEHICLES. Specific names of individual books, planes, trains, buses, cars, spacecraft, and so on can be treated like book titles, but not model names: *Enola Gay, Palmetto,*

Silver Bullet, Red Baron, Apollo IV, Titanic. But note: "The singer drove an Accord."

TITLES IN QUOTATION MARKS

Shorter written works—songs, short poems, stories, articles, chapters, and the like—are capitalized in the same way book titles are, but they are set off in *quotation marks* rather than being underlined or italicized: "Every Move You Make," "Ode on a Grecian Urn," "The End of History," "The Middle Years."

Titles set off in quotes have *commas* and *periods* within the quotes if that punctuation ends a *clause* or the *sentence*: "I was singing, 'Every Move You Make.' " If the title itself ends with a punctuation mark (*exclamation point* or *question mark*), then no punctuation follows the quotes that end the title, even at the end of a sentence: "The actor recited 'A Call to Arms!' " If the sentence ends with a question mark or exclamation point that is not part of the title, that punctuation goes outside the quotes: "Were you singing 'Every Move You Make'?" *Colons, semicolons,* and *parentheses* that are not parts of titles go outside quotes surrounding titles: "The actor recited 'Ode on a Grecian Urn'; that was followed by 'Memory' (a major Russian work); finally came 'The Raven': Did you hear all that?"

To, too, two. Don't confuse these words that sound alike but are spelled differently (*homonyms*) and have different meanings.

TO. The *preposition* "to" suggests motion toward or attribution to something: "I went to Denver and gave a speech to an association." "To" also appears in verb *infinitives*: "To err is human."

TOO. "Too" is an *adverb* that intensifies words or adds things: "That is too dark for this room. It is big, too." See *intensifier*.

TWO. The *number* "two" (2) is always just that: "Look, two eagles. That is too exciting not to report to the rest of the group."

Told. See *tell.*

Tone. The spirit of what is said, its attitude, is called "tone." Severe, playful, ironic, intense, wheedling, ingratiating— there is no real limit to tone nor any clear guidance about where it is appropriate. One can seek consistency of tone, use abrupt tone shifts to make a point, or intentionally vary tone throughout a statement for all sorts of purposes. The careful writer stays aware of tone and how it is used, how it might be received by different *audiences,* and how expectations of tone can be manipulated. See, for example, *style, emphasis, irony, rhetoric,* and *colloquial.*

Too. See *to.*

Took. See *take.*

Tore. See *tear*.

Torn. See *tear*.

Toward. *Preposition* governing the *objective case*: "The infant crawled toward the door." Do not spell with an "s." WRONG: "Move towards the rear, please."

Transitive. *Verbs* that transmit or convey their action to other words (*objects* or *indirect objects*) are said to be "transitive": "The camper chopped wood." Some verbs have no objects and are used intransitively: "The camper chopped." Other verbs can only be used as *intransitives*: "The guest arrived." See *voice* and *reflexive pronoun*.

Two. See *to*.

Typeface. Writers were once limited to typewriters that produced only one shape of letter on paper. Now there are various machines that produce differently shaped letters, which are said to be in "typefaces." Typefaces (fonts) do not affect words in any way; they do not cause any variation in their use or the grammatical *rules* that govern them. But careful writers will observe the same principles of *parallelism*, consistency, and restraint that they apply to other aspects of writing when they have the opportunity to use typefaces in documents. (The emphatic and defining force of typefaces and variations among them is lost if too many faces appear in one document, if incompatible faces are put together on the same page just because they are available to use and not because they have a purpose, or if bad choices are made among possible faces.

If you can use many typefaces, be careful not to abuse that freedom and leave your reader's eyes weary. See also *italics*, *bold type*, and *emphasis*.

U

Under. A *preposition* governing the *objective case*: "The boat rocked under them."

Unique. Don't use "very," "more," or any other *modifier* with "unique," which means one of a kind and therefore cannot vary as a modifier might suggest.

Up. A *preposition* governing the *objective case*: "The ladybug crawled up the scout's leg."

Upon. See *on*.

Upper case. Capitalized letters (in large, special forms) are said to be "upper case." Letters not capitalized are called "*lower case*." Capitals start sentences and perform other functions (see *capitalization*).

U.S. This *abbreviation* for "United States" is properly used only as an *adjective*: "That is U.S. territory." However, many less formal *styles* accept the abbreviation in place of the full name of the country: "Colorado is in the U.S." Some styles prefer "USA" if the whole name is not given: "New York is part of the USA."

Usage. Unlike grammatical *rules*, principles of usage are more flexible, depending on the *audience*, purpose, and occasion of a statement for guidance as much as on the strictures arrived at by academics or others. Many entries in this book suggest how best to use certain words, constructions, or devices. But in almost every instance, alternative patterns, circumstances, or considerations are noted to give some sense of the range of possibilities and choices available to the writer or speaker.

Special *dictionaries, style* books, and guidebooks on usage can be consulted for further insight into this complex stylistic issue. When in doubt, look for a reliable, authoritative source that is accepted by the audience being addressed.

V

've. An *apostrophe* and "ve" can be added to *pronouns* to create *contractions* of *past tense* constructions using "*have*": "I've been an editor for twenty years." Ordinarily such contractions are not used in formal *standard English* writing.

Verb. Words that convey action, condition, and similar aspects of statements are called "verbs": "There <u>are</u> many verbs in English, <u>ranging</u> from vivid words like '<u>cannonball</u>' to blander verbs like '<u>appear</u>.' All verbs <u>depict</u> action or status, <u>rendered</u> into <u>varying</u> forms." In the example, all the verbs are underlined. The rest of this entry characterizes the common properties of verbs and basic *rules* and suggestions for their use. Consult entries on specific verbs as well as those for *tense, voice, mood, intransitive, transitive, passive, active voice, imperative, subjunctive, linking verbs, agreement,* and so on for further explanations and examples.

CONJUGATION, TENSES, AND INFLECTION

Verbs change forms to reflect the *person* doing the acting (*I, you, we, he, she, it,* they), how many things or people are acting (*number*), and when something happens (*tense*). The changes in form can mean the addition of letters to the basic form of the verb or its *root* (the core letters that contain its meaning, such as "-vis-" in "envision," a root that conveys the sense of seeing or being seen); such changes are called *inflection*, and the patterns of changes are called *conjugations*. Verb changes of this kind can produce different person, number, or tense: "I talk, he or she talks, they talked, we talked." Some verbs make the main tenses in different patterns (adding "es" rather than "s" in the present tense) or are altogether *irregular verbs*.

Other words are also combined with verbs or forms of them to produce different tenses: "I talk, you will talk, he has talked, we will have talked, you had talked, they are talking." See the entries on *tenses* for further information. The added verbs are called "*auxiliary* verbs."

Some of the forms that combine to make new tenses are specially inflected forms of verbs: the present *participle* ("ing" form: "talking") and the past participle ("ed" or "d" form, usually the same as the past tense form). The participles can function outside verbal constructions, becoming *gerunds*, *adjectives*, and even *nouns*: "Swimming is enjoying a revival, predicated on raised expectations." All the underlined words in the example are participles.

VOICE

Verbs also have a property called "*voice*" that indicates where action is directed. *Active voice* verbs convey action directly to *objects* or *indirect objects*: "I hand the book to the librarian." *Passive* voice verbs depict action that does not pass to an object but is reflected back on the *subject* of a *sentence*: "The book was handed to the librarian by me." The passive voice is usually disdained in *standard English* because it often omits agents and doesn't make causation clear: "It will be done." But this flaw of obscurity is sometimes prized by writers who want to deflect attention from the agent of an action for whatever reason. Voice is a property of *transitive* verbs, those able to transmit action to an object. *Intransitive* verbs do not convey action to an object but usually express condition: "It happens, one becomes used to something and simply vegetates." All the verbs (underlined) in the example are intransitive.

Mood

Verbs convey the writer's or speaker's attitude or stance by changing "*mood*" as reflected in differing verb forms. The indicative mood is the common form that states facts or presumed facts: "That is so; the lions are eating the antelope." The *imperative* mood issues commands or requests: "Pick up your room!" The *subjunctive* mood is used to make statements that are contrary to fact or are wishes, requests, and demands: "If your younger brother were taller, I'd ask that he help put up the decorations with us."

Linking Verbs

A major category of verbs is called "*linking verbs*": "*be*," "*become*," "appear," and the like do not convey action so much as condition or status. They take no objects but can be followed by *nouns* or *adjectives* that are called predicate *nominatives* or *subject complements*: "Jan is an executive and is creative as well as insightful." See *predicate*.

ADVERBS

Words that modify verbs or add to their meaning are called "*adverbs*": "The dancer quickly exited the stage." Most adverbs end in "*-ly*," as does "quickly" in the example. But some do not: "The cat almost ate the canary." See *modifier*.

AGREEMENT

It is critical that verbs agree with their *subjects* in *person* and *number*. WRONG: "Kim are right, and I is wrong." RIGHT: "Kim is right, and I am wrong." In a simple example like this one, the error seems obvious. But in longer, more complex sentences, it is easy to lose sight of the original subject or its number or person, particularly if *phrases* or *clauses* in a different number or person come between the subject and verb. WRONG: "The lion, having eaten many chimpanzees, which are common on the plains of the area and often live in enormous troops in the trees, are hungry." There is only one lion, and it *is* hungry. Positioning of verbs near their subjects and *objects* helps keep *sentences* clear and makes it easier to be sure subjects and verbs agree.

FRAGMENTS

Large, involved collections of words can contain several verbs, *subjects, objects,* and so on but still not be *sentences* at all. If the main subject has no verb (or vice versa), even the longest collection of words remains an incomprehensible *fragment*: "The tiger, having eaten many chimpanzees, which are common on the plains of the area and often live in enormous troops in the trees, deciduous and palmlike depending on the microclimate, which can vary enormously and cause severe fluctuations in the tiger population." The example is not a sentence, despite all the verbs, subjects, and so on, and even in spite of the double appearance of the tiger. The first tiger does nothing, so there is no sentence here.

PARALLELISM

Although there is no formal grammatical *rule* that calls for consistency or *parallelism* in verb use, it is generally beneficial to writing to maintain the same or similar *tenses, moods, voices,* and so on from *sentence* to sentence, *paragraph* to paragraph, and beyond. Of course, monotony is not a goal of writing, and variety can come from all sorts of changes in tense or any other verb property. Just be certain that such shifts leave an understandable, easily followed statement for the reader.

Verbs are important parts of sentences, and there are many entries in this book that discuss various aspects of how they are formed, function, and are best used. Be sure to consult all the italicized topics if you have more questions about any aspect of verbs that is outlined in this entry.

Vocabulary. The choice of words in statements is all-important. The storehouse of words you command is called your "vocabulary." The bigger it is, the more choices you have when you are searching for the right word. See, for example, *style, colloquial, dialect, audience, scientific language,* and *standard English* for more information about how to chose the right vocabulary for your needs.

Voice. *Transitive* verbs normally suggest action directed to or carried out on something or someone, which is their *object*: ''The batter hit the ball.'' In this form *verbs* are said to be in the ''*active voice.*'' But transitive verbs can be made to reflect action back on their *subject* and convey no action to their object; this is called the ''*passive* voice'' of transitive verbs: ''The ball was hit by the batter.''

Passive voice forms usually add a *linking verb* element to distinguish them from the active forms in corresponding *tenses* or *moods*: ''The child watches. The child is/was/will be/would have been watched.''

Generally, writing today favors the use of the active voice, since it is more conversational, more lively, and clearer. Its *clarity* comes from the fact that the active voice states the subject and object more directly and explicitly than does the passive—we know from an active sentence who did what to whom. Passive sentences are more obscure: ''Pollution has not been cleaned up.'' The sentence points to a condition but does not indicate who caused the pollution, who should be cleaning it up, or who should be concerned. Most writing should avoid this sort of fuzzing of cause and effect or responsibility when possible.

Some *styles,* however, rely on the passive's veiling of subjects and objects to produce a specific effect. *Scientific language,* for instance, has often favored the passive in the belief that the absence of personal agents (subjects) makes information more objective, more verifiable. Some critics of science and scientific style argue that the predominance of the passive voice merely hides the role of the scientist. These critics believe it is important to keep in mind that a scientist may have brought assumptions, preconceptions, prejudices, or other distorting attitudes or opinions to work that cannot be considered objective or verifiable just because it is reported in the passive voice.

Other observers of language and style have frequently pointed out that government documents commonly use the passive voice to obscure responsibility for unpopular decisions: "Taxes are being raised." Who raised them? It is sometimes in the interests of politicians or bureaucrats to mask the source of policies or practices by using the passive voice.

The general guideline suggesting avoidance of the passive is a good one to follow. However, when circumstances call for the disappearance or masking of a subject, the passive can be a handy tool. That is, choice of voice can be a stylistic or *rhetorical* option of great value in gaining *emphasis,* variety, or other effects. The passive should be used sparingly in most situations, but at times it can be very effective.

Vowel. The letters "a," "e," "i," "o," and "u" are called "vowels" and are differentiated from *consonants* because of the way we produce their sounds when we speak. Recognizing which letters are which can be important when dividing a word into *syllables* in order to *hyphenate* it.

W

Wake, woke (waked), woke (waked, woken). An *irregular verb* in its main, *past tense*, and past *participle* forms. The forms in *parentheses* are used to distinguish *transitive* from *intransitive usages* of this *verb*. The transitive sense (with an *object*) uses "wake, woke, woken": "Chris wakes Jan"; "Chris woke Jan"; "Chris had woken Jan every morning." The intransitive uses "wake, woke (or waked), waked (or woken)" and usually includes "up": "I wake up; I woke up; I had woke [waked, woken] up."

Waked. See *wake*.

Was. First-*person* and third-person singular *past tense* of "*be*": "I, he/she/it was."

Wasn't. This *contraction* of "was not" is not normally accepted in *standard English* writing.

Way, ways. "Ways" is a *colloquial* form of "way" that should not appear in most formal or *standard English* writing.

Ways. See *way*.

We. The first-*person* plural *personal pronoun*.

Wear, wore, worn. An *irregular verb* in its main, *past tense*, and past *participle* forms.

Well. See *good*.

Went. See *go*.

Were. Second-*person* singular and first-, second-, and third-person plural *past tense* of "*be*": "You, we, they were."

When, where. Be sure that "when" refers to time, and "where" refers to place. It is wrong to use these words to designate a situation or case that does not suggest a particular time or place. WRONG: "Democracy is when the people rule." RIGHT: "Democracy is the rule of the people."

Where. See *when*.

Which. See *that* and *who*.

Who, whom; whoever, whomever. Ah, the pain of choosing between "who" and "whom"! It really isn't that hard if you remember that "who" is always and only a *subject,* and "whom" is always and only an *object*: "Who hits whom?" "Who does what to whom?" "Who is that?" "That is who?" "With whom did you talk?" "You talked with whom?"

Each of the examples uses the *pronouns* "who" and "whom" properly. The only confusing part is when "who" appears after certain *verbs*, like "*is*" and other *linking verbs* ("appear," "*become*," and so on). The right choice is "who" because linking verbs do not have objects; they have *subject complements* (also called "*predicate* nominatives"). Subject complements are in the same form (and *case*) as subjects.

A further confusion arises when "who" or "whoever" is the subject of a *clause*. Since clauses can themselves be the *objects* of other things (like *prepositions*), the correct subject form of "who" might look odd in what seems to be a place that requires an object: "Give the bat to whoever is up next." "Whoever" is correct here because it is the subject of "is up" and not the object of "to." The whole clause "whoever is up next" is the object of "to," but "whoever" plays a role within that clause that requires it to be in the subject form (*nominative* case). "To whom do I give the bat?" "To whoever is up next."

In everyday speech or writing, the grammatical distinction between "who" and "whom" is weakening and even becoming a sign of pretension. "Who is that for?" sounds right, while "For whom is that?" might get an odd look, even though it is technically correct because "whom" is the object of "for." Of course, if your everyday circle of friends or *audience* is made up of English professors, then the first example might be worse than the second. Similarly, in all formal writing, it is important to maintain the *standard English* usage and observe the grammatical *rules*. Just how far speech or writing can deviate and still be comprehensible and acceptable is a matter for each speaker or writer to judge. See also *grammar, usage,* and *style.*

Note also that "who" refers to people, whereas "which" refers to things.

Whoever. See *who*.

Whom. See *who*.

Whomever. See *who*.

Who's, whose. "Who's" is a *contraction* of "who is." "Whose" is a *possessive* pronoun that modifies a *noun*, at least implicitly: "Whose house is this?" "Whose is it?" See also *pronoun* and *modifier*.

Whose. See *who's*.

Will. See *shall*.

Win, won, won. An *irregular verb* in its main, *past tense*, and past *participle* forms.

Wind, wound, wound. An *irregular verb* in its main, *past tense*, and past *participle* forms.

With. A *preposition* governing the *objective case*: "I went with them."

Without. A *preposition* governing the *objective case*: "We'll have to manage without them."

Woke. See *wake*.

Woken. See *wake*.

Won. See *win*.

Worse, worst. The comparative and *superlative* of "*bad*" and "*badly*" and "*ill*." See also *comparison*.

Worst. See *worse*, *bad*, *ill*, and *superlative*.

Wound. See *wind*.

Write, wrote, written. An *irregular verb* in its main, *past tense*, and past *participle* forms.

Written. See *write*.

Wrote. See *write*.

XYZ

You. Second-*person* singular and plural *personal pronoun*. See also *number*.

Your, you're. Although these words sound alike (*homonyms*), "your" is a *possessive* pronoun that modifies a *noun*: "How is your dog?" "You're" is a *contraction* of "you are." See also *pronoun* and *modifier*.

You're. See *your*.

Yourself. See *-self*.

Zero. This *number* should usually be written out in text, but its corresponding figure ("0") can be used if the *emphasis* of the writing is on the numerical amount: "The accountant's instructions read, 'If the remainder is 0 to 50 cents, round down to the dollar.' "

Key Word Index of Grammatical Terms